STUDIES
IN ANGLICAN
HISTORY

SERIES EDITOR
Peter W. Williams, *Miami University*

*Sponsored by the Historical Society
of the Episcopal Church*

THE

NATURE

OF

SALVATION

THE

NATURE

OF

SALVATION

THEOLOGICAL CONSENSUS

IN THE EPISCOPAL CHURCH,

1801–73

ROBERT W. PRICHARD

University of Illinois Press

Urbana and Chicago

Publication of this book has been supported by a grant from the Historical Society of the Episcopal Church.

© 1997 by the Board of Trustees of the University of Illinois
Manufactured in the United States of America
C 5 4 3 2 1

This book is printed on acid-free paper.

Library of Congress Cataloging-in-Publication Data

Prichard, Robert W., 1949–
The nature of salvation : theological consensus in the Episcopal
Church, 1801–73 / Robert W. Prichard.
p.   cm. — (Studies in Anglican History)
Includes bibliographical references and index.
ISBN 0-252-02309-9 (alk. paper)
1. Episcopal Church—Doctrines—History—19th century. 2.
Anglican Communion—United States—Doctrines—History—19th
century. 3. White, William, 1748–1836. I. Title. II Series.
BX5930.2.P75   1997
283'.73'09034—dc20   96-25380
CIP

To my father,
with thanks for his support for this project

SERIES
EDITOR'S
PREFACE

Peter W. Williams

Studies in Anglican History is a series of scholarly monographs sponsored by the Historical Society of the Episcopal Church and published
by the University of Illinois Press. It is intended to bring the best of
contemporary international scholarship on the history of the entire
Anglican Communion, including the Church of England and the Episcopal church in the United States, to a broader readership.

Robert Prichard, who teaches church history at the Virginia Theological Seminary, goes back in this volume to the formative years of
the Episcopal church in the United States. Where scholars since the
1930s have emphasized the liturgical aspects of the deep and often
vitriolic disputes that divided American Episcopalians into high-
church and evangelical parties, Prichard instead emphasizes the theological conceptions that both parties shared. In doing so he highlights
the intellectual contributions of Bishop William White of Philadelphia
and the teaching of the professors of divinity at the several Episcopal seminaries. The result of this study is a fresh picture of the first
three-quarters of the nineteenth century in which the intellectual heritage of American Anglicanism is distinguished more by commonality than by disagreement.

Contents

ACKNOWLEDGMENTS

I wish to thank E. Brooks Holifield of Emory University, Peter Williams of Miami University of Ohio, Elizabeth Dulany and Bruce Bethell of the University of Illinois Press, Allen Guelzo of Eastern College, Nancy Brown, who is the faculty secretary at Virginia Seminary, and E. A. Prichard for their considerable assistance in bringing this book to publication.

Chapter 2 and a portion of chapter 1 appeared in an earlier published form. They are reprinted with permission from *Anglican and Episcopal History/The Historical Magazine of the Protestant Episcopal Church* 51, no. 1 (Mar. 1982): 23–51.

INTRODUCTION

Americans of the nineteenth century worried about their salvation. They had neither an ancient national religious tradition nor a single predominant denomination to comfort them; worse yet, they had to contend with conflicting proposals about how they could know they were among the saved, and the mélange of answers fed their anxiety all the more. The conservative groups among the Reformed churches—the "old" factions of the Presbyterians, Congregationalists, and Dutch and German Reformed churches—sought assurance in a sense of seriousness about religion and in an appreciation for the Reformed theological formulations: God had mysteriously predestined the individual to salvation, but the individual who truly trusted Christ need not be troubled further. The revivalist Protestants—the Methodists, Baptists, and the various "new" groups in the Reformed churches—sought their assurance in the personal experience of conversion. Roman Catholics looked for assurance through sacramental grace and the authority of their church's hierarchy. Members of Christian sects, such as the Mormons, found comfort in their leaders' claims of divine knowledge. Episcopalians sought assurance from two sources: from baptism and from what they referred to as "the renewed life."

One task of theologians in the nineteenth century was to make sense of their denominational claims about assurance. The theologians of the Reformed tradition tried to modify and explain the doctrine of predestination at a time in which free will was the common assumption. Revivalist Protestants attempted to create a theological road map with which to understand and prepare for conversion. Roman Catholics adopted formulas intended to buttress their church's claim of divine authority. Christian sects expounded theological views that limited the full enjoyment of salvation to those who accepted their particular dogmas.

Episcopalians wrestled with their own form of this question of assurance. Their theologians defined a distinctive understanding of the
baptismal covenant and expounded an adult renewal of which good
works were a sign and a conversion experience was a possible, but not
necessary, concomitant. They neutralized the anxiety-provoking issue
of predestination and painted an eschatological picture in which judgment was on works. The Episcopal theologians combined these propositions into a consistent view of assurance: Christians were assured
of salvation by baptism, which opened a covenant relationship with
God, and by good works, which were the only sure sign of renewal.
Christians did not need to worry about predestination and did not need
to emulate any particular pattern of conversion experience.

Church historians have made much of the difference between the two
predominant church parties in the nineteenth-century Episcopal church,
the high-church and evangelical parties. Even before the nineteenth
century came to a close, S. D. McConnell suggested that a kind of in-
ternecine warfare among Episcopalians had commenced in 1811 and
continued until late in that century.[1] This thesis has been refined in the
present century with the division of this ecclesiastical war into various
periods, but it has remained largely unquestioned. William Manross,
for example, accepted the division of the church as a major strand for
his narration of the nineteenth century in his *History of the American
Episcopal Church* (1935).[2] Six years later George DeMille subdivided
the high-church movement into three periods (1811–40, 1840–60, and
after 1860).[3] E. Clowes Chorley incorporated this subdivision in his
Men and Movements in the American Episcopal Church (1946), a work
that continues to be one of the better histories of the denomination.[4]

James Thayer Addison and Raymond Albright, whose histories of
the Episcopal church extended the story of the denomination into the
twentieth century, did not significantly change the party approach to
nineteenth-century Episcopal history, although the longer time spans
covered in their works did suggest that it functions best within certain
chronological limits.[5] More recent historians have given a new emphasis
to the church-party approach, however, for they have found it to be
useful in explaining the relationship of nineteenth-century Episcopalians to American society at large. Bruce Mullin (*Episcopal Vision/
American Reality,* 1986) and Richard Rankin (*Ambivalent Churchmen
and Evangelical Churchwomen,* 1993), for example, have described the
interplay between the high-church party of DeMille's first period and

a background American culture that was revivalist and evangelical.[6] Diana Butler did something similar for the evangelicals in her *Standing against the Whirlwind* (1995), in which she traced the conflict between evangelical bishop Charles Pettit McIlvaine of Ohio and a radical American evangelical revivalism.[7]

My book's focus on a sense of assurance that was shared across Episcopal party lines is intended as a corrective to this emphasis on division. I do not suggest that the divisions between the two church parties were insignificant or nonexistent, however. Indeed, I have used a revised form of the church-party approach both here and in my *History of the Episcopal Church*.[8] Nevertheless I am convinced that the frequent use of a church-party approach does demand an accompanying exposition of what Episcopalians held in common; the lack of such an exposition leaves the reader asking why Episcopalians managed to remain united to the degree to which they did.[9]

I argue in this work that high-church and evangelical Episcopalians were linked by certain theological ideas. This premise does not rule out the existence of other uniting elements. Some authors have suggested, for example, that high-church and evangelical Episcopalians were united primarily by social and economic factors.[10] My own suspicion is that several factors were at work.

My focus here is on one particular link, a common view of assurance that was taught to and by Episcopal clergy in both church parties. Clergy did disagree as to emphasis. High-church Episcopalians put the most emphasis on the baptismal covenant as a basis for assurance. Evangelical Episcopalians placed greater emphasis on the doctrine of renewal. Both groups nevertheless shared the same theological explanations for those sources of assurance, relied on the same authors, and used the same examples. They differed only in emphasis.

The four theological chapters that constitute the center of this work—chapters 2 through 5—follow the individual from before the cradle until after the grave. Chapter 2 deals with the question of divine predestination of the believer's salvation. Chapter 3 deals with baptism and entrance into the covenant; chapter 4, with adult renewal; chapter 5, with death and resurrection.

The question of assurance runs through all these chapters. Chapter 2 chronicles the Episcopal rejection of a rigid Reformed doctrine of predestination as destructive of assurance. Chapter 3 traces the work of Episcopal authors who described the baptismal covenant as a basis for assurance. Chapter 4 details how Episcopalians defined personal renewal as a ground for assurance against the background of the continued revivals of the Second Great Awakening. Finally, chapter 5 deals with Episcopal rejection of the common notion of rewards conferred immediately on death, preferring another eschatological view more in accord with their understanding of renewal and assurance.

Ideas do not exist in isolation from the persons who held them. The framework of this book is therefore not only theological but also historical. The first and final chapters trace the theologians who achieved the consensus on assurance and those who later dismantled it. Bishop William White (1748–1836) of Pennsylvania was the thinker primarily responsible for the consensus. At the beginning of the nineteenth century, he induced the church to adopt the Thirty-nine Articles of Religion as a statement of faith. He designed the standard Course of Ecclesiastical Studies, which would be used in the church for the preparation of ordained ministers for most of the century. He wrote, preached, and presided over the church's General Convention well into the century's fourth decade.

The story of White's work is the topic of the first chapter and of the work as a whole. Indeed, the internal organization of each of the central chapters demonstrates his importance. Each chapter begins with an explanation of an author that Bishop White designated or a position he took, followed by an indication of how the theme developed in the light of high-church and evangelical emphases.

The English Oxford movement was responsible for dismantling the agreement about assurance that White helped to establish. Americans who subscribed to the Oxford theology rejected the prevailing understanding of both the renewed life and the baptismal covenant. The first generation of Oxford adherents, maturing before the Civil War, perceived the church's hostility toward their views and left for the Roman Catholic church. After the war ended, members of second generation stayed and won a place for their views in the church. Their efforts and the reaction they provoked among evangelicals brought an end to the theological consensus of the first three-quarters of the century and left the church with a broader theological pluralism.

This work covers a period extending between two symbolic dates. In 1801 Bishop White persuaded the General Convention to adopt the Thirty-nine Articles as the standard for the American Church. The heated debate over the Oxford movement ended in 1873. In that year a relatively small number of evangelicals, unwilling to accept a theological statement by the House of Bishops, withdrew to form the Reformed Episcopal Church. During these seventy-two years there was a consensus among Episcopalians about the assurance of salvation. The individual could be assured of salvation by the experience of personal renewal and the fact of baptism.

This consensus has been overlooked for reasons that have more to do with the twentieth-century Episcopal church than with the nineteenth-century one. Episcopalians have come to treasure the theological pluralism that begins at the end of the period I describe and to believe that it has been a constant throughout their history. A common apologetic approach is to suggest that Queen Elizabeth I established a liberal set of ground rules for theological inquiry that has remained in force ever since.[11] Such an apologetic overlooks the real differences between the first two-thirds of the nineteenth century and the last third of the twentieth.

Bishop White exercised his leadership in an era when Episcopalians were uncertain of their future. They lacked colleges and seminaries and were suffering from the withdrawal of missionary society and state support that the Revolution had brought. Some of their number predicted the denomination's demise. Division and disagreement would have fulfilled such predictions. Consensus meant life. When the consensus dissolved late in the century, it had already served its purpose. The Episcopalians of the 1870s, looking back on a century of growth and a firmly fixed American liturgical tradition, lived with a theological pluralism that would have spelled disaster for the young church of 1801.

NOTES

1. S. D. McConnell, *History of the American Episcopal Church from the Planting of the Colonies to the End of the Civil War* (New York: Thomas Whittaker, 1890).

2. William Manross, *History of the American Episcopal Church* (New York: Morehouse, 1935).

3. George DeMille, *Catholic Movement in the American Episcopal Church* (Philadelphia: Church History Society, 1941).

4. E. Clowes Chorley, *Men and Movements in the American Episcopal Church* (New York: Scribner's, 1946).

5. James Thayer Addison, *The Episcopal Church in the United States,*

1789–1931 (New York: Scribner's, 1951); Raymond Wolf Albright, *A History of the Protestant Episcopal Church* (New York: Macmillan, 1964).

6. R. Bruce Mullin, *Episcopal Vision/American Reality: High Church Theology and Social Thought in Evangelical America* (New Haven, Conn.: Yale University Press, 1986); Richard Rankin, *Ambivalent Churchmen and Evangelical Churchwomen: The Religion of the Episcopal Elite in North Carolina, 1800–1860* (Columbia: University of South Carolina Press, 1993). Mullin concentrated on New York, and Rankin focused on North Carolina; both were states in which the high-church party would predominate.

7. Diana Hochstedt Butler, *Standing against the Whirlwind: The Evangelical Party in Nineteenth-Century America* (New York: Oxford University Press, 1995). The radical evangelical revivalism was only the first of a series of "whirlwinds" against which Butler described McIlvaine as fighting. The other whirlwinds were tractarianism, the Civil War, internal schism in the evangelical party, and liberalism.

8. Robert W. Prichard, *A History of the Episcopal Church* (Harrisburg, Pa.: Morehouse, 1991).

9. Allen Guelzo has recently warned of the "'myth of synthesis,' which, in varying proportions, pervades the standard histories of the Episcopal Church in the United States." This myth, he explained, "involves the suggestion that Episcopalian history, unlike the schismatic and divisive histories of other American denominations, is genetic and comprehensive rather than controversial—that the Episcopal Church has managed to exceptionalize itself, to synthesize 'Catholic' and 'Protestant,' 'Liberal' and 'Evangelical,' and disarm the potentially confrontational elements of American religions in a tolerant and elegant embrace" (Allen C. Guelzo, "Ritual, Romanism, and Rebellion: The Disappearance of the Evangelical Episcopalians, 1853–1873," *Anglican and Episcopal History* 62 [Dec. 1993]: 553).

As I hope the final chapter of this work shows, I have tried not to overlook the differences between evangelical and high-church Episcopalians. The fiercest fights are often between family members and friends, however. The great deal they hold in common serves to highlight their significant points of difference: "If you agree with me thus far, how can you be so perverse as not to agree completely?" The fact that high-church and evangelical Episcopalians shared a number of theological ideas does not mean that they were somehow immune to disagreements of the sort that divided other American Protestants.

10. Kit and Frederica Konolige's *Power of the Glory, America's Ruling Class: The Episcopalians* (N.p.: Wyden, 1978) suggested something of this sort, but the book was flawed by not seriously considering the social standing of other American denominations.

11. For an example of this approach, see David L. Holmes, *A Brief History of the Episcopal Church* (Valley Forge: Trinity, 1993), 7–18.

1   The Influence of William White

~

The General Convention of the Episcopal Church that met in Trenton, New Jersey, in September 1801 was not an impressive gathering. The church was young; it had come into being as an independent denomination only twelve years earlier. None of the states represented sent the full delegation to which it was entitled. One of the largest states—Virginia—sent no delegation at all. The news that the bishops and deputies shared about the church was not entirely auspicious.

By the time of this gathering, William White of Pennsylvania already had emerged as something of an elder father within the church. The generation of church leaders that had received theological education and ordination in England was rapidly passing, and at the convention of 1801 a new generation of clergy was coming of age, a generation for whom the English colonial church was only a vague memory. It was to William White that this generation would look for guidance.

As a young man in the 1780s White had provided the blueprint for the formation of an American denominational structure. He had led the way in adapting a British religious establishment to the conditions of the new American republic. Now in the last three decades of his long life, he attempted to provide leadership of a different sort. With major organizational issues behind him, he attempted to sketch out his denomination's theological principles.

The young clergy at the General Convention meetings from 1801 to 1834 brought youth and enthusiasm to the propagation of the principles that they learned from Bishop White. They recognized a tension within the bishop's teaching and developed two conflicting schools of interpretation: the high-church and the evangelical parties. Nevertheless members of both parties were his theological children. When it came to answering the difficult questions of faith—To what did they

turn within their tradition in expounding the Good News of Jesus
Christ? In what ways could they hold out the assurance of salvation
to the individual believer? How did they regard themselves in relation
to other denominations?—they invariably turned to White's words, to
the texts that he accepted as standard, and to the authors whom he
designated as appropriate interpreters of the faith. Bishop White guided
his denomination to a theological understanding of what it meant to
be a Christian within the Episcopal church.

BISHOP WHITE AND THE EPISCOPAL CHURCH

Bishop White's stature at the General Convention meeting of 1801,
and the skill and moderation with which he took advantage of it, had
not emerged overnight. He had served a long apprenticeship, first as
parish priest and leading promoter of a unified national church and then
as a participant in a curious minuet in which three bishops consecrated in England and one consecrated in Scotland attempted to avoid
treading on one another's prerogatives. He made his share of errors but
profited from the experience, and when he finally stood alone at the
helm of the church, he was ready to provide a firm but understanding
hand. He would interpret his own efforts, and the whole history of the
fledgling denomination, for those who would follow.

The Prologue: The Years prior to 1801

Born in Philadelphia in 1748, William White was the son of Thomas White, a prosperous lawyer and land speculator. Growing up in his
parents' home and in schools in Philadelphia and England, White came
in touch with the leading intellectual lights of his age. He befriended
American painter Benjamin West (1738–1820) and was introduced by
his two English aunts to Oliver Goldsmith (1728–74) and Samuel
Johnson (1709–84). His sister married wealthy colonial merchant
Robert Morris (1734–1806), and he himself wed the daughter of Philadelphia's mayor.[1]

White was baptized as an infant in the United Parish of Christ
Church and St. Peter's. During his student years Philadelphia was
caught up in the sweep of the religious revival that Americans have since
called the Great Awakening. White's father was an active layman and
brought some of the leaders of the awakening into his home. Many
Philadelphians had the opportunity of seeing Anglican evangelist

George Whitefield (1714–70) preach; William White dined with him. Although White was only a child, the encounter left a lasting impression on him.

After graduating from the College of Philadelphia (known later as the University of Pennsylvania) and traveling to England in 1770 for theological studies and ordination, White became an assistant clergyman at the United Parish of Christ Church and St. Peter's.[2]

White's first seven years at the United Parish passed in the customary obscurity of the junior clergy, but in 1779 the American Revolution catapulted him into a position of prominence. The rector of the United Parish, Jacob Duché (1737–98), was a chaplain to the Continental Congress and an early supporter of the war. When the British occupied Philadelphia, however, he renounced the patriots' cause and fled to England. Faced with the departure of many senior clergy and the unlikelihood of any English ordinations in the near future, the vestry of the United Parish took the only reasonable course of action open to it. In April 1779 it unanimously elected White rector.[3] The Continental Congress soon followed suit, electing him as a chaplain in Duché's stead. At the age of thirty-one White was both the rector of the largest Episcopal parish in the largest city of the new nation and the chaplain to the nation's Congress.[4]

In this prominent position, surrounded by members of Congress attempting to shape a new government, White was acutely aware of the disorganized state of his own denomination. Its organizational structure had been tied to the Church of England, a church in what was now a hostile nation. Three years after his election as rector, White addressed the church at large in a pamphlet titled *The Case of the Episcopal Churches Considered,* in which he suggested that the organization of the denomination on a national level could not wait for peace with England or for an English decision to consecrate bishops for the American church.[5] His proposal provided a needed catalyst; Episcopalians in the middle states began meeting to form a charter for a national organization. A separate group led by Connecticut clergy took another approach. Rather than concentrate on the legislative body, they centered their efforts on procuring a native episcopate. They elected one of their number, Samuel Seabury (1729–96), and sent him to England with the request that he be consecrated a bishop. These two groups would combine in 1789.

White was successful organizationally, but he did not enjoy the same initial success in matters theological. From 1782 until 1787 White explored the limits of his own church in a theological process of trial and error. At first he perceived the denomination's theology to be pliable. He believed that he was able to reshape the doctrines of the body in whatever way he felt appropriate. As long as he held to the basic doctrines of the Trinity and justification by faith alone, he could alter traditional material at will. He prepared a revision of the English Book of Common Prayer of 1662, which was in use in the American colonies at the time of the Revolution, and of the Thirty-nine Articles of Religion with William Smith (1727–1803), a priest who had been one of his teachers at the College of Philadelphia.[6] The two men removed the Athanasian Creed because of its condemnatory language. They rejected the Nicene Creed because of its technical trinitarian language. They discarded the difficult doctrine of Christ's descent into hell.[7]

English theologians had for over a century dreamed of what they could do if only their monarchs would allow them a free hand at revising the Thirty-nine Articles and the Prayer Book of 1662. By the second half of the eighteenth century, English authors had produced a whole genre of booklets suggesting ways to modernize church standards, and White and Smith had just such a pamphlet in their hands when they made their revisions.[8]

White and Smith's revision of the prayer book, although approved at the middle states convention in 1785, proved to be a failure. Their edition, known as the *Proposed Book,* was rejected by the English bishops, by the participants in the competing Connecticut attempt to form an American church, and by rank-and-file worshipers in the middle states.[9] Moreover the attempted revision produced another, unforeseen result. Charles Miller of King's Chapel, Boston, regarded White and Smith's effort as an invitation for yet more radical revision of the prayer book. White and Smith had fallen short of a thorough revision, Miller argued. Should not the doctrine of the Trinity be removed along with other passages? Failing to find such changes, Miller and his congregation withdrew from the Episcopal church to become Unitarians.[10]

White would not forget the experience of failure. He had received a practical lesson in theology and tradition. Thereafter he would exercise a more moderate hand in dealing with the church's liturgy and the theology. Tradition could not be wholeheartedly rejected, nor could standards easily be set aside.

The middle states convention accepted the obvious and abandoned

White and Smith's revision of the prayer book and Articles of Religion. The members of the 1786 General Convention reversed their earlier approval of the *Proposed Book* and adopted a brief list of changes to be made in the English 1662 edition of the Book of Common Prayer. They postponed any action on the Articles of Religion.

The New England and middle states groups united in 1789. At that point there were three Episcopal bishops in the United States; Samuel Seabury had been consecrated bishop of Connecticut in Scotland in 1784, whereas White of Pennsylvania and Samuel Provoost (1742–1815) of New York were consecrated in England in 1787.[11] A fourth bishop, James Madison (1749–1812) of Virginia, was consecrated in England in 1790.

White had been the acknowledged leader of the middle states convention at the time of the merger with the Connecticut group.[12] After 1789 his status in the newly created House of Bishops was less clear.[13] The three who had been consecrated prior to the merger—Seabury, White, and Provoost—adopted a rotating presidency. Seabury presided at the convention of 1789, Provoost would chair the 1792 meeting, and White would follow in 1795. This somewhat unwieldy arrangement was complicated by the fact that Seabury and Provoost disliked each other. Only through White's considerable skills in diplomacy could they cooperate to the degree to which they did. For example, White was able to arrange for the consecration of Bishop Thomas Claggett (1743–1816) of Maryland in 1792 by scheduling two meetings of the House of Bishops, Seabury attending one meeting and Provoost attending the other.[14]

Theologically matters were equally difficult during the 1790s. Seabury feared that the Thirty-nine Articles were too Calvinist. Madison and Provoost, if not outright deists, were at least hostile to any further creeds for the church. White alone among the first four bishops had an interest in the adoption of the articles. He suspected that theological decisions avoided on a national level would revert to the parish. Had not the congregation of King's Chapel, Boston, declared itself to be Unitarian? White therefore argued that the General Convention must act.[15]

Yet no significant action could take place. The bishops simply were in too great disagreement about theology. Madison and Provoost felt that the less said, the better. Seabury's thought was shaped by his considerable dislike of Congregationalist ideas about conversion, predestination, and election. White's own thoughts must have still been in flux. He had demonstrated in his freewheeling revision of the prayer book that his first instinct had been toward a rationalistic, nonsacramental understanding of the church, but his appreciation for church tradition was constantly growing. The events of the convention of 1799 were to clarify his understanding of the church's theology.

Provoost, White, and Edward Bass (1726–1803), the newly conse-crated bishop of Massachusetts, were in the House of Bishops at the convention of 1799. Seabury had died, and Madison and Claggett could not attend. A continuation of the rotating presidency would have giv-en the chair to Samuel Provoost. Provoost was losing enthusiasm for the church, however; in any case his major interest in presiding had been in denying the position to Seabury. He allowed White, who had chaired the previous convention, to continue to preside.

Even with White presiding, the bishops were unable to come to any agreement on the Articles of Religion. The House of Clerical and Lay Deputies consequently decided to take the matter in hand. In 1799 the Reverend Ashbel Baldwin of Connecticut convinced the deputies to establish a committee to revise the articles. That committee, led by William Walter (1737–1800) of Christ Church, Boston, followed the path that White and William Smith had taken fourteen years earlier; committee members boldly rewrote the articles. Their revisions, with the exception of the positions taken on predestination and the neces-sity of episcopal ordination, were similar to those made in the *Proposed Book*.[16]

The Walter committee draft was presented too late for action in the convention. It was printed with the General Convention *Journal,* and action on it was deferred until 1801. The report's publication appar-ently lent it something of an official appearance, but like the earlier *Proposed Book,* it was decried by the church's rank and file. For Bish-op White it was a demonstration of a lesson he had learned firsthand. The standards of the church were not pliable.

The eighteenth century closed with theological confusion in the Episcopal church. Eleven years after the formation of a unified national denomination, the church still had not taken an explicit position on the Thirty-nine Articles. Help was on the way, however, because Bish-op White, tutored by his own trial and error and by years of delicate compromise, would soon be able to proffer a solution.

Bishop White and the Second Generation of the Church

Those who attended the seventh meeting of the General Convention of the Protestant Episcopal church in Trenton, New Jersey, in September 1801 could not fail to recognize the change in leadership that was taking place in the church. Many familiar faces were gone. Three of the four original bishops were absent: Seabury had died, and Madison and Provoost had both withdrawn from an active role in the church. With the exception of White, the bishops who came had been consecrated in America. Claggett of Maryland had been consecrated in 1792; he had then joined with White and Provoost in consecrating Abraham Jarvis (1739–1813) to fill the vacancy left in Connecticut by Seabury's death. In the early days of the convention, White, Claggett, and Jarvis would consecrate Benjamin Moore (1748–1816) to replace the inactive Provoost.

There was also a turnover among the lay and clerical deputies. Of the twenty-eight deputies at this meeting, only eight had been at the General Convention meeting two years before. Not a single member of the Massachusetts, Maryland, or New York delegations and only one member of the Connecticut delegation could recall that earlier gathering firsthand.

Many of the clergy present had studied for orders and had been ordained since 1785. They were accustomed only to an American church. Joseph G. J. Bend (1762–1812) was one; he had been ordained by Bishop Provoost in 1787.[17] Soon after his ordination Bend had accepted a call to serve as an assistant to Bishop White at the United Parish in Philadelphia. The placement would prove to be fortunate for Bend. He gained not only a lifelong friendship with White but also a prominent position in the small denomination. Within four years he was elected rector of St. Paul's Church in Baltimore, a congregation that would grow rapidly under his leadership. By 1801 he was representing the diocese of Maryland at the General Convention.[18]

John Henry Hobart (1775–1830) was another such newcomer. Born in Philadelphia, he was among the earliest students of the city's Episcopal Academy, of which Bishop White was a trustee. He graduated from Princeton at the top of the class of 1793. The college offered him a position as a tutor. When it became clear that he need not become a Presbyterian, he accepted, corresponding with Bishop White and studying for the Episcopal ministry while he taught. He was ordained by White in 1798 and moved rapidly through a series of small parishes, claiming the need for time for private study, but not unmindful of the possibilities of advancement. In 1800 he was called as an assistant at Trinity Church, New York, one of the oldest, wealthiest, and most prestigious of Episcopal parishes. One year later he represented the diocese of New York at the General Convention meeting.[19]

Of course, there were some older hands at the convention; Boston clergyman Samuel Parker (1744–1801) was a notable example.[20] By and large, however, the body was young and relatively inexperienced in matters of polity and theology.

The solution that White held out to this body in regard to the still unadopted Thirty-nine Articles was in keeping both with his own experience with the *Proposed Book* and with his perception of the Church of England. Could not the General Convention give up the effort thoroughly to revise the articles, drop political references to the monarchy and England, and concentrate on the issue of interpretation?

In his earlier discussions with Seabury about the Thirty-nine Articles, White had begun to suspect that interpretation was the critical issue.[21] After all, the articles were not an unambiguous theological standard. Composed in initial form during the reign of Edward VI (1547–53), and then refined under Elizabeth I (1558–1603), they were intended to fulfill both a political and a theological purpose. By excluding from the ministry of the Church of England two groups whose loyalty to the Tudor monarchs was suspect—Roman Catholics and Anabaptists—the articles were intended to preserve the public peace. Much of the material they contained was restrictive rather than systematic: Christians were not to believe in supererogation, sacramental adoration, the necessity of a celibate priesthood, the acceptability of worship in an unintelligible language, or the jurisdiction of the bishop of Rome over England; they were not to deny Christ's descent into hell, the appropriateness of the Apocrypha for example of life and manner, the three creeds, the impropriety of self-appointed preachers, the impossibility of perfection, the correctness of Christian service in the military, or the appropriateness of private ownership.[22]

There was moreover a chronological reason for the interpretative questions about the articles. They were composed prior to the Reformed Synod of Dort, in which the Continental church refined its position on predestination. Anglicans after Dort would have a great deal of difficulty not reading the decisions of that synod, or their dissatisfaction with them, into their understanding of the articles.

When British monarchs repeatedly refused to allow the rewriting of the articles to iron out such interpretative difficulties, Anglican authors took the only course open to them. They produced works explaining to their own satisfaction precisely what the articles were meant to say. By 1801 Bishop White could look back on a two-century tradition of interpretation. The interpreters ranged widely in opinion. White could have chosen from among them fierce anti-Calvinists, faithful adherents to Dort, militant high-church sacramentalists, gracious compromisers, or a host of other figures. Unlike the eighteenth-century authors to whom White and Smith had referred in writing the *Proposed Book,* these interpreters did not suggest revisions in the text of the articles.

The solution to the American church's impasse on the articles was clear to White: adopt the Thirty-nine Articles with an absolute minimum of change while at the same time according a special status to a particular line of interpretation. Rewriting the articles to fit one's theological preferences proved to be impossible; interpreting them along those lines proved to be quite a different matter.

Moving in cooperation with his friend Samuel Parker and his former assistant Joseph Bend, White soon accomplished his goal. At the opening session of the 1801 convention, members of the House of Bishops formally revised their rules of order to abandon the rotating presidency. White presided and, as senior active bishop by date of consecration, would continue to do so until his death. Later that same day White and the other two bishops present—Jarvis and Claggett—adopted a "form and manner of setting forth the Articles of religion, and agreed that the same be sent to the House of Clerical and Lay Deputies for their concurrence."[23]

The House of Deputies already had before it the Walter committee draft revision of the Articles of Religion from the previous session of the General Convention. Walter had died, however, and the negative response to the proposal in the years between conventions left the deputies less than anxious to act. The deputies therefore chose to act on the bishops' resolution rather than on Walter's draft. Samuel Parker was appointed chair of a committee on the articles. The committee recommended several additional changes.

The Parker committee proposal provided for the adoption of the Thirty-nine Articles with four political changes: the omission of article 11, on the respective authority of princes and church councils; the amendment of article 35 to note that, although good explanations of doctrine, the English Homilies were not binding in matters of law in America; the alteration of article 36 to refer to the American rather than English ordinal; and the removal of references to the monarchy in article 37.[24] In addition the Parker committee recommended amending article 8 to remove reference to the Athanasian creed, since the creed had already been removed from the prayer book in 1789.

The House of Deputies accepted the Parker committee report. The bishops gave their consent.[25] Sixteen years after the first meeting of the General Convention, American Episcopalians had finally agreed on a form of the Thirty-nine Articles.

As soon as the House of Deputies had adopted the articles, Joseph Bend asked for the floor. Would not it be wise, he asked, to establish a list of preferred texts for those who were preparing for the ministry of the church? Would not the bishops of the church be most qualified to establish such a course of ecclesiastical studies? The deputies concurred, and their request was sent on to the upper house.[26]

The bishops entrusted the work to White, who was given three years to complete the task. He returned to the following convention in New York in September 1804 with his mission completed. The list he presented contained approximately fifty texts divided into seven categories: apologetics, biblical study, ecclesiastical history, systematic divinity, homiletics, liturgics, and pastoral theology.[27]

In the area of systematic divinity White designated five texts. Only one was a full-fledged commentary on the Thirty-nine Articles. This was Gilbert Burnet's (1643–1715) *Exposition of the Thirty-nine Articles of the Church of England.*[28] The Episcopal church, which until 1801 had been unable to act on the Thirty-nine Articles, now had both an American version of the articles and a designated interpreter.

The importance of this change is difficult to overemphasize. A denomination that had no college or theological seminary, that since the opening of the Revolution had adopted no position on its parent denomination's statement of faith, and that had no long-standing tradition of training its own clergy had for the first time a statement of faith and an author to which it could turn. White, acting with the conventions of 1801 and 1804, provided what he had come to recognize the denomination needed—not a new statement of faith, but an exposition of the tradition it had received.

What had begun as White's quest for a consistent position on the articles, moreover, now had connotations that extended far beyond that single document. The convention's charge had been for an entire course of ecclesiastical studies. White had specified not only the commentary on the articles but also numerous other texts. The other texts in theology were Bishop John Pearson's (1613–86) *Exposition of the Creed,* Thomas Stackhouse's (1677–1752) *Complete Body of Divinity,* an anthology edited by William Jones of Nayland (1726–1806) titled *The Scholar Armed,* and George Prettyman Tomline's (1750–1827) *Elements of Christian Theology.* Pearson's work was a solid Anglican explanation of the creed; like Burnet's *Exposition of the Thirty-nine Articles,* it would prove to be a consistently influential theological text in the nineteenth-century Episcopal church. Stackhouse's *Divinity* soon would be left by the wayside, however. White recommended it as the one text in theology for the student unable to complete a more thorough course, and some students did use it, but it was published in an expensive folio edition, difficult to obtain, and too encyclopedic to be popular.[29] Moreover Stackhouse relied on and cited the earlier works by Burnet and Pearson on several critical issues. Similarly *The Scholar Armed* and *Elements of Christian Theology* would not rival Burnet's and Pearson's texts as perennial favorites. As White himself had noted, all that they contained might well be gleaned from a judicious reading of Scripture and scriptural commentaries.[30]

Pearson's and Burnet's works, and many others on White's list, were written in the second half of the seventeenth century. White found in them a tone different from that of the tracts suggesting revision of the articles to which he and William Smith had referred in the 1780s. English authors in both periods had a rationalistic tone, but whereas the writers of the later eighteenth century used that rationalism to critique such traditional doctrines as the Trinity and Christ's descent into hell, the seventeenth-century authors had primarily devoted their rationalism to bolstering traditional doctrine.[31] It was primarily on the troublesome issue of predestination that the earlier divines had begun to suggest certain compromises in traditional doctrine.

White's seventeenth-century authors had a second important characteristic. They wrote before the Great Awakening. They therefore were not directly concerned with the frequent postawakening revivalist assertion that the assurance of salvation resulted from a recountable conversion experience, nor did they always follow postawakening linguistic conventions. Assurance of salvation came for them from a renewed moral life and from the normal participation in the church that commenced at baptism. Nineteenth-century Episcopalians would gain this vision of assurance from White and his reading list.

Later sessions of the General Convention would fill in some gaps in Bishop White's theological program. The conventions of 1808 and 1817, for example, would call the clergy's attention to the catechism in the prayer book, and the convention of 1814 would provide for the publication of the Homilies. The foundation had already been laid, however. White emerged in the first decade of the century as the church's theological mentor. Some disagreement about theological issues would continue in the denomination, but increasingly the new generation of church leaders would address those issues in the same terms—the terms of the Thirty-nine Articles, of Burnet's commentary, of Pearson's *Exposition of the Creed,* and of the increasing quantity of material from White's own pen.

The measure of White's influence might be best illustrated by two fragments from later in the century, a piece of church legislation and a Sunday school text. The legislative evidence came from the General Convention in 1889. A committee of the House of Bishops had been appointed in 1856 to examine and revise White's Course of Ecclesiastical Studies. Thirty-three years later the committee reported to the General Convention that the committee members "were unanimous in their opinion that the original draught of a course of studies, signed by Bishop White and adopted by the House of Bishops in 1804, is a document of permanent value and ought not to become obsolete."[32] To back up its conviction, the committee then reprinted the list in its entirety.

The Sunday school text was a slim volume published in 1846 in Baltimore. The anonymous Episcopalian who prepared the work was identified only as a "lady . . . [who] has been for many years faithfully and successfully engaged in" the Sunday school of the Episcopal church.[33] She explained in a few short sentences what had taken the General Convention sixteen years to resolve—the adoption of the Thirty-nine Articles.

After repeated discussion and propositions, it had been found, that the doctrines of the gospel, as they stand in the Thirty-nine Articles of the Church of England, were more likely to give general satisfaction, than the same doctrines in any new form that might be devised. They were therefore adopted by the two houses of convention. In all the deliberations of the several conventions, the object kept in view, says Bishop White, "was the perpetuating of the Episcopal Church, on the ground of the general principles which she had inherited from the Church of England; and not departing from them, except so far as local circumstances required, or some very important cause rendered proper."[34]

The author was convinced that the discussion and delay had been matters only of strategy. Certainly, she reasoned, there had been agreement about matters of doctrine; only the form of the statement was in question. It was from Bishop White—in this case from his *Memoirs of the Protestant Episcopal Church*—that she had gained this comforting assurance. For her and for Episcopalians during the better part of a century, White had helped to project an image of theological agreement and harmony.

BISHOP WHITE'S THEOLOGICAL CHILDREN

As I argue in detail in the coming chapters, the consensus that Bishop White helped to foster contained within it a certain ambiguity.[35] On the critical question of assurance, White suggested two sources rather than just one: the individual could be assured by the experience of personal renewal and by the fact of baptism.

The relationship of the two could be approached from either of two directions. One could emphasize the baptismal covenant as a permanent relationship that would lead in the normal course of events to adult renewal and salvation, or one could emphasize adult renewal as the culmination of a relationship begun in the baptismal covenant.

Within a theological vacuum this difference in emphasis might have been only a minor matter. Within an age of Protestant revivalism, however, the implications of the two approaches became crucial. The first emphasis put a greater value on baptism than that accorded to it by most other Protestants. To adopt this approach would be to call attention to the distinctiveness of Episcopal doctrine.[36] The second emphasis would be more in keeping with other Protestant churches and their preoccupation with the faith of the adult believer.

Bishop White tried to balance the two emphases, often through his own example. He advised against mixed worship with other Protestants while at the same time serving as local president of the ecumenical Bible Society. He taught that the episcopacy was not a necessary order of the church while becoming a virtual incarnation of the episcopate for nineteenth-century Episcopalians—the senior active bishop for a third of the century.

The younger Episcopalians who looked to White recognized the ambiguity in his position. Some, such as White's theological students William Augustus Muhlenberg (1796–1877) and John Henry Hopkins (1792–1864), emulated his attempt to balance the stress on baptism and that on personal renewal. Many more would choose to emphasize one or the other of White's sources of assurance. Those who chose to stress baptism and therefore to accent their differences with other Protestants were known as high-church Episcopalians; they glorified and held high the church and particularly the apostolic succession of the denomination's bishops as the source of assurance. Those who stressed personal renewal were called evangelical Episcopalians because of their affinity with other Protestant evangelicals.

Of course, the existence of high-church and evangelical parties long antedated the nineteenth century. White could lay no claim to initiating such distinctions. The party tradition in Anglicanism dated back to the Reformation, if not before. Nevertheless White could justifiably claim to have influenced the specific groups of evangelical and high-church Episcopalians who came after him. In seeking to understand their faith, whatever their emphasis, they turned to him and to the authors and standards he helped to establish.

The High-Church Episcopalians

At the time of the convention of 1801, John Henry Hobart was undergoing an important change in his thought. He was both a personal friend and a former student of Bishop White. After his move to New York in 1800, however, Hobart adopted a militant insistence on the episcopacy that would impose a priority on White's belief in two sources of assurance.

The change in the young Hobart is understandable for three reasons. First, the change in locale was extremely important. Philadelphia, in which representatives of every major American denomination could be found, had a long history of religious toleration. The atmosphere in New York was very different. Episcopalians there had found themselves to be the object of considerable criticism in the public press, particularly in the years immediately before the American Revolution. Presbyterians and some other non-Episcopalians had denounced plans for a colonial episcopate as a tyrannical English plot.[37] Although the conclusion of the Revolution and the introduction of bishops who lacked the political powers of their English counterparts led some to change their attitudes toward Episcopalians, others remained critical. Hobart would not find in New York the brotherly welcome he might have expected in Philadelphia.

A second cause lay in Hobart's marriage. He recently had wed Mary Gooden Chandler, daughter of Thomas Bradbury Chandler (1726–90).[38] Although they married after the death of her father, Hobart found in the memory of his father-in-law an important element that had been missing in his own life. Hobart was young when his own father died. Chandler had been a distinguished Anglican clergyman, an author and public spokesman for the church. His memory was still held in general esteem. Dr. Chandler had been a leading American advocate of a colonial episcopate. Hobart, possibly gaining his position at Trinity on the strength of his father-in-law's reputation, chose to make Chandler's concern his own. At all costs, he held, the Episcopal church must stress the importance of the episcopate and the error of those denominations that lacked it.

A third cause was pragmatic. As an assistant at Trinity Church, Hobart stood a chance of becoming the bishop of New York. By 1801 the parish already had the reputation of a maker of bishops. The fourth rector of the parish, Charles Inglis (1734–1816), was a British loyalist who was rewarded for his constancy with appointment as the first bishop of Nova Scotia.[39] Both the fifth and sixth rectors, Samuel Provoost and Benjamin Moore, had served simultaneously as rector of the parish and bishop of New York. It was extremely likely that an assistant minister at Trinity would one day succeed Moore as bishop.

Trinity Church was a large parish with several assistants, however, so that one needed a public following to be the favored candidate. Whether by design or chance, Hobart found in the episcopacy an important public platform. He wrote a pamphlet on the merits of the Episcopal church, a copy of which fell into the hands of John M. Mason (1770–1829). Mason, a Reformed divine instrumental in the formation of Union Seminary, was the editor of the *Christian's Magazine*. Searching for a topic of public interest, he reopened the episcopacy

controversy by criticizing Hobart's pamphlet. Hobart responded with
a series of articles of his own. These were later collected and published
as *An Apology for Apostolic Order.*[40]

The effect of Hobart's advocacy for apostolic order was to tip the
balance of White's formula for assurance of salvation in favor of baptism. Theologically the episcopacy had little bearing on Hobart's view
of the renewed life, but it had an important tie to his understanding of
the baptismal covenant. If the episcopacy was a necessary element for
the existence of the church, and if baptism was the entrance into the
church, might not the episcopacy be a necessary part of the baptismal
covenant? Hobart strongly hinted that it was so and discouraged participation in ecumenical events and organizations with denominations
that lacked the vital component. He suggested that to join the covenant in the way in which Christ ordained, one must enter the community in which his duly chosen representatives—the bishops in apostolic succession—were found.

For Hobart the renewed life was the second element in the pursuit
of assurance. One joined the apostolic church in baptism, and then, as
a natural though not inevitable result, one came to live the renewed
life.

Hobart's single-minded advocacy of the episcopacy proved to have
the desired effect on his career. When Benjamin Moore's declining
health created the need to elect an assistant bishop, Hobart was chosen. Consecrated in 1811, Hobart used his episcopal prestige and authority to extend his own views and influence. He sought and helped
to secure parish positions for those who held a high view of the episcopacy and questioned the validity of other Protestant denominations.
He discouraged those who did not and even rid himself of their influence by finding positions outside his diocese for some of them. For
example, when Hobart became convinced that Gregory Townsend Bedell (1793–1834) questioned his ban on ecumenical organizations, he
withdrew an offer of an assistantship and suggested Bedell's name to a
vestryman from Fayetteville, North Carolina.[41]

Hobart's influence might be gauged best by the success of those who
served as his assistants. Six were later elected bishops: Thomas C.
Brownell (1792–1865), bishop of Connecticut; Jonathan M. Wainwright
(1792–1854), provisional bishop of New York; George Upfold (1796–
1872), bishop of Indiana; William DeLancy (1797–1856), bishop of
western New York; Benjamin T. Onderdonk (1791–1861), bishop of

New York; and George Washington Doane (1799–1859), bishop of New Jersey. In addition to these assistants, two other future bishops were within Hobart's circle of influence: Levi Silliman Ives (1797–1867), who was his son-in-law; and Henry U. Onderdonk (1791–1861), the brother of Hobart's assistant Benjamin.[42]

Hobart also left his mark on the first Episcopal theological seminary. In 1813 he became convinced that a seminary was needed to provide clergy for his diocese. Theological seminaries were relatively new institutions at the time; a group of Congregationalists had founded the first three-year postgraduate Protestant seminary at Andover, Massachusetts, just five years earlier. Nonetheless Hobart was not the only Episcopalian to recognize the importance of such institutions. In 1814 Christopher Gadsden (1785–1852), later the bishop of South Carolina, suggested that the General Convention establish and control a single national seminary. Hobart resisted at first, wanting an institution exclusively under his own supervision, but financial considerations eventually softened his opposition. Wealthy builder Jacob Sherrod, who died in 1821, left money in his 1821 will with the stipulation that it be used for a "general" seminary in the city of New York. The General Theological Seminary was established as provided for by the will, but Hobart was able to gain a desired concession. His assistant, Benjamin T. Onderdonk, was entrusted with the teaching of ecclesiastical polity at the new institution.[43]

Onderdonk's presence on the faculty guaranteed proper emphasis on the episcopate, but the addition of another member of the faculty ensured that the tie to Bishop White would be strong. Bird Wilson (1777–1859) would teach systematic divinity from the founding of the General Theological Seminary until 1850, when he retired. Wilson had studied theology with Bishop White. Like Hobart, he remained a lifelong friend of the bishop. His most notable publication was a biography of White, and were it not for a few votes, he would have been elected to succeed White as bishop of Pennsylvania. Not only would Wilson teach from the texts listed by White in 1804, as the charter required, but he also would add works by White written after that date. The students who attended General Seminary received White's theology from Wilson, with Hobart's added emphasis on the episcopate coming from Onderdonk.

Wilson taught the General Seminary students who in time came to be the professors of divinity in a second generation of seminaries with a high-church orientation. William Adams (1813–97) of the class of 1841 joined several of his classmates to found Nashotah Theological Seminary in Wisconsin in 1842; he would teach divinity at the institution until the last decade of the century. John Williams (1817–99), who entered General Seminary with the class of 1838 but did not graduate, held the chair of systematic divinity at Berkeley Divinity School in Connecticut from the time of the school's separation from Trinity College in 1854 until the 1890s. Solon W. Manney (d. 1869) and Samuel Buel (1815–92), both of the class of 1837, taught divinity at Seabury Theological Seminary in Minnesota (founded in 1860), as did John Steinfort Kedney (1819–1911), who graduated from General Seminary in 1841.

When Wilson retired, his position was filled from the ranks of his former students. Samuel Roosevelt Johnson (1802–73), a graduate of the class of 1823 and the brother of the school's first graduate, and Samuel Buel, who had taught at Seabury, successively filled the chair of divinity from 1850 until 1888.[44]

Hobart's powerful personality, his skill as a writer and polemicist, the pervasive influence of his former assistants, and his influence on the General Theological Seminary combined to make his theological stance the standard for the high-church party in the first half of the nineteenth century. Borrowing the two sources of assurance from Bishop White, but adding his own emphasis on the episcopacy, he taught that one was assured of salvation because of entrance into the baptismal covenant in a church with apostolic succession and because of the adult renewal that followed. It is not surprising that historians have begun to refer to the pre–Civil War high-church theology as the "Hobartian Synthesis" or "Hobartian High-Churchmanship."[45]

Evangelical Episcopalians

In the sessions of the General Convention after 1804 White witnessed the rising influence not only of Hobart and the group of high-church Episcopalians who rallied around him but also of a second group who called themselves evangelicals. Initially smaller and less well organized, the evangelicals benefited from dissatisfaction with Hobart. Meeting at General Convention sessions and elsewhere, they soon formed a bloc to balance Hobart's high-church party. The high-church Episcopalians had found their geographical center in New York. For the evangelicals, Washington, Maryland, and Virginia provided a similar kind of center. Although never the sole area of evangelical activity, this region served as a communication center and meeting point for evangelical Episcopalians from throughout the country, particularly in the years prior to the Civil War.

The evangelicals were in many ways like the countervailing high-church party. They, too, were indebted to Bishop White for their understanding of Episcopal authors and doctrine. They matured in a denomination of which White was the clearly identifiable leader. Like their high-church colleagues, they accepted White's premise about the sources of assurance but altered White's careful balance between the baptismal covenant and adult renewal.

High-church Episcopalians assigned a priority to the baptismal covenant and emphasized the difference between the Episcopal church and other Protestants groups. Evangelicals adopted the complementary approach, giving priority to adult renewal. Since adult faith was the major preoccupation for nineteenth-century Protestants, evangelicals were able to affirm their basic unity with members of other denominations. They rejected Hobart's opposition to ecumenical organizations, and, while claiming that apostolic succession was the best form of church government, they denied that episcopal ordination was necessary for valid baptism.

William H. Wilmer (1782–1827) was a conspicuous member of this evangelical party. Eleven years younger than Hobart, he was among the first to prepare for the ministry after the adoption of the Course of Ecclesiastical Studies in 1804. As Wilmer's *Episcopal Manual* of 1815 would demonstrate, he took seriously the theological texts chosen by White.[46]

White was acquainted with the Wilmer family long before he met William. In 1785 he had met William's uncle, Maryland clergyman James J. Wilmer, a deputy to the first session of the middle states General Convention. William's older brother, Simon, was a priest as well and a regular fixture at the General Convention, appearing at every meeting from 1808 to 1820.[47]

Bishop Claggett of Maryland ordained William Wilmer in 1808. That same year the General Convention met in Baltimore. Local clergy were invited to attend, and it is likely that Wilmer was there.[48] He passed up the 1811 convention in New Haven but attended every other General Convention meeting during his life. In 1817 he was elected president of the House of Deputies, a position he held until his death.

Richard Channing Moore (1762–1841) also attended the convention of 1808. A deputy from New York, he would be less than comfortable with the rising fortunes of John Henry Hobart. Moore would support Trinity assistant Cave Jones (1769–1829) rather than Hobart in the election for bishop in 1811. Hobart won; Moore, on the other hand, was not elected to return to the General Convention in that year. In 1814 Wilmer would have little trouble in convincing Moore to leave New York for the greener pastures of Wilmer's area.

An important element in Hobart's success as a party leader lay in his ability to provide jobs for sympathetic clergy. The state of New York offered both an urban center with a number of well-established parishes and an expanding western field for missions. Wilmer would recognize a similar potential in his own area. Maryland and Virginia both had established churches before the Revolution. The war had ended the establishment of the Church of England, and subsequent legislation in Virginia had led to the loss of some of the larger holdings of church land. A number of parishes that could support clergy remained, however. There had been no strong leadership in the Virginia church since the war, for Bishop Madison proved to be more interested in the College of William and Mary than in the diocese under his charge. Few new clergy had been ordained, so that retirement or lack of interest had left a number of vacancies. The church in Maryland had benefited from stronger leadership and from the attention of several clergy who had moved from Pennsylvania, but there was in Maryland, as in Virginia, possible employment for clergy. Between Maryland and Virginia lay the District of Columbia, a growing city with a need for new churches and the allure of a national capital.

In 1812 Wilmer was called to serve as rector of St. Paul's, Alexandria. Now in the diocese of Virginia, he soon befriended William Meade (1789–1862), a young clergyman who shared his evangelical views. Bishop Madison died in 1812, and the two men convinced the clergy of the state that they should pass over John Bracken (1747–1818), Madison's successor as the president of the College of William and Mary, and choose Richard Channing Moore of New York as bishop instead.[49] Moore was consecrated in 1814.

The diocese of Maryland also elected an assistant bishop in 1814. Evangelicals there hoped to duplicate the accomplishment of their counterparts in Virginia, but their candidate, George Dashiell, lost to James Kemp (1764–1827), who had high-church sympathies. Dashiell was not a gracious loser. He challenged the legality of the election, and when the challenge failed and he found himself the object of charges of immorality, he withdrew from the Episcopal church to form his own small denomination. Only three other evangelical clergy followed.[50] The whole episode embarrassed and discredited the Maryland evangelicals who remained within the Episcopal church. They would never again approach the numerical strength needed to elect an evangelical candidate for bishop. Nonetheless, despite episcopal displeasure and their status as a minority, evangelicals would remain a viable element within the diocese of Maryland.

Virginia and Maryland evangelicals found open positions for like-minded clergy. In many cases clergy or candidates for ordination who were unhappy with Hobart's leadership came from New York or New England. Bishop Moore persuaded Benjamin Allen (1787–1829) and his brother Thomas G. Allen to leave New York for Virginia.[51] Stephen H. Tyng (1800–1885) applied first to Hobart for a job before coming to Washington in search of placement.[52] John P. K. Henshaw (1792–1852) left New England to accept a call from St. Peter's Church in Baltimore. Reuel Keith (1792–1842) moved to Virginia because of health.[53] Charles Pettit McIlvaine (1799–1873) followed his father, a U.S. senator, to Washington.

Bishop White shared many of the convictions of the growing evangelical bloc. With them he doubted the absolute necessity of the episcopate for the church and the wisdom of Hobart's ecumenical ban. In New York Hobart forbade his clergy to join an interdenominational Bible society; in Philadelphia Bishop White served as an officer of a similar organization.

At the same time, there were some differences of opinion between White and the evangelicals. White did not share their enthusiasm for revivalistic methods of promoting renewal. Nonetheless he encouraged and supported the evangelical clergy, just as he had the high-church clergy. It was to White that James Milnor (1773–1845), a congressman who became interested in the evangelical movement while in Washington, turned for assistance when he decided to enter the ordained ministry, and it was as White's assistant that Milnor's new ministry began.[54] It was White who came to the defense of Stephen H. Tyng when the latter came under attack for his Sunday evening prayer services.[55] It was with White that Wilmer worked as president of the House of Deputies. It was, as was already mentioned, also White who drafted the list of texts with which those evangelical clergy who studied after 1804 prepared themselves for the ordained ministry.

The evangelical clergy recognized the value of a theological seminary, but they were not anxious to devote their wholehearted efforts to a national seminary in Hobart's backyard. While paying lip service to the cause of the General Seminary, they went about forming their own institution. After unsuccessful attempts in Maryland and in Williamsburg, the evangelicals founded the Protestant Episcopal Theological Seminary in Virginia in 1823.[56] White's influence pervaded the school. Wilmer, who was chosen the first professor of divinity, reported to the board of trustees after his first year of classes. Wilmer himself was a trustee; the other clerical members were Bishop Moore, William Meade, Reuel Keith, and John S. Ravenscroft (1772–1830), who would later be bishop of North Carolina. Wilmer told them that his students had read from Burnet and Pearson and that he was following White's list of recommended texts. The board approved his report and adopted a regulation by which only the books on White's list could be used unless faculty approval was obtained and advance notice given.[57]

Wilmer did not long hold the chair of systematic divinity. Reuel Keith, the first full-time professor of the seminary and originally a teacher of biblical studies, gradually moved into teaching in that area. After Keith's death in 1842, William Sparrow (1801–74) took over.

Like the General Seminary, Virginia Seminary, as the evangelical school was commonly called, inspired the formation of other schools of similar orientation. In 1832 Charles McIlvaine, the second bishop of Ohio, brought the theology department of Kenyon College, which had been founded in 1824 by his predecessor Bishop Philander Chase (1775–1853), firmly into the evangelical fold. The three most important professors of divinity at Kenyon were William Sparrow, Thomas Mather Smith (1796–1864), and John J. McElhinney (1810 or 1811–95). Sparrow and McElhinney later moved to positions at Virginia Seminary.

When the Civil War effectively closed Virginia Seminary to northern students, evangelicals in Pennsylvania founded the Philadelphia Divinity School (1862), calling James May (1805–63), who had been the professor of ecclesiastical history and polity at Virginia, to teach divinity. After an early death he was replaced by Daniel Raynes Goodwin (1811–90), who would hold the chair of divinity until the 1880s.

Massachusetts evangelicals, in turn, called John Seeley Stone (1795–

1882), a respected evangelical who had lectured at Philadelphia, to be the first professor of divinity at the Episcopal Theological School (1867).[58]

With a geographical base in the Washington area, a seminary of their own, and increasing numbers of clergy, the members of the evangelical party began to enjoy a success in advancement similar to that of Hobart's assistants. Meade, McIlvaine, and Henshaw were elected bishops of Virginia (1829), Ohio (1832), and Rhode Island (1843), respectively. Wilmer was elected president of William and Mary in 1826, and had not death ended his career in 1827, he would certainly have been elected bishop as well. Tyng would follow Milnor as rector of the increasingly important St. George's Church, New York.

~

In the second and third decades of the nineteenth century, Bishop White lived to see the formation of two interest groups within the church over which he had so long presided. Younger Episcopalians, sensing the tension in White's dual insistence on the baptismal covenant and the adult experience of personal renewal as the grounds for assurance, sought to establish a clear emphasis. Hobart and the high-church party argued for greater emphasis on the baptismal covenant and therefore on the distinctive nature of the church. Wilmer, Meade, and Moore argued for greater emphasis on renewal.

The adherents of both parties were still strongly indebted to Bishop White. They shared his belief in a double source of assurance. Their leaders were in regular communication with him. All the clergy who prepared for the ministry after 1804 studied under the provisions of White's course. The seminaries adopted White's list as the basis for their teaching. They turned to White and his *Memoirs* for their recollections of their denomination's history. They were all White's theological children.

NOTES

1. John F. Woolverton, "Philadelphia's William White: Accommodation in the Post-Revolutionary Period," *Historical Magazine of the Protestant Episcopal Church* 43 (Dec. 1974): 281–82.

2. Ibid.

3. For a discussion of the ways in which clergy were selected for Anglican congregations during the colonial era, see Borden W. Painter, "The Anglican

Vestry in Colonial America" (Ph.D. diss., Yale University, 1965). Virginia vestries chose their own rectors. In Maryland the governor made the choice. In Pennsylvania and many of the remaining colonies the bishop of London and an English missionary society that provided funds for clergy salaries (the Society for the Propagation of the Gospel in Foreign Parts) exercised considerable influence over clergy choices. The influence of the society and of the bishops of London was effectively ended by the onset of the Revolution, however. The Virginia pattern would then prevail.

4. Bird Wilson, *Memoir of the Life of the Right Reverend William White, D. D., Bishop of the Protestant Episcopal Church in the State of Pennsylvania* (Philadelphia: James Kay, Jun., and Brother, 1839), 62.

5. William White, *The Case of the Episcopal Churches Considered*, in *Readings from the History of the Episcopal Church*, ed. Robert W. Prichard, 61–80 (Wilton, Conn.: Morehouse-Barlow, 1986).

6. S. D. McConnell, *History of the American Episcopal Church from the Planting of the Colonies to the End of the Civil War* (New York: Thomas Whittaker, 1890), 245.

7. Peter Hall, ed., *Reliquiae Liturgicae: Documents Connected with the Liturgy of the Church of England*, vol. 5, *The American Prayer Book* (Bath: Binns and Goodwin, 1847), 260–70.

8. William White, *Memoirs of the Protestant Episcopal Church* (New York: E. P. Dutton, 1880), 120.

9. Massey Hamilton Shepherd, *The Oxford American Prayer Book Commentary* (New York: Oxford University Press, 1973), xv. Shepherd characterized the attitude of the church's rank and file toward the *Proposed Book* as "cool" and that of New England church leaders as "distinctly hostile." Shepherd did note, however, that the effort in 1785 was "not entirely fruitless." Some elements of the book "were incorporated into the final draft of the Book [of Common Prayer] of 1789."

More recently, Marion Hatchett has expanded this latter judgment about the influence of the *Proposed Book* on the 1789 Book of Common Prayer. While recognizing that the *Proposed Book* was never widely used, he argues that it did serve as the initial draft with which the members of the General Convention would work in 1789. See *The Making of the First American Book of Common Prayer* (New York: Seabury, 1982).

10. Letter from Charles Miller to William White dated January 8, 1786, printed in Wilson, *White*, 329–36.

11. A change in English law was required in order to consecrate clergy without an oath of allegiance to George III. In August of 1784, Parliament allowed for that omission in the ordination of deacons and priests, and two candidates from Maryland were ordained.

Members of Parliament were not yet willing to make a similar allowance for the consecration of bishops, however. The Episcopal clergy of Connecticut had elected Seabury, but they had done so in a secret meeting without lay involvement. Moreover the state of Connecticut had an established Congregational church. Seabury, who had been in England since 1783, was unwilling to await further parliamentary action. He went to Scotland, where he was consecrated by nonjuring bishops, the successors to the Scottish bishops who had been displaced in 1689 by William and Mary's decision to accept a presbyterian government in the Church of Scotland.

In 1786 Parliament adopted further legislation providing for the consecration of three bishops for the middle states.

For a discussion of the organization of the Episcopal church and the reunion of the Connecticut and middle states bodies, see Robert W. Prichard, *A History of the Episcopal Church* (Harrisburg, Pa.: Morehouse, 1991), 73–103.

12. William Smith had shared much of the leadership with White early on, but he suffered from alcoholism that limited his effectiveness as a leader. Elected bishop of Maryland, Smith was not consecrated because of questions about his character.

13. The middle states convention had been a unicameral body. A separate body, the House of Bishops, was created in 1789 as one of the conditions for Bishop Seabury's participation in the General Convention.

14. Clara O. Loveland, *The Critical Years: The Reconstitution of the Anglican Church in the United States of America, 1780–1789* (Greenwich, Conn.: Seabury, 1956), 279–83.

15. White, *Memoirs*, 192–94, 213.

16. William Stevens Perry, ed., *Journals of General Conventions of the Protestant Episcopal Church in the United States, 1785–1835*, 3 vols. (Claremont, N.H.: Claremont Manufacturing, 1874), 1:231–34.

17. Arthur Pierce Middleton, "Prayer Book Revision Explained: Sermons on the Liturgy by Joseph Bend, Rector of St. Paul's, Baltimore, 1791–1812," *Anglican and Episcopal History* 60 (Mar. 1991): 58.

18. William B. Sprague, *Annals of the American Pulpit: Or Commemorative Notices of Distinguished American Clergymen of Various Denominations from the Early Settlement of the Country to the Close of the Year Eighteen Hundred and Fifty-five with Historical Introductions*, 9 vols. (New York: Robert Carter and Brothers, 1857–1869), 5:353–55. Bend had attended the General Convention meeting of 1789 as a deputy from Pennsylvania.

19. William Berrian, introductory memoir to John Henry Hobart, *The Posthumous Works of the Late Right-Reverend John Henry Hobart, D.D., Bishop of the Protestant Episcopal Church in the State of New York*, 3 vols. (New York: Swords, Standford, 1833), 1:5–15, 34–67, 76.

20. Parker, a New England clergyman who was sympathetic to the middle states convention, had played an important role in 1789; see Loveland, *Critical Years,* 236–72 and 287–88.

21. White, *Memoirs,* 213.

22. For a text of the Thirty-nine Articles, see *The Book of Common Prayer and Administration of the Sacraments and Other Rites and Ceremonies of the Church, together with the Psalter or Psalms of David, according to the Use of the Episcopal Church* (New York: Church Hymnal, 1979), 867–76. The best historical commentary on the articles was written in the nineteenth century by Charles Hardwick: *A History of the Articles of Religion: to Which Is Added a Series of Documents, from* A.D. *1536 to* A.D. *1615; together with Illustrations from Contemporary Sources* (Philadelphia: H. Hooker, 1852).

23. Perry, *Journals, 1785–1835,* 1:273.

24. Ibid., 1:266–68, 279–80.

25. Ibid., 1:264, 266, 276.

26. Ibid., 1:268.

27. Ibid., 1:315–20.

28. Another designated text, George Prettyman Tomline's *Elements of Christian Theology,* was a two-volume work whose second volume did contain a commentary on the articles. The second volume was never published in the United States, however, and White's comment on it makes it unlikely that he knew of or intended that section of the second volume. "Works of this sort," he wrote, were "principally confined to arrangement" of material "from the Scripture" (Perry, *Journals, 1785–1835,* 1:317). This is an accurate description of the first volume, but not of the second.

29. Samuel Seabury III was one who was able to obtain a copy of Stackhouse; the copy, which he read in 1820, may have been from the library of Bishop Seabury, who was his grandfather. See *Moneygripe's Apprentice: The Personal Narrative of Samuel Seabury III,* ed. Robert Bruce Mullin (New Haven, Conn.: Yale University Press, 1989), 130, 132.

30. Perry, *Journals, 1785–1835,* 1:317. The textbooks in the remaining six of White's categories—apologetics, biblical studies, ecclesiastical history, homiletics, liturgics, and pastoral theology—are of secondary interest in this work. I refer to them only insofar as they shed light on the theological issues under discussion in the divinity texts. Thus, for example, William Sherlock's (1641–1707) works on eschatology, listed by White in an appendix of "devotional and practical" reading, are discussed in chapter 5 because of their pertinence to Pearson's discussion of death.

For a general treatment of the books on the reading list, see George L. Blackman, *Faith and Freedom: A Study of Theological Education and the Episcopal Theological School* (New York: Seabury, 1967).

31. Henry F. May has used the terms *Moderate Enlightenment* and *Skep-*

tical Enlightenment to contrast the attitudes of these seventeenth- and eighteenth-century authors; see his *Enlightenment in America* (New York: Oxford
University Press, 1976).

Many of the specific seventeenth-century authors that White chose were
those who have been commonly designated as "latitudinarian." The term has
had negative connotations in many church histories written since the 1870s,
but some authors are now calling for a reexamination. See Donald Green,
"Latitudinarism Reconsidered: A Review Essay," *Anglican and Episcopal
History* 62 (June 1993): 159–74.

32. *Journal of the Proceedings of the Bishops, Clergy and Laity of the Protestant Episcopal Church in the United States of America, Assembled in a General Convention* (Printed for the Convention, 1890), 748.

33. *A Catechism of the Thirty-nine Articles of the Protestant Episcopal
Church* (Baltimore: James Young, 1846), 3.

34. Ibid., 26.

35. Other authors have called attention to this ambiguity in White's
thought; see, for example, Harvey Hill, "Worship in the Ecclesiology of William White," *Anglican and Episcopal History* 62 (Sept. 1993): 319–20.

36. Several recent works devoted to nineteenth-century Episcopal theology have focused on this distinctiveness. See, for example, Robert Bruce Mullin, *Episcopal Vision/American Reality: High Church Theology and Social
Thought in Evangelical America* (New Haven, Conn.: Yale University Press,
1986); and Richard Rankin, *Ambivalent Churchmen and Evangelical Churchwomen: The Religion of the Episcopal Elite in North Carolina, 1800–1860*
(Columbia: University of South Carolina Press, 1993).

37. See Carl Bridenbaugh, *Mitre and Sceptre: Transatlantic Faiths, Ideas,
Personalities, and Politics, 1689–1775* (Oxford: Oxford University Press,
1962), for a description of the pre-Revolutionary debates in New York.

38. Berrian, memoir to Hobart's *Works*, 1:71.

39. Philip Carrington, *The Anglican Church in Canada* (Toronto: Collins,
1963), 46.

40. John Henry Hobart, *An Apology for Apostolic Order and Its Advocates, in a Series of Letters Addressed to the Rev. John M. Mason*, 3d ed. (New
York: Standford and Swords, 1844).

41. Stephen H. Tyng, biographical sketch to Gregory T. Bedell, *Sermons
by the Rev. Gregory T. Bedell, D. D., Rector of St. Andrew's Church, Philadelphia*, 2 vols. (Philadelphia: William Stavely, John C. Pechin, 1835), 1:xlii–
xliii.

42. Michael Taylor Malone, "Levi Silliman Ives: Priest, Bishop, Tractarian, and Roman Catholic" (Ph.D. diss., Duke University, 1970), 10.

43. See Powel Mills Dawley, *The Story of the General Theological Seminary: A Sesquicentennial History, 1817–1967* (New York: Oxford University

Press, 1969), for details. For a brief period before the Sherrod bequest there were two competing schools: a diocesan seminary established by Hobart and a General Convention seminary. The latter began in New York City but moved briefly to Connecticut. The two combined to form the General Theological Seminary.

44. Here and in all subsequent discussions of Episcopal seminaries, I limit my remarks to those institutions that were strong enough to survive until the twentieth century. Other, less-successful efforts in the period before 1874 include Ravensworth Seminary (Columbia, Tenn.), the theological department of Jubilee College (Ill.), the diocesan seminary in South Carolina (Camden), the theological department of Griswold College (Dubuque, Iowa), Nebraska Divinity School, DeLancy Divinity School (Geneva, N.Y.), and the theological department of Burlington College (N.J.). The Theological School in Lexington, Kentucky, which failed at midcentury, was revived in 1951. The School of Theology of the University of the South (Sewanee, Tenn.), although planned before 1860, did not have its first dean until 1878.

45. Mullin, *Episcopal Vision,* 60; Rankin, *Ambivalent Churchmen,* 79.

46. William H. Wilmer, *The Episcopal Manual: A Summary Explanation of the Doctrine, Discipline, and Worship of the Protestant Episcopal Church, in the United States of America,* new and improved ed., ed. John Coleman (Philadelphia: R. S. George, 1841), 57, 106.

47. Sprague, *Annals,* 5:515–19.

48. Perry, *Journals, 1785–1835,* 1:339.

49. David L. Holmes, "The Revival," in Interdiocesan Bicentennial Committee of the Virginias, ed., *Up from Independence: The Episcopal Church in Virginia,* 78–85 (Orange, Va.: Green Publishers for the Interdiocesan Bicentennial Committee of the Virginias, 1976).

50. Diana Hochstedt Butler, *Standing against the Whirlwind: The Evangelical Episcopalians in Nineteenth-Century America* (New York: Oxford University Press, 1995), 14.

51. Thomas G. Allen, *Memoir of the Rev. Benjamin Allen, Late Rector of St. Paul's Church, Philadelphia* (Philadelphia: Latimer, 1832), 93.

52. Charles Rockland Tyng, *Record of the Life and Work of the Rev. Stephen Higginson Tyng, D. D. and History of St. George's Church, New York to the Close of His Rectorship* (New York: E. P. Dutton, 1890), 51.

53. Joseph Packard, *Recollections of a Long Life* (Washington, D.C.: Byron S. Adams, 1902), 94.

54. John S. Stone, *A Memoir of the Life of James Milnor, D.D., Late Rector of St. George's Church, New York* (New York: American Tract Society, 1840), 200–201.

55. Tyng, *S. H. Tyng,* 93–94.

56. W. A. R. Goodwin, *History of the Theological Seminary in Virginia and*

Its Historical Background, 2 vols. (New York: Edwin S. Gorham, 1923), 1:120–46.

57. Ibid., 2:595–96.

58. The Philadelphia Divinity School and the Episcopal Theological School merged in 1974 to become the Episcopal Divinity School of Cambridge, Massachusetts.

2 PREDESTINATION

THE STUDENT following Bishop White's Course of Ecclesiastical Studies had to come to terms with Gilbert Burnet, whose *Exposition of the Thirty-nine Articles* was the main commentary on the Articles of Religion to which American candidates for the ministry were exposed. The articles were the official statement of theology of the American Episcopal church; Burnet was the only officially designated interpreter of their meaning.

In his introduction Burnet made clear to his readers what he personally believed to be the most important element of his work: "There is no part of this whole work, in which I have laboured with more care, and have writ in more uncommon method, than concerning *predestination*. For, as my small reading had carried me further in that controversy than in any other whatsoever, both with relation to ancients and moderns, and to the most esteemed books in all the different parties; so I weighed the Articles with that impartial care that I thought became me; and have taken a method, which is, for aught I know, new."[1] Burnet regarded his discussion of the seventeenth article, which was on predestination, as the portion of his volume that made the greatest contribution to Anglican scholarship.

As the student quickly learned, Burnet's claim to novelty rested on his moderation. Following decades of commentators who proclaimed earnestly that the Church of England was bound to either a Calvinist or an Arminian understanding of predestination, Burnet suggested that the language of the articles permitted either position. Most Anglicans readily embraced the latitude that Burnet allowed.

Burnet had declared in the introduction to the *Exposition of the Thirty-nine Articles*, however, that he personally adhered to neither the Arminian nor the Calvinist understanding of predestination. He subscribed to a third position, which he characterized as a more ancient Greek view that presumably was also allowed by the language of the Thirty-nine Articles.[2] This aspect of his argument did not receive the same immediate attention as did his call for toleration of Calvinist and Arminian views. By the nineteenth century, however, a number of Anglicans began to explore this third approach. One such individual was Richard Laurence (1760–1838), who was the archbishop of Cashel in the Church of Ireland. Laurence used the 1805 Bampton lecture to describe a more ancient view of predestination to which he believed the English reformers had subscribed.

In America Bishop White, fascinated by Laurence's argument, produced his own commentary on predestination. White, Laurence, and Burnet could not agree on the precise content of the more ancient view they promoted, however, so that theological students did not readily adopt a third view until the 1860s, when a new English commentary on the Thirty-nine Articles by Edward Harold Browne appeared in the United States. Browne authoritatively summarized the half-century debate since Laurence advanced his version of a view to which Brown gave the title "ecclesiastical election." During the latter half of the nineteenth century most Episcopal theological students read both Burnet's argument on neutrality and Browne's explanation for that neutrality.

The theological student who read Burnet, or Burnet and Browne, was in one sense extremely fortunate. Burnet's moderation helped to shield members of the Episcopal church from the serious division over predestination that characterized not only the seventeenth-century Anglican church but also many of the American Protestant churches of the nineteenth century.

BISHOP WHITE AND GILBERT BURNET

Bishop White had not chosen Gilbert Burnet's *Exposition of the Thirty-nine Articles* for the Course of Studies of 1804 casually. He designated the English work both out of an awareness of the historical divisiveness of the predestination issue and out of an appreciation for Burnet's success in dealing with that division. White's choice would help to spare American Episcopalians from the predestination controversies so often found among their fellow Protestants.

The Divisive Issue

In 1801, the year the General Convention adopted the Thirty-nine Articles, White presided over a church whose members were in wide disagreement over the issue of predestination. The presence in America of a large number of Congregationalists, Presbyterians, and Reformed Christians, who advocated a Calvinist understanding of predestination, and the possibility of rewriting the Thirty-nine Articles threatened to reopen the Calvinist-Arminian division that had been resolved for most members of the Church of England. There were advocates of both a more explicitly Calvinist and a more explicitly Arminian position for the church at the convention. In addition there were those who favored an eighteenth-century interpretation of predestination known as nationalism. Still others suggested that the church should take no stance on the issue.

The inability of the advocates of these four positions to reach a consensus was the primary obstacle to the adoption of the articles in 1785–89 and the reason for the delay in the efforts of Ashbel Baldwin and William Walter in the House of Deputies in 1799. Had he been unable to bridge these differences in 1801, White would have faced the prospect of future divisions in his flock.

Episcopal Calvinists   Uzal Ogden (1744–1822), the rector of Trinity Church, Newark, was the most prominent Calvinist at the early sessions of the General Convention. Like White, he had been a participant in the earliest efforts to organize an American Episcopal church. Unlike White, however, he had been a supporter of the Anglican phase of the Great Awakening, which had begun about 1760.[3]

In common with most of the colonial Anglican supporters of the awakening, Ogden did not initially differentiate between the Calvinism of Whitefield and the Arminianism of John Wesley. He preached in both Presbyterian and Methodist churches.[4] When that difference became clear to him, however, his sympathies lay with the Calvinist side of the argument.[5]

Ogden's position was one with considerable historical precedent. Not only was the belief that God predestined certain persons to respond to his love and receive everlasting life a biblical doctrine, but it was also a position that had been embraced to a greater or lesser degree by all the major Reformation groups. Anglicans had adopted a statement on predestination in 1553 as the seventeenth article of King Edward VI's Forty-two Articles and had reaffirmed the position as the seventeenth article of Queen Elizabeth's Thirty-nine Articles. The first paragraph of Elizabeth's article declared:

> Predestination to Life is the everlasting purpose of God, whereby (before the foundations of the world were laid) he hath constantly decreed by his counsel secret to us, to deliver from curse and damnation those whom he hath chosen in Christ out of mankind, and to bring them by Christ to everlasting salvation, as vessels made to honour. Wherefore, they which be endued with so excellent a benefit of God, be called according to God's purpose by his Spirit working in due season: they through Grace obey the calling: they be justified freely: they be made sons of God by adoption: they be made like the image of his only-begotten Son Jesus Christ: they walk religiously in good works, and at length, by God's mercy, they attain everlasting felicity.[6]

The position was a logical inference from the doctrine of grace. If individuals were saved by grace alone and not by their own merit, only God could have determined who was to be saved.

Objections to this doctrine came not so much from alternative readings of the same passages of Scripture as from an awareness of the practical implications of such a doctrine. The Christians of the first generation of the Reformation found a belief in predestination, as the seventeenth article had gone on to say, "full of sweet, pleasant, and unspeakable comfort."[7] They had undergone the concrete experience of leaving the Roman Catholic fold and were able to see their departure as a sign of God's election. God had called out of the corrupt church those whom he chose to save. Once denominational lines stabilized, however, and most new members came from birth rather than conversion, individuals could no longer point to the concrete experience of leaving what they regarded as a corrupt church. Reared in a church from birth, the second-generation Protestant did not know exactly how to be sure of election.

Most Reformed theologians and some theologians of the Church of England, such as William Perkins (1558–1602), came to regard such questions as signs of backsliding. Any doubt about election was the result of inadequate faith and self-examination. In 1619 representatives of the major Reformed churches of Europe gathered in Holland at the

Synod of Dort and adopted a rigid predestinarian document, declaring that the "saving efficacy" of Christ's death extended only to the elect, that God called the elect "effectually" (i.e., irresistibly), and that for the elect there was a "certainty of perseverance."[8] Nineteenth-century Christians referred to the doctrines endorsed at Dort as "Calvinism," a somewhat misleading label since the synod was held fifty-five years after John Calvin's death. Dort rejected the alternative explanation known from the works of Jacob Arminius (1554–1609) as "Arminianism." The advocates of the Arminian view believed that God elected those "'who repent[ed] and believe[d] in Christ'" but did so on the basis of "'foreknowledge of . . . which persons should believe according to the administration of [word and sacrament].'"[9]

Anglican representatives sent by James I did sign the first of the articles adopted at Dort. Despite the interest of a number of Anglicans, however, the Church of England never officially adopted the statement. On the contrary, James's son, Charles I, turned to an Arminian, William Laud (1573–1645), as his choice for the archbishopric of Canterbury. The Calvinist sympathizers, predominantly members of the Puritan party, gained control of Parliament and in the years of interregnum replaced the Thirty-nine Articles by adopting the Westminster Confession, which followed the tenets of Dort on predestination.[10]

With their return to power in 1660, the English monarchs restored the Thirty-nine Articles, and the Puritans were faced with the choice of abandoning their gains of the past twenty years or leaving the established church. Many left, forming the dissenting Presbyterian and Congregationalist churches, but some remained, continuing the thread of Calvinist Anglicanism. Such figures as Dr. John Edwards (1637–1717), George Whitefield, and Augustus Montague Toplady (1740–78; remembered for his hymn "Rock of Ages") would keep the tradition alive into the eighteenth century.

Uzal Ogden therefore had a long tradition to which to turn in advocating a Calvinist position. Ogden's hand was strengthened, moreover, by events within his own diocese. In August 1798 the New Jersey convention elected him bishop. The action of the diocesan convention needed only the approval of the General Convention before the consecration could take place.

If matters had proceeded at their accustomed rate, Ogden would have been consecrated a bishop in 1799, and White would have had a Calvinist within the relatively small House of Bishops. White was able to buy time with a stalling tactic, however. His brother-in-law, Robert Morris, joined with two others in the diocese in questioning the propriety of Ogden's election. Although they did not raise doubts about his moral character, they asked "how far the 'sufficiency in good learning' of the Rev. candidate may enable him to perform the duties of his station."[11] The phrase probably indicated a dissatisfaction with the nature of the learning that Ogden had acquired, not its level. The General Convention of 1799 sidestepped this complaint, however, and called for a new election based on a procedural question.[12] Ogden was again elected in New Jersey, but the issue had been postponed until the 1801 meeting of the General Convention.[13]

Episcopal Arminians   A sizable portion of the Episcopal clergy was Arminian in sympathy, particularly in areas in which there were significant numbers of Presbyterians and Congregationalists. Episcopal clergy in such areas often adopted an Arminian position to exploit a growing dissatisfaction with the Calvinism of the Westminster Confession. This tactic contributed to the church's growth in New England and the middle states.

Like the Calvinists, the Arminians had some historical justification for their position. Although the Thirty-nine Articles contained a predestinarian position with at least strong affinities with Calvinism, the Book of Common Prayer failed to emphasize the doctrine. The promises to the candidates in baptism, for example, were not explicitly conditional on God's previous election. Indeed, a note added to the Book of Common Prayer in 1662 explicitly rejected the idea, at least in the case of infants. The note declared that "it is certain by God's Word, that Children which are baptized, dying before they commit actual sin, are undoubtedly saved."[14] In addition the Anglican Church, from Laud onward, had been replete with Arminians. They held the prominent positions in the church, especially after the 1662 departure of the dissenting Puritans.

The apparent Calvinism of the seventeenth article remained an annoyance to the sizable number of Anglican Arminians. Dissenters in England, Presbyterians and Congregationalists in America, and Calvinists within the Anglican church itself all pointed to the article to suggest that Arminians were disloyal to the doctrine of their own denomination.

In the decade before the American Revolution, Thomas Bradbury

Chandler approached Samuel Seabury with a suggestion about a way to meet this charge of disloyalty. Both were advocates of an Arminian theology, and Chandler apparently believed that it would be possible to write a historical essay demonstrating that the church had never been Calvinist. Perhaps Seabury did not agree about the possibility of writing such an essay; in any case he never followed through with Chandler's suggestion.[15] When the Revolution made it possible for Americans to reconsider the status of the articles, Seabury chose a different tactic. He simply opposed their adoption.[16]

After Seabury's death in 1796, some fellow high-church clergy pursued a different strategy. The desire to correct the Episcopal church's position on predestination was one of the chief reasons that clerical deputies Ashbel Baldwin and William Walter called for revising the Thirty-nine Articles at the 1799 meeting of the General Convention. Although the Walter committee was unable to complete its work, it did prepare a proposed revision, which was printed in the convention's *Journal.* The revised article declared that predestination was "universal in intention," although "the wickedness of mankind . . . render[ed] it [partial] in . . . application."[17] God's call was neither effectual nor limited.

Like the election of Uzal Ogden for bishop, the newly rewritten seventeenth article would be an item for discussion at the General Convention meeting of 1801.

Advocates of Silence or Ambiguity   In addition to avowed Arminians and Calvinists, there was a sizable group of Episcopalians who felt that the wisest course of action was simply to avoid saying anything. The church should either adopt a nebulous statement that left its stance in doubt or refuse to make any statement on the issue.

The middle states General Convention of 1785 had chosen the first of these two opinions. Bishop White, who played a role in rewriting the Articles of Religion for the *Proposed Book,* which was authorized by that meeting of the convention, later characterized the rewritten form of the article as one that "professes to say something on the subject, yet in reality says nothing."[18] The article had begun "Predestination of life, with respect to every man's salvation, is the everlasting purpose of God, secret to us," but it had contained no further explanation of how the doctrine was to be understood.[19]

Like the Arminians and Calvinists, the advocate of silence could claim precedent in the Anglican tradition. Charles II, for example, had sought to deal with the predestination debate by outlawing public discussion. His approach met with at best only temporary success, however.[20]

The rewritten article of the 1785 convention had also been short-lived. It was set aside by two later events: the rejection of the *Proposed Book,* to which the articles were attached, and the union in 1789 with the New England Episcopalians, necessitating a readoption of church doctrine and discipline. Nonetheless, if one could characterize the mood that prevailed between 1789 and 1800 on the issue of predestination, it was one of silence or ambiguity. Many members at General Convention meetings during this period felt that the less said, the better.

Bishop White's Nationalism   In his *Memoirs of the Protestant Episcopal Church,* William White suggested that during the 1785 middle states' General Convention meeting he was neither an Arminian nor a Calvinist. He favored a position popularly known as nationalism. The theory, which later Anglicans would incorrectly attribute to John Locke (1632–1704), revolved around the interpretation of Romans 9, where St. Paul clearly advocated a doctrine of predestination.[21] In it Paul recalled the choice of Jacob over his brother Esau and the hardening of the pharaoh's heart to explain why God had chosen the Gentiles to receive Christ at a time when Jews had not uniformly accepted him: "What then are we to say? Is there injustice on God's part? By no means! For he says to Moses, 'I will have mercy on whom I have mercy, and I will have compassion on whom I have compassion.' So it depends not on human will or exertion, but on God who shows mercy. . . . He has mercy upon whomever he chooses, and he hardens the heart of whomever he chooses."[22] Most later interpreters would regard this passage as referring to God's choice of individuals. God selected the individual Jacob and rejected the individual Esau. He chose Moses and rejected the pharaoh. Nationalists believed that such interpreters misunderstood Paul. They argued that the use of individuals in the passage was intended only as illustrative. Paul's major concern was for nations and ethnic groups. What Paul wanted to know was why God had chosen the Gentiles and not used the nation of Israel as the sole vehicle of his glory. The whole discussion of personal predestination was therefore based on a false premise. God chose whole nations to hear his Gospel and to respond, while other nations did not hear the Gospel and thus lacked the possibility of an explicit response.

White felt in 1785 that this was the solution to the predestination
question. He was nevertheless aware that his opinion was not widely
held. Indeed, the only concrete action that the 1785 General Convention took was to reject nationalism. No one reading the article on predestination would have had the slightest clue as to whether Episcopalians were endorsing Arminianism or Calvinism; it was clear that the
article applied predestination to the individual, however, thereby elim-
inating a nationalist understanding. The article began "predestination
to life, with respect to every man's salvation."[23] Between 1785 and 1801
the sentiments in the church toward nationalism did not alter appre-
ciably. The opinion was no more popular in 1801 than it had been in
1785.

As the convention of 1801 approached, White was faced with dis-
comfiting prospects: the possibility of a Calvinist member of the House
of Bishops, the discussion of an Arminian rewriting of the Thirty-nine
Articles in the House of Deputies, and the absence of any noticeable
support for his nationalism.

A glance at other Protestant denominations could hardly be reassur-
ing. Methodists in the United Kingdom had divided into Calvinist and
Arminian branches in the eighteenth century. Presbyterians and Congregationalists in the United States argued whether the Calvinist doctrine of predestination proved to be an impediment to personal conversion. A group of "new" elements—New Side Presbyterians, New
Light Congregationalists, and New Divinity Men—answered yes. Too
great a dependence on predestination had discouraged the individual
from responding to the call to conversion. There was a need to modify traditional statements such as Dort and Westminster to spur individual action. A corresponding group of "old" elements within the
Presbyterian and Congregationalist churches answered no. To abandon traditional doctrine was to allow too great a role for delusive personal emotions. In 1801 the debate still raged, and it continued to do
so for most of the nineteenth century. The experience of other Protestants would offer White little assurance that the issue could be met
easily or that it would be wisely ignored. Action was needed.

The Great Compromiser

By 1801 William White recognized that Gilbert Burnet's commentary on the Thirty-nine Articles offered a solution to the Episcopal
church's divisions over the question of predestination. A resolution on

predestination would allow the church finally to act on the Thirty-nine Articles.

Burnet and the Latitudinarians   William White may have felt some personal affinity with Gilbert Burnet. Although the two men lived a century apart, there were strong similarities in their circumstances. Both were clearly identified with political revolutions: Burnet as a chaplain to William of Orange during the Glorious Revolution of 1688 and White as chaplain of the Continental Congress during the American Revolution. Both were advanced to the episcopate following the revolutions with which they were associated. Both valued unity and advocated tolerance for divergent views.

Gilbert Burnet was part of a circle of clergy active in London that also included John Tillotson (1630–94), Simon Patrick (1627–1701), and Edward Stillingfleet (1635–99). Members of the group became known as latitudinarians. The term, in part derisive, had been applied first to a group of Cambridge scholars also known as the Cambridge Platonists. Most of the members of the London circle studied at Cambridge, and the title passed to them.

Burnet and the other latitudinarians advocated toleration for divergent views on the two issues that most divided Protestants of their day— predestination and ordination.[24] They were unwilling to accept Roman Catholicism in England, however. They opposed James II's reintroduction of Roman Catholicism and gave their support to William and Mary's campaign to remove him.[25]

When the Glorious Revolution succeeded, William and Mary rewarded the latitudinarians by appointing them to the episcopate. Tillotson became the archbishop of Canterbury; Burnet, the bishop of Salisbury; Patrick, the bishop of Chichester; and Stillingfleet, the bishop of Worcester. As bishops they continued to speak in public for wider toleration of Protestants.[26]

Burnet's *Exposition of the Thirty-nine Articles* was an academic attempt to advance toleration in one specific area. Although the work covered all thirty-nine articles, the most important discussion in the book, as Burnet acknowledged in the introduction, was his chapter on predestination. The tack he took depended on a close reading of what the article said and a careful examination and classification of existing views on the issue.

Burnet identified four positions on predestination: the supralapsarian, the sublapsarian, the Arminian, and the Socinian. The supralapsarians, of whom John Calvin was the prime example, followed the doctrine to its logical limits: before the fall of humanity, God predestined both the fall and the salvation and damnation of individual persons. The sublapsarians took a less rigidly logical position, believing God to have permitted but not caused the fall and to have provided for the salvation of the elect afterward. The Arminians believed that God chose a source of salvation (Jesus Christ) and the means to obtain it (word and sacrament) but chose specific individuals only on the basis of their use of the means of salvation. The Socinians believed that the individual's voluntary obedience apart from God's grace was sufficient for salvation.

Burnet accepted Calvin's contention that the first two positions were logically the same. He dismissed the final position as unworthy of comment and then discussed the remaining options (sub- or supralapsarianism and Arminianism) at length. The critical issue between the two, Burnet suggested, was the question of whether God's decrees were absolute or whether they were based on foreknowledge of human response.[27] The formularies of the Church of England, he noted, did not explicitly address this question of foreknowledge. Burnet believed that the first generation of English reformers had embraced Calvin's position. Nonetheless, he argued, the article's silence on foreknowledge and the Church of England's unwillingness to alter the language once the issue had been more clearly defined at Dort left a freedom of conscience to either Calvinist or Arminian: "It is very probable that those who penned it [the seventeenth article] meant that the decree was absolute; but since they have not said it, . . . [the Arminians] may subscribe to this Article without renouncing their opinion . . . I leave the choice free to my reader."[28] Since the articles were not explicit on the question debated at Dort, both Arminians and Calvinists could subscribe to them.

A fiery Scot whose meddling in politics was not always appreciated, Burnet was at times contemptuous of his peers' intellectual abilities. He earned the dislike of a good number of his fellow clergy.[29] Anglicans welcomed his commentary, however, with its offer of an escape from the partisan Arminian-Calvinist debate. Fierce partisans of the Arminian and Calvinist positions were still to be found in the two centuries that followed, but the level of their debate was lower. Virtually no one argued that the formularies of the English church denied fellowship to those who disagreed with them.

Works by the latitudinarians proved to be popular with Anglicans in colonial North America.[30] William White shared that opinion and chose a historical text for his Course of Ecclesiastical Studies that identified the latitudinarians in quite positive terms. The text, a translation by Archibald MacLaine of John Lawrence Mosheim's *Ecclesiastical History,* introduced the latitudinarians in this way:

> The public calamities, that flowed from these vehement and uncharitable disputes about religion [i.e., disputes about predestination and the episcopacy] afflicted all wise and good men, and engaged several, who were not less eminent for their piety than for their moderation and wisdom, to seek after some method of uniting such of contending parties as were capable of listening to the dictates of charity and reason, or at least of calming their animosities, and persuading them to mutual forbearance. These pacific doctors offered themselves as mediators between the more violent *episcopalians* on the one hand, and the more rigid *presbyterians* and *independents* on the other; and hoped that, when their differences were accommodated, the lesser factions would fall of themselves. The contests that reigned between the former turned partly on the forms of church government and public worship, and partly on certain religious tenets, most especially those that were debated between the arminians and calvinists. To lessen the breach that kept these two great communities at such a distance from each other, the arbitrators, already mentioned, endeavoured to draw them out of their narrow enclosures, to render their charity more extensive, and widen the paths of salvation, which bigotry and party rage had been labouring to render inaccessible to many good Christians. This noble and truly evangelical method of proceeding, procured to its authors the denomination of latitudinarians.[31]

Burnet, to whom the text at this point referred in a footnote, had with the other latitudinarians acquired a positive reputation among eighteenth-century American Anglicans. Bishop White's decision to turn to Burnet in the conventions of 1801 and 1804 helped to preserve that positive reputation for the first half of the nineteenth century.[32]

The Conventions of 1801 and 1804   Circumstances came to White's rescue in 1801. The death in 1800 of William Walter, the Massachusetts deputy who had chaired the deputies' committee on the articles, stripped the Arminian advocates of an able spokesman. The indiffer-

ence of Bishops Provoost and Madison in the gathering in Trenton in
1801 removed two advocates of inaction. The continued agitation by
White's brother-in-law and other lay persons in the diocese of New
Jersey provided a justification for the convention again to reject the
hapless Uzal Ogden, who once more had been elected bishop by the
New Jersey diocesan convention.[33] White was the presiding bishop and
the preacher at the convention's opening service. He was the former
bishop or rector of many deputies and had been a consecrator of all
the other bishops who were present. The largely inexperienced members of the convention looked to White. He was in an undisputed position of leadership.

It was at this point that White, now drawing on his understanding
of Burnet, suggested adopting the Thirty-nine Articles without any
alteration of the wording of the seventeenth article. As soon as the
convention agreed, White's former curate, Joseph G. J. Bend, introduced
the resolution that authorized White to designate the textbooks for
candidates for the ordained ministry. When White presented his list to
the convention in 1804, it included only one text devoted entirely to
commentary on the newly adopted Articles of Religion—Burnet's *Exposition of the Thirty-nine Articles*. The General Convention accepted
White's recommendation.

The still luckless Ogden would soon lose his parish position. The
1804 General Convention adopted a canon specifically to deal with his
situation—that of a tenured rector in dispute with a vestry. The canon
allowed a parish to dismiss such a rector provided that it secured the
consent of the diocesan bishop or, if there were none (as in the case of
New Jersey), of the state convention. A special New Jersey convention
met in December of 1804 and consented to the dismissal. In the following year Ogden was accepted as a presbyter by the presbytery of
New York.[34]

Evangelical Episcopalians: Sympathetic Neutrality   The Washington evangelicals, most of whom matured in the church after 1804,
accepted Burnet's statement of their church's position on predestination as standard. They found in Burnet a justification for a stance that
might be called sympathetic neutrality, a refusal to take sides in the
Calvinist-Arminian debate, combined with a strong sympathy for
those other denominations, particularly the Reformed churches, that
felt otherwise. William Holland Wilmer's *Episcopal Manual* (1815)

set the tone. There were exceptions, the most notable being Reuel
Keith of Virginia Seminary. Most evangelicals followed Wilmer's lead,
however.

Wilmer's *Manual* summarized the doctrines and teachings of the
Episcopal church. Wilmer referred to Burnet in framing his position on
predestination:

> The 17th Article does, indeed, recognize the doctrine of predesti-
> nation; and so do the Scriptures. But the main question, *in what sense*
> it is to be received, the article does not undertake to decide. "That
> in which the knot of the whole difficulty lies (says Bishop Burnet) is
> not defined in the article, that is whether God's eternal purpose or
> decree was made, *according to what he foresaw his creatures would
> do*, or purely upon *absolute will*, in order to his own glory." The ques-
> tion, in fact, is too mysterious for human apprehension, and too
> awful to be considered without the profoundest reverence. In order
> to apprehend, and to explain it aright, we must possess the spirit and
> language of angels. . . . The Articles do not appear to have been in-
> tended so much to set forth a precise scheme of doctrine, as to em-
> body in a short compass the very language of the Bible itself. It is,
> therefore, as hopeless a labour to extract from them a regular sys-
> tem, either of Arminianism or Calvinism, as from Scripture.[35]

In spelling out the historical positions on predestination, Burnet had
carefully cited the scriptural evidence for each. What was an implicit
argument for him—that both Calvinism and Arminianism were in some
sense scriptural but that neither view captured all the biblical message—
became an explicit position for Wilmer.

This was not to say that either view was frivolous or entirely false.
On the contrary, the affirmations of both views—Calvinism's claim that
God ruled over his creation and Arminianism's claim that human choice
and action have an importance—were valuable. Limited human understanding could not reconcile the two or discard either affirmation,
however. One would need, as Wilmer argued, "the spirit and language
of angels" to do so.

This carefully qualified stance of neutrality provided Wilmer and his
fellow evangelicals a useful theological tool. While asserting the absence
of any single biblical doctrine, they were able to pursue either position
in a limited sense. As Charles Simeon, the Cambridge don who for many
Americans symbolized nineteenth-century Anglican evangelicalism,

commented, "No dissenter dares to preach as I do, one day Calvinist, another day Arminian, just as the text happens to be."[36]

When the Washington evangelicals began publishing the *Washington Theological Repertory* in 1819, they outlined this qualified neutrality. Although they did not cite Burnet by name, his thought clearly lay behind their affirmation: "For ourselves, we profess to be neither Calvinist nor Arminians. We believe, that the articles of our church, taken in connection with her liturgy and homilies, do not 'so much set forth a precise scheme of doctrine . . . as they speak the very language of the Bible itself; and that it is therefore, as hopeless a labour to extract from them a regular system, either of Calvinism or Arminianism, as from scripture.'"[37] The members of the editorial board of the *Repertory* quoted the *Episcopal Manual,* which in turn had relied on Burnet for an adequate exposition of predestination.

When the Washington evangelicals succeeded in founding the Protestant Episcopal Theological Seminary in Virginia, in 1823, Wilmer became the first professor of divinity. Wilmer, abiding by the decision of the school's trustees to follow White's 1804 Course of Ecclesiastical Studies, chose Burnet's commentary as his primary text on the Thirty-nine Articles. The work remained one of only a handful of texts used in systematic divinity at Virginia: prior to the Civil War only three books were used in addition to the *Homilies* and the Bible.

William Sparrow, an exceedingly popular divinity professor at Virginia Seminary from 1841 until 1874, continued in the course that Wilmer had so carefully charted. He told his students that too close an investigation into a logical doctrine of predestination was something never attempted "by one who rightly understood that high spiritual subject."[38]

Sparrow's neutrality on predestination resembled that of another important teacher of evangelical Episcopal divinity. John Seeley Stone became the first professor of divinity at the Episcopal Theological School in Cambridge, Massachusetts, at the age of seventy-two. He shared with Sparrow an interest in the use of Burnet and a belief that no single, logical doctrine of predestination was possible or desirable.[39]

Sparrow, Wilmer, and Stone were neutral in regard to the Arminian-Calvinist debate, yet they regarded that dispute as a serious one and the debaters as fellow Christians. The best illustration of this sympathetic stance—particularly toward the Reformed denominations—was the personal relationship that united evangelical professors of divinity to Congregationalist Leonard Woods (1774–1854) of Andover Seminary in Massachusetts.

Andover, the first three-year postgraduate Protestant seminary, was founded by members of two theological parties in the Congregational church: Old Calvinists and the followers of Samuel Hopkins (1721–1803). The Old Calvinists favored traditional Reformed statements, such as the Westminster Confession; the followers of Hopkins accepted Hopkins's modification in Calvinist doctrine to give a larger role to the will.[40] Both took strong exception to the Unitarian leanings of Harvard University, however. They joined forces to combat what they saw as the spread of infidelity. Their new institution would not go the way of Harvard; to safeguard their principles, the founders adopted a creed that Andover's professors were to sign at regular intervals. Although silent on the disagreement between the Old Calvinists and the Hopkinsians as to whether God elected some to damnation or simply allowed them to receive the proper reward for human sinfulness, the creed declared that God effectually called those who believed, and it included Arminians by name among those groups of heretics against whom the professors were to pledge their opposition.[41]

As professor of divinity from the founding of the school in 1808 until 1846, Woods carefully followed the founders' creed. In the mid-1820s his student Thomas Mather Smith prepared a detailed description of Woods's lectures and references as an aid to others.[42] As Smith's outline made clear, Woods explicitly rejected both Arminianism and the nationalism to which Bishop White had once subscribed.[43]

Andover and Woods greatly influenced other Protestants. By 1831 there were twenty-two theological seminaries following the Andover three-year plan of study, with a total of fifty-one professors, many of whom had received training at Andover.[44] Episcopalians were no exception to the prevailing pattern of enthusiasm for Andover. With no theological seminaries in England, Episcopalians turned to Andover for a model for theological education. The list of Episcopal seminary professors who attended Andover was a long one. The divinity professors, all of whom taught at evangelical seminaries, included Reuel Keith (the second professor of divinity at Virginia), Thomas Mather Smith (professor at Kenyon from 1845 until 1863), and Daniel Raynes Goodwin (of the Philadelphia Divinity School from soon after its founding in 1862 until the 1880s). John Seeley Stone did not attend the school as a student, but as a priest from nearby Boston he met regularly on campus with Episcopal students.[45]

Of Woods's former students, Thomas Mather Smith had the most intimate relationship with the professor. A descendant of the New England Mather family, he entered Andover in 1817 to prepare for the Congregational ordained ministry. After completing his course of study and briefly serving as an evangelist in western New York, he returned to Andover to prepare the detailed outline of Woods's lectures. During this period he married Woods's daughter. When he returned to the parish ministry, he invited his father-in-law to preach his installation sermon. In the later 1830s Smith moved to a congregation in New Bedford, Rhode Island, that was badly divided by revivalism. Worn down by parish infighting, he left his congregation for a job with the ecumenical Sunday School Union in Boston. Gradually coming to the conviction that a fixed liturgy and an episcopal polity could protect a congregation from excess emotionalism, he approached Episcopal bishop Manton Eastburn (1801–72) of Massachusetts.

Eastburn quickly passed the word to other evangelical Episcopalians. Stephen Tyng, a former member of the group of Washington evangelicals who was then in New York at St. George's Church, took an interest. St. George's had endowed a chair of divinity at Kenyon seminary; because of Sparrow's move to Virginia, the chair was vacant. Tyng wrote to his friend Charles McIlvaine, who then called Smith to Kenyon. Bishop McIlvaine took a strong interest in the teaching of theology at his diocese's seminary. He was quickly satisfied of the appropriateness of Smith's joining the faculty. Indeed, McIlvaine was soon confident enough about Smith's teaching to move his residence away from the seminary.[46]

William Sparrow, who did not attend Andover, was an example of yet another tie to Andover and Woods. Sparrow's predecessor at Virginia Seminary, Reuel Keith, had introduced a text translated by Woods, George Christian Knapp's *Lectures on Christian Theology*. Sparrow found the text to be a useful tool for an end not intended by Keith. He used it to advocate the neutral position on predestination.

Woods's introduction to Knapp's *Lectures* noted that Knapp's view differed from "the opinion commonly received by Theologians in this country . . . in the doctrine of Decrees."[47] In his lectures Keith had followed Woods's notes concerning the point at which the text varied from the Andover position. Sparrow followed the text on the point of divergence, however, finding in the German author a useful complement to Burnet's neutrality.[48] Knapp argued that "on the one hand, the freedom of the human will is unimpaired by the government of God; and on the other, the government of God is unobstructed and undisturbed by the free actions of men. . . . That men are free in what they do, is every where assumed in the Bible, and must be presupposed in every system of morals. . . . Still, however, the free actions of moral beings are under the most minute inspection, and the most perfect control of God."[49] The use of Knapp's ideas was a sign of the evangelical Episcopalians' paradoxical relationship to other evangelical Protestants: Knapp's book was translated by Woods at Andover, first introduced in an Episcopal seminary by a man who had studied with Woods, and used to teach a doctrine that differed from the Congregationalists on the question of predestination. Four evangelical seminaries—Virginia, Kenyon, Philadelphia, and the Episcopal Theological School in Cambridge—used the book. Mutual respect, but courteous disagreement, characterized the relationship between Episcopal evangelicals and Protestants of the Reformed tradition in America. To the evangelical Episcopalians it seemed that Calvinism was a doctrine with elements of truth and partial biblical support. They rarely if ever criticized other Protestants for their stance on the issue of predestination. Within their own fold, however, they would be somewhat less tolerant.

An outright advocate of Calvinism, Reuel Keith threatened an evangelical tradition of neutrality that had brought peace to the church since 1804. Bishop White's designated text had made the denomination's position clear: neither Calvinist nor Arminian was to be excluded from the church. Reuel Keith was the only major divinity professor to question this stance. For him only Calvinism was allowable. His recalcitrance on the issue led some in the church to question his sanity.

A graduate of Middlebury College, Vermont, in 1814, Keith came under the influence of John P. K. Henshaw, who had graduated from Middlebury six years earlier. Henshaw baptized Keith, probably in 1815 or early 1816, after Henshaw's ordination to the diaconate by Bishop Griswold of Rhode Island but before Henshaw's decision to accept a call to St. Peter's Church in Baltimore. After baptism Keith headed to King George County, Virginia, where he served as a lay reader and a private tutor. He returned to the North in 1816, where he wavered between completing a course of study at Andover and studying for orders with Henshaw, who was at the time serving at St. Ann's Church in Brooklyn.

Bishop Moore of Virginia, anxious to fill vacant churches in his diocese, expressed a willingness to ordain Keith after only a brief period
of study, and Keith headed south once again. Keith served briefly in
Georgetown and in Williamsburg (in the unsuccessful attempt to rees-
tablish the teaching of religion at the College of William and Mary).
In 1823 he moved to Alexandria to become the first full-time professor at Virginia Seminary.

Wilmer was the part-time professor of divinity; Keith was the professor of pulpit eloquence and pastoral theology. In 1826, however,
Wilmer left Alexandria, lured by the presidency of William and Mary,
and Keith gradually assumed the role of professor of divinity.

Keith retained Burnet on the reading list, but he supplemented the
bishop's view with his own series of lectures. Whatever the standards
of the church might allow, he taught that only one view was allowed
by Scripture. "The Scripture declares the will of God to be absolute,
especially in respect to predestination, election, and reprobation."
Arminianism "is entertained by so many wise and good men, that it
ought to be thoroughly examined, and its utter repugnance to the word
of God clearly pointed out."[50] Keith had clearly gone beyond the neutrality of Burnet and of Wilmer, Sparrow, and Stone. Keith rejected all
positions but his own as unscriptural.

Keith presented something of an embarrassment to his fellow evangelicals. Joseph Packard, who would also teach at Virginia, reported
that Keith's immoderate views were accompanied by signs of depres-
sion. Keith "would often sit for days together in his house without
saying a word, and leaning his head upon the back of his chair."[51] After
the death of his wife in 1840, Keith became so depressed that he could
no longer teach. A century before, Methodists had circulated rumors
about the death of Augustus Toplady, an Anglican Calvinist antagonistic to Wesley. Toplady's death had been one of despair, they charged,
the natural result of his Calvinist views.[52] Colleagues of Keith would
take a similar tack. "His mind," Packard reported, "was thrown off
its balance" by fear of perdition.[53] At his death he was replaced by the
more moderate William Sparrow.

Keith's story and his rapid replacement by Sparrow indicate the limited appeal that strict Calvinism held for most Episcopal evangelicals.
To be sure, Calvinism was a serious doctrine and bore serious examination; other Protestants who held such views were not to be ridiculed.
Episcopal standards were neutral in the Calvinist-Arminian debate,

however, and Episcopal evangelicals had a freedom in regard to it that few were willing to surrender.

High Church Episcopalians: Critical Neutrality   The evangelicals, with few exceptions, had not been Calvinists. Nevertheless they had a sympathy for Calvinists that was often grounded in personal friendship. The high-church Episcopalians shared with the evangelicals their neutrality. They were largely unwilling to commit themselves to either an Arminian or a Calvinist system. They brought a very different spirit to that neutrality, however. For the evangelicals Burnet's affirmation that the theses of the Thirty-nine Articles were acceptable to either Arminian or Calvinist meant that there was a measure of truth in Calvinism. For the high-church Episcopalian it meant the opposite; there was a measure of error.

In his commentary on the seventeenth article, Burnet had pointed out both the similarities and the dissimilarities of Calvinism and Anglicanism. High-church Episcopalians used Burnet's account of the differences to emphasize their denomination's distance from the Calvinist system. Burnet noted, for example, that the Anglican reformers did not explicitly adopt the belief that God had selected those not chosen for salvation for damnation as a logical corollary of their belief in election. Burnet pointed out that the seventeenth article did not "make any mention of reprobation, no, not in a hint; no definition is made *concerning it.*"[54] G. T. Chapman, the high-church rector of Christ Church, Lexington, would simply paraphrase this comment in his own discussion of Episcopal church doctrine. Of the seventeenth article, he observed, "not one syllable does it contain of individual reprobation or preterition."[55]

A second observation by Burnet was related to this argument about the absence of reprobation from the seventeenth article. The Anglican church, he suggested, had rejected the doctrine of limited atonement: "the universal extent of the death of Christ seems to be very plainly affirmed in the most solemn part of all the offices of the Church: for in the office of Communion, and in the Prayer of Consecration, we own, that Christ, 'by the one oblation of himself, once offered, made there a full, perfect, and sufficient sacrifice, oblation, and satisfaction for the sins of the whole world. . . .' And there are yet more express words in our Church Catechism to this purpose."[56] Contrary to the later position of the Synod of Dort, the Anglican reformers declared that Christ's death was for all humanity.

Writing in 1847, William Adams, the professor of divinity at Nashotah House, could look back on the issue of Christ's atonement as one
about which debate had died down, at least in the West. In the course
of an argument about baptism, Adams referred to the debate as a thing
of the past:

> Of old there was a dispute as to whether Christ died for all or only
> for the elect. The doctrines certain persons had taken up, rendered
> it very necessary for them to assert that Christ had made atonement
> only for some few. This was a limitation of the atonement established
> by the tradition or doctrine of man against the plain words of holy
> scriptures. Men who had more confidence in the word of God than
> in these so called "doctrines," protested against such a limitation;
> they protested too in the face of a majority, for they knew that truth
> was on their side, and will make room for itself amidst overpower-
> ing numbers. The advocates for an atonement made for all men have
> been successful, the advocates for a limited atonement are in a mis-
> erable minority.[57]

Limited atonement was not the doctrine of the Anglican church, and
Adams was therefore free to criticize it.

Like other high-church divinity professors, Adams used Burnet's
Exposition of the Thirty-nine Articles in his classes. He had attended
General Seminary, where he had used the book as a student in Bird
Wilson's classes. When Adams revised his texts and course of study in
the late 1860s, he listed Burnet's work in such a way as to leave no
doubt about the work's primary usefulness. Second-year seminary students were to read "Burnett [sic] on the Seventeenth Article."[58]

Students at other high-church seminaries also studied Burnet's *Exposition of the Thirty-nine Articles*. Their church, they read, was not
committed to either a Calvinist or an Arminian position. Their professors linked Burnet's observations on predestination with a high-church
emphasis on the first of Bishop White's sources of assurance, the baptismal covenant. Episcopalians could be sure of salvation because they
joined an apostolic covenant in baptism. Other Protestants lacked not
only the apostolic element of the covenant but also a reasonable and
biblical doctrine of predestination.

Evangelicals, emphasizing the second of Bishop White's two sources of assurance, disagreed. According to the evangelicals, although
Christians entered the covenant relationship in baptism, they drew their

strongest assurance from adult renewal. As long as other Protestants taught the importance of adult faith, evangelicals felt no need to call attention to difficulties in their doctrines of predestination.

LAURENCE AND ECCLESIASTICAL ELECTION

Both high-church and evangelical Episcopalians found Gilbert Burnet's *Exposition of the Thirty-nine Articles* to be a useful summary of their church's position. The evangelicals saw a neutrality sympathetic to Calvinism; the high-church Episcopalians espied a neutrality antagonistic to Calvinism. Both groups were able to use the text in their own ways, with a license that had been extended by Burnet. No heated debate developed within the church, however, and in contrast to several other American denominations, the Episcopal church did not divide over predestination.

Bishop White nevertheless was not entirely satisfied. Burnet had ably argued that the Anglican church had not exclusively chosen either Arminianism or Calvinism. Such a position was valuable in avoiding division, but it also had its limitations, for it presented the church as indecisive on an issue of major theological importance. White began to believe that neutrality was not enough; the church needed a consistent position on predestination.

In 1805, just one year after White designated the Burnet text, a British author offered some new hope for a systematic explanation of the church's doctrine. Richard Laurence (1760–1838), the archbishop of Cashel in Ireland, addressed the question of predestination when he was chosen the Bampton lecturer.[59] The course that Laurence took was an extension of Burnet's argument. Burnet had suggested that the Anglican reformers had adopted a statement that could be signed in good conscience by either Arminian or Calvinist. He had further suggested that he himself subscribed to neither view but rather to a position that he described as "the doctrine of the Greek Church."[60] Laurence simply joined these two propositions with a historical argument. The Anglican reformers had adopted a neutral stance on the Arminian-Calvinist debate because they too had subscribed to a position held by the early church.

Burnet was circumspect about his own understanding of the "Greek" doctrine of predestination. In a convoluted paragraph tucked in the midst of his commentary on the seventeenth article, he defined the view in terms more of individual advocates than of its logical components. The Greek doctrine was that advocated by "Gregory Nazianzen and St. Basil. . . . Chrysostom, Isidore of Damiete, and Theodoret."[61] In it, "freedome of the will is very fully set forth."[62] Beyond this, Burnet said little.

Laurence, in contrast, placed great importance on this pre-Augustinian understanding of predestination and took great pains to describe it. He argued that early Christians used the word *election* to refer to God's choice of the church. It did not mean the choice of specific individuals for salvation or damnation. Laurence moreover suggested that this doctrine not only was that of the early church but also was in "perfect conformity with the less abstruse, and more scriptural opinions of the Lutherans. With them it teaches an election of Christians out of the human race."[63]

Laurence's argument had several advantages. It provided the church with a position that allowed for some compromise between free will and God's choice. Further, it provided a historical interpretation in which the Reformed doctrine of predestination was a minority view that could be contrasted with a more widely held view that was accepted by early Christians, the Greeks (i.e., Orthodox Christians), Lutherans, and Anglicans.

In addition the position Laurence took was in keeping with a general nineteenth-century rapprochement between Lutherans and Anglicans. In the United States Lutherans and Episcopalians discussed the possibility of union on at least two occasions.[64] William White's own parish in Philadelphia included several Lutherans who came to the Episcopal church seeking English-language services that their children could understand.[65] In Europe in 1841 the English Parliament would accept a Prussian suggestion that a joint bishopric be established in Jerusalem and staffed by either Anglicans or Lutherans.[66] On another missionary front, the Society for the Promotion of Christian Knowledge employed Lutherans alongside their Anglican missionaries in India.[67] These nineteenth-century signs of cooperation helped to buttress Laurence's argument about the sixteenth century.

William White was impressed by Laurence's exposition. He found in the work the great advantage that had once attracted him to nationalism. Laurence, like the nationalists, interposed an element between the individual and salvation to lessen the conflict between human choice and divine election. For the nationalists that element was the nation: God chose a nation and then chose to save certain individuals within it. For Laurence it was the church: God chose the church and elected certain of its members to salvation. By doubling the terms involved, it was possible to allow God's absolute choice in one area and a choice dependent on human initiative in another.

There was one difference between the theories of Laurence and the nationalists, however.[68] The nationalist theory could not be reversed; it made sense only if the choice of the nation was absolute.[69] Yet a divine choice of nations, the salvation of whose citizens was dependent on their respond to God's choice, did not square with the language of the seventeenth article. Its language was consistent with the election of individuals rather than of nations and of a choice for salvation rather than a choice for the *possibility* of salvation. This may have been the roadblock that led Bishop White to abandon nationalism after 1785.

Laurence's view was more flexible. It was possible to speak of God's absolute choice on either of the terms in the theological equation. God could *absolutely* choose individuals for the *visible* church, while then basing the choice of those members of the visible church for salvation on foreknowledge of their response; or God could base the choice of individuals to the *invisible* church on the foreknowledge of their response, and then *absolutely* elect the invisible church to salvation. Thus it was possible to explain Laurence's view in language that accorded with the seventeenth article, thereby avoiding the criticism leveled at nationalism. God's choice was in the first sense of individuals and in the second sense to salvation.

Bishop White decided to write his own work on predestination incorporating the insights of both Burnet and Laurence. The two-volume work, *Comparative Views of the Controversy between the Calvinists and the Arminians,* appeared in 1817. The influences of Burnet and Laurence were evident throughout. From Burnet White borrowed the assertion that the authors of the seventeenth article were silent on the question of foreknowledge. "This is the knot of which bishop Burnet justly remarks, that the whole difficulty lies in it; and that, in the articles, is not defined." He also picked up Burnet's comments on the existence of a Greek view on predestination. The authors of the article, White argued, would not frame "their institutions so rigorously, as to exclude a Chrysostom or a Nazianzen, if they had been their contemporaries, from their communion."[70]

White went to considerable lengths to acknowledge his reliance on Bishop Laurence. White told his readers of:

60 THE NATURE OF SALVATION

a work lately edited in England, by Richard Lawrence [*sic*] D. D.;
being eight sermons delivered at the Bampton Lecture, with ample
notes attached to them. It is here conceived to be a work of great merit, and is mentioned as such, partly because other readers may be
thereby induced to gather from it, as the author of this has done,
much information on the subject; and also, because of the use which
will be made of the notes, in what is to follow. They contain extracts
from literary works, not accessible by the present writer, and perhaps
not to be had in the United States: to which notes, accordingly, there
will be a reference, where it may be deemed pertinent to the present
purpose.[71]

At one point White noted, "This remark is Dr. Laurence's. At least, it
is not here recollected to have been met with in any other writer."[72] The
American bishop was so reliant on Laurence that he was convinced that
information not traceable to other authors must be Laurence's.

White followed Laurence in using the church as the intermediate term
in the equation of salvation. White argued that Lutherans and Anglicans
believed God's decree to salvation to be a "decree to respect a church
chosen among the human race."[73] The decree was of the individual, but
it was made because of that individual's participation within the church.
White explained this in a comment on a phrase in the seventeenth article: "When the article, instead of specifying individual election, speaks
of a body; it leaves to the reader the liberty of interpretation, that God,
having accommodated the whole proceeding to the corporate character,
chose the individual, because of his falling within the descriptive prop-
erties of it."[74] God elected individuals but did so because they were part
of the church. The proper understanding of predestination therefore did
not solve "the old controversy of liberty and necessity, which has exercised the wits and pens of speculative men from very remote times to the
present."[75] God's election was of the church. Belief in that choice did not
entail any particular understanding of divine foreknowledge or the degree to which individuals exercised their free will. The universal "sense
of liberty," however, led White to suggest that "we are so far free, as is
requisite to responsibility."[76]

White found in Laurence a complement to Burnet that enabled him
to adopt a position with the advantages of his previously held nationalism but without its weaknesses. He discovered Laurence's work too
late to include it within the Course of Ecclesiastical Studies, but his own

Comparative Views would introduce the theory, which came to be called "ecclesiastical election," to the theological seminaries. It provided a basis for the more technical discussions of predestination at the seminary level for much of the remainder of the century.

Ecclesiastical Election and High-Church Episcopalians

High-church and evangelical Episcopalians had differed in the emphasis they brought to their reading of Burnet's *Exposition of the Thirty-nine Articles;* they differed also in their use of the doctrine of ecclesiastical election, which White suggested as a complement to Burnet. The high-church Episcopalians stressed ecclesiastical election as the primary view of the Anglican church, a view that the Anglican reformers charitably had not imposed on their less-enlightened Arminian and Calvinist coreligionists but one that was particularly Anglican nonetheless. The evangelicals, on the other hand, greeted the position as yet another acceptable view of the subject.

Bird Wilson, a friend of Bishop White who taught divinity at General Seminary, added *Comparative Views* to the texts specified for the Course of Ecclesiastical Studies. Wilson used the text during his entire tenure at General Seminary, and his successor, Samuel Roosevelt Johnson, initially used the work as well. The text was slow reading, however, and the professors in the second generation of high-church divinity schools, which began to open in the 1840s, were hesitant to use *Comparative Views* with their students.

In 1854 Johnson made a discovery that would increase the acceptance of the doctrine of ecclesiastical election within the church. Johnson found that his students were able to absorb the argument from a popular new English commentary on the articles more easily than they could do so from White's often laborious restatement of Laurence. Johnson quietly dropped White's *Comparative Views* from his book list and added Bishop Edward Harold Browne's *Exposition of the Thirty-nine Articles*. Browne's prose, unlike the often convoluted product of Bishop White's pen, was clear and concise. It was Browne, moreover, who provided the simple label—ecclesiastical election—that was lacking in both Laurence and White.[77] Despite this new text, however, Johnson continued to have his students read Gilbert Burnet's commentary on the articles.

Other high-church seminaries soon copied Johnson's choice of texts. By 1860 William Adams was using Browne's commentary with that of

Burnet at Nashotah House. Bishop John Williams of Connecticut, who doubled as the professor of divinity at Berkeley Seminary from 1854 until the 1890s, produced an American edition of Browne's commentary in 1865. General Seminary graduates Solon Manney, Samuel Buel, and John Steinfort Kedney introduced Browne to their students at Seabury Seminary in Minnesota.

In 1871 Samuel Buel moved from Seabury to General Seminary to fill the chair of divinity vacated by Samuel Johnson. His lectures, published in 1890, indicated his continued advocacy of ecclesiastical election. Election was, he wrote,

> without question . . . the election of individuals. The election into the Church is the election of individuals, and therefore the election to the end of everlasting salvation, for which the Church was founded, is and must be an election of individuals. . . . It cannot be explained, this foreknowledge of God, side by side with free creaturely determination—and yet must be admitted. . . . Neither Calvinist nor Arminian will accept the truth with its counter-truth, the predestination of God with the free-will and accountability of men. Both must be accepted, because both are true and revealed.[78]

At the end of the century Buel was still teaching General Seminary students the advantages of a view to which Bishop White had turned in 1817. Ecclesiastical election provided a valuable complement to Bishop Burnet's neutrality. Burnet argued that the seventeenth article could be signed by either a Calvinist or an Arminian. Laurence, White, and Browne suggested that the reason such a liberty was granted was that the Anglican reformers believed in ecclesiastical election. God chose individuals to belong to the church and chose the church for salvation; Christians need not solve the quandary of whether the ultimate salvation of individuals depended on their own will or God's choice.

Ecclesiastical Election and the Evangelicals

Although evangelical Episcopalians lacked the direct personal contact with Bishop White on the seminary level of the sort that Bird Wilson had, they nonetheless were influenced by White's *Comparative Views*. The evangelical seminaries moved somewhat more slowly to supplement Gilbert Burnet's neutrality with the ecclesiastical election doctrine of Laurence and Browne, but within ten years of the high-church seminaries' adoption of Browne's *Exposition of the Thirty-nine*

Articles, the text was in use at the majority of evangelical seminaries as well.

Charles McIlvaine, who had been one of the Washington evangelicals, was an enthusiastic evangelical promoter of the ecclesiastical view. While writing a work denouncing the English Oxford movement in the 1840s, he came across the writings of George Stanley Faber (1773–1854). Like McIlvaine, Faber had warned about the dangers of Oxford; Faber had also written a theological work on predestination. Faber's reasoning and language were his own—he felt the matter turned on the question of ideality (i.e., the goal for which a thing was done). His conclusion was the same as that of White and Laurence, however. Browne's later summary of the position of the Anglican church referred to both Laurence and Faber.

Like Laurence, Faber suggested an affinity between the views of Anglicans and Lutherans. He thought that the Lutheran reformer Philipp Melanchthon held "the true ancient Ideality of Election," that is,

> an Election of individuals, out of the great corrupt mass of mankind into the pale of the visible Church, with God's morally-acting purpose and intention, that the Elect profiting by their privileges of Election should finally obtain everlasting felicity . . . a system professedly adopted from the pure sources of primitive Christian antiquity! Such, therefore, was the System, which Cranmer acting by the advice of Melanchthon and in consequence of his own diligent researches into the same antiquity, embodied in the seventeenth article of the Church.[79]

When McIlvaine's own anti-Oxford work appeared, he confidently told his readers that the claims of the Thirty-nine Articles "were constructed for the most part on the Lutheran System."[80]

Faber's anti-Oxford works were used at Philadelphia and the Episcopal Theological School. McIlvaine's work, *Oxford Divinity,* was used at Kenyon and Philadelphia. Together the two authors helped to prepare the way for the introduction of Edward Harold Browne's *Exposition of the Thirty-nine Articles,* the text that was instrumental in disseminating the ecclesiastical election view at high-church seminaries. By the late 1860s Kenyon, Philadelphia, and the Episcopal Theological School were using the text. Sparrow, trying to undo what Calvinist Reuel Keith had done before him at Virginia, delayed introducing it; it was added to the course lists by his successors ten years after his death in 1874.

Even after Browne was introduced to evangelical students, there were differences in the way their professors handled the material. Samuel Buel at General Seminary taught ecclesiastical election as the view of his church. Daniel Raynes Goodwin at Philadelphia lectured to his students about four views on predestination: Calvinist, Arminian, nationalist, and ecclesiastical. Whereas Buel left his students with the caution that neither the Calvinist nor the Arminian position could ever be entirely true, Goodwin left the distinct impression that all the views he discussed were faulty.[81] Ecclesiastical election was one view, and it may have had some support among the reformers, but it was not the only acceptable understanding. Nor was it immune from the difficulties that confronted any view attempting to deal with humanity's relationship to the divine.

Evangelical Goodwin and high-churchman Buel in the 1870s held something in common with Wilmer and Wilson of the 1820s. All were strongly influenced by Bishop William White. White's selection of Gilbert Burnet for special emphasis in the course of Ecclesiastical Studies of 1804 provided for peace in the church by establishing that either a Calvinist or an Arminian position was acceptable. His further discussion of the predestination issue in 1817 introduced a complementary interpretation that, particularly in the years after midcentury, allowed divinity professors to restate the church's position. Evangelical and high-church Episcopalians brought their own emphases to White's texts, but they worked with the same books and were indebted to the same man. William White laid out the path for them.

NOTES

    1. Gilbert Burnet, *An Exposition of the Thirty-nine Articles of the Church of England,* new ed. (London: Thomas Tegg, 1827), x–xi.
    2. Ibid., xi.
    3. Most colonial Anglicans opposed the revivalist preaching of George Whitefield during the 1740s and early 1750s because of his attitudes on episcopal authority. By 1760, however, a new generation of colonial clergy was coming of age; these men had more positive ideas about Whitefield and the Great Awakening. Even Trinity Church, New York, began to seek a "sound Whitfilian" for the position of assistant. Ogden was part of this new genera-

tion. For details see Robert C. Monk, "Unity and Diversity among Eighteenth-Century Colonial Methodists and Anglicans," *Historical Magazine of the Protestant Episcopal Church* 38 (Mar. 1969): 51–69; and Robert Prichard, *A History of the Episcopal Church* (Harrisburg, Pa.: Morehouse, 1991), 55–59.

4. John N. Norton, *Life of Bishop Croes of New Jersey* (New York: General Protestant Episcopal Sunday School Union and Church Book Society, 1859), 93.

5. Ogden's sympathies became clear in 1804 when he withdrew from the ministry of the Episcopal church. Despite cordial relations with Methodists in his area, it was to the Presbytery of New York that he applied for admission as a clergyman. See Norton, *Croes*, 96–97, and Monk, "Unity and Diversity," 59–61. Note, however, that Monk, who was interested in relationships between Anglicans and Methodists, entirely overlooked Ogden's Presbyterian ties. He mentioned neither Ogden's preaching in Presbyterian churches nor his admission to the Presbyterian ministry.

6. *The Book of Common Prayer and Administration of the Sacraments and Other Rites and Ceremonies of the Church, together with the Psalter or Psalms of David, according to the Use of the Episcopal Church* (New York: Church Hymnal, 1979), 871.

7. Ibid.

8. Henry Petersen, *The Canons of Dort: A Study Guide* (Grand Rapids, Mich.: Baker, 1968), 95–111.

9. Jacobus Arminius, *Declaration of Sentiments,* quoted in Carl Bangs, *Arminius: A Study in the Dutch Reformation* (Nashville: Abingdon, 1971), 351–52.

10. Owen Chadwick, *The Reformation,* vol. 3 of *The Pelican History of the Church,* ed. Owen Chadwick (Great Britain: Penguin, 1977), 233–40.

11. The Reverend Mr. Waddell, Robert Morris, and J. M. Wallace, circular letter to standing committees, quoted in Norton, *Bishop Croes,* 92.

12. The General Convention resolution cited a possible lack of a quorum as the reason for invalidating the election. See William Stevens Perry, ed., *Journals of General Conventions of the Protestant Episcopal Church in the United States, 1785–1835,* 3 vols. (Claremont, N.H.: Claremont Manufacturing, 1874), 1:228.

13. Norton, *Croes,* 91–92.

14. *The Book of Common Prayer and Administration of the Sacraments and Other Rites and Ceremonies of the Church according to the Use of the United Church of England and Ireland: Together with the Psalter or Psalms of David* (Oxford: Clarendon, 1819), 153.

15. Bruce E. Steiner, *Samuel Seabury, 1724–1796: A Study in High Church Tradition* (Athens: Ohio University Press, 1971), 123.

16. William White, *Memoirs of the Protestant Episcopal Church* (New York: E. P. Dutton, 1880), 119.

17. Perry, *Journals, 1785–1835,* 1:233.

18. White, *Memoirs,* 119.

19. Peter Hall, ed., *Reliquiae Liturgicae: Documents Connected with the Liturgy of the Church of England,* vol. 5, *The American Prayer Book* (Bath: Binns and Goodwin, 1847), 265.

20. Gerald R. Cragg, *From Puritanism to the Age of Reason: A Study of Changes in Religious Thought within the Church of England, 1660 to 1700* (Cambridge: Cambridge University Press, 1960), 18–19.

21. Among the works that attributed nationalism to John Locke were Edward Harold Browne's *Exposition of the Thirty-nine Articles, Historical and Doctrinal,* 1st American ed. from 5th English ed., ed. J. Williams (New York: H. B. Durand, 1865), 402; and Daniel R. Goodwin's *Syllabus of Lectures on Systematic Divinity, on Apologetics, and on the Canon, Inspiration, and Sufficiency of Holy Scripture* (Philadelphia: Caxton Press of Sermons, printed for the use of the students, 1875), 101.

22. Romans 9:14–16, 18 (NRSV).

23. Hall, *Reliquiae Liturgicae,* 5:265.

24. During Charles II's reign (1660–85) the Church of England ceased to be the comprehensive national church that it once had been. Twenty percent of the clergy and 300,000 lay persons refused to accept the terms of the religious settlement worked out at the Savoy conference (1661). They withdrew from the Church of England to form dissenting Presbyterian and the Independent (Congregational) churches. It was these dissenting Protestants that Gilbert Burnet and his companions hoped to bring back to the Church of England. For figures on the size of the dissenting churches, see Robert Currie, Alan Gilbert, and Lee Horsley, *Churches and Churchgoers: Patterns of Church Growth in the British Isles since 1700* (Oxford: Clarendon, 1977), 27; and Gordon Donaldson, *James V–VIII,* vol. 3 of *The Edinburgh History of Scotland,* ed. Gordon Donaldson (Hong Kong: Wilture Enterprises, 1965), 366.

25. Charles II, who died in 1685, made a profession of Roman Catholicism on his deathbed. His brother James II, who followed him to the throne, converted well before his accession. James pursued a religious policy that included toleration of Roman Catholicism, the reception of a papal nuncio at court, the introduction of a Roman Catholic episcopate in England, and the imprisonment of Anglican bishops opposed to his policies. Such actions led to widespread popular opposition, and in June of 1688 seven members of the House of Lords wrote to William and Mary in Holland requesting their intervention. Mary, who was James's eldest daughter, and William, who was her spouse and a grandson of Charles I, were both committed Protestants. William invaded England. When some of James's troops defected to William, James fled without any pitched battle. In January of 1689 Parliament declared the throne deserted and offered it to William and Mary.

26. Pedro Thomas Meza, "Gilbert Burnet's Concept of Religious Toleration," *Historical Magazine of the Protestant Episcopal Church* 50 (Sept. 1981): 227–42.

27. Carl Oliver Bangs argued in *Arminius: A Study in the Dutch Reformation* (Nashville: Abingdon, 1971) that later interpreters have overemphasized the importance of foreknowledge in Arminius's thought. If his premise is correct, Burnet's insistence on foreknowledge—an insistence that is pivotal to his argument on the interpretation of the article—may play a role in the history of interpretation and in that overemphasis.

28. Burnet, *Exposition of the Thirty-nine Articles,* 175–77.

29. John Hunt, *Religious Thought in England from the Reformation to the End of the Last Century,* 3 vols. (London: Strahan, 1870–73), 2:145.

30. John Woolverton has noted, for example, that the Cambridge Platonists and the latitudinarians were "widely represented in colonial Episcopalian libraries in the [Chesapeake] bay area." It is his judgement that "in the last third of the seventeenth century, these became more representative of colonial Episcopal thought throughout the American colonies than any other group of theologians in the Church of England." See John Frederick Woolverton, *Colonial Anglicanism in North America* (Detroit: Wayne State University Press, 1984), 44.

31. John Lawrence Mosheim, *An Ecclesiastical History, Ancient and Modern from the Birth of Christ, to the Beginning of the Present Century in Which the Rise, Progress, and Variations of Church Power Are Considered in Their Connexion with the State of Learning and Philosophy and the Political History of Europe during That Period,* trans. Archibald MacLaine, 4 vols. (New York: Collins and Hannay, 1821), 4:108.

32. By the end of the nineteenth century, some Episcopalians had come to see Burnet and other latitudinarians in a different light. This was particularly true of Anglo Catholics, who were highly critical of the latitudinarian willingness to reach some accommodation about the episcopacy. For a recent example of such a negative portrayal, see Bonnell Spencer, *Ye Are the Body: A People's History of the Church* (West Park, N.Y.: Holy Cross, 1950).

33. Perry, *Journals, 1785–1835,* 1:264.

34. Norton, *Bishop Croes,* 91–96.

35. William H. Wilmer, *The Episcopal Manual: A Summary Explanation of the Doctrine, Discipline, and Worship of the Protestant Episcopal Church, in the United States of America,* new and improved ed., ed. John Coleman (Philadelphia: R. S. George, 1841), 57, 60–61.

36. Charles Simeon quoted in Hugh Evan Hopkins, *Charles Simeon of Cambridge* (Grand Rapids, Mich.: William B. Eerdmans, 1977), 191.

37. *Washington Theological Repertory* 3 (Aug. 1821): 2.

38. William Sparrow, *Sermons by the Rev. William Sparrow, Late Profes-*

sor of Systematic Divinity and Evidences of Christianity in the Theological Seminary of the Protestant Episcopal Church in the Diocese of Virginia (New York: Thomas Whittaker, 1877), 62.

39. George Blackman, *Faith & Freedom* (New York: Seabury, 1967), 251–52.

40. Hopkins made a distinction between regeneration, which was the work of the Holy Spirit, and conversion, which was based on human response; see Sydney E. Ahlstrom, *A Religious History of the American People* (New Haven, Conn.: Yale University Press, 1972), 408–9.

41. Edward A. Park, *The Associate Creed of Andover Theological Seminary* (Boston: Franklin, 1883), 22–23.

42. W. S. P.[erry], *A Memorial of the Rev. Thomas Mather Smith* (Cambridge, Mass.: H. O. Houghton, 1866), 7.

43. Thomas Mather Smith, *Outline of the Course of Study Issued by the Students of the Theological Seminary, Andover, in the Department of Christian Theology* (Andover, Mass.: Flagg and Gould, 1825), 20.

44. Robert Wood Lynn, "Notes toward a History: Theological Encyclopedia and the Evolution of American Seminary Curriculum, 1808–1968," *Theological Education* 17 (Spring 1981): 118–23; "View of the Theological Seminaries in the United States, 1831," *Quarterly Register of the American Education Society* 3 (May 1831): 303.

45. In areas other than divinity, former Andover students were found in both evangelical and high-church seminaries. These other professors included Edward Abiel Washburn (1819–81), professor of polity at Berkeley in the 1850s; Edwin Harwood (1822–1902), Berkely professor of New Testament; Frederick Jordan Goodwin (1811–90), Berkely professor of apologetics; John Anketell (1835–1905), Seabury biblical languages professor; Joseph Packard (1812–1905), Virginia Old Testament professor; Joseph Meunscher, professor of sacred literature at Kenyon; Lucius Whiting Bancroft (b. 1827), Kenyon and Philadelphia professor of history, polity, and liturgics; Edward Totterson Bartlett, Philadelphia history professor; and Alexander Viets Griswold Allen (1841–1905), Episcopal Theological School professor of history.

46. Perry, *Smith*, 3–27.

47. Leonard Woods Jr., introduction to George Christian Knapp, *Lectures on Christian Theology*, trans. Leonard Woods Jr., 2 vols. (New York: G. & C. & H. Carvill; Andover, Mass.: Flagg and Gould, 1831–33), 1:xxix.

48. Joseph Packard, *Recollections of a Long Life* (Washington, D.C.: Byron S. Adams, 1902), 171–72.

49. Knapp, *Theology*, 1:519.

50. Reuel Keith, *Lectures on Those Doctrines in Theology Usually Called Calvinistic* (New York: J. Inglis, 1868), 9, 32.

51. Packard, *Recollections*, 97.

52. *Dictionary of National Biography* (1917–), s.v. "Augustus Montague Toplady," by Henry Bennett.

53. Packard, *Recollections*, 96–97.

54. Burnet, *Exposition of the Thirty-nine Articles*, 175.

55. G. T. Chapman, *Sermons upon the Ministry, Worship, and Doctrine of the Protestant Episcopal Church and Other Subjects* (Lexington, Ken.: Smith and Palmer, 1828), 183.

56. Burnet, *Exposition of the Thirty-nine Articles*, 176.

57. William Adams, *Mercy to Babes: A Plea for the Christian Baptism of Infants, Addressed to Those Who Doubt and Those Who Deny the Validity of that Practice* (New York: Stanford and Swords, 1847), 17–18.

58. *Catalogue of the Officers and Students of Nashotah Theological Seminary* (Milwaukee: Burdick and Armitage, Church Printers, 1871), 14.

59. John Bampton (d. 1751), a canon of Salisbury, had endowed a series of Oxford lectures. Initiated in 1785, the series rapidly became an important forum for Anglican theological and biblical thought.

60. Burnet, *Exposition of the Thirty-nine Articles*, xi.

61. Ibid., 152.

62. Ibid.

63. Richard Laurence, *An Attempt to Illustrate Those Articles of the Church of England Which the Calvinist Improperly Consider As Calvinistical* (Oxford: Oxford University Press, 1805), 159.

64. William Manross, *History of the American Episcopal Church* (New York: Morehouse, 1935), 207; Lawrence Foushee London and Sarah McCulloh Lemmon, *The Episcopal Church in North Carolina, 1701–1959* (Raleigh: Episcopal Diocese of North Carolina, 1987), 139–41.

65. Alvin W. Skarden, *Church Leader in the Cities: William Augustus Muhlenberg* (Philadelphia: University of Pennsylvania Press, 1971), 5.

66. Desmund Bowen, *The Idea of the Victorian Church: A Study in the Church of England, 1833–1889* (Montreal: McGill University Press, 1968), 75–76.

67. E. Clowes Chorley, *Men and Movements in the American Episcopal Church* (New York: Scribner's, 1946), 276.

68. Some Episcopal authors, particularly those writing for the general public, never really grasped the difference between nationalism and ecclesiastical Election. The confusion was understandable. Both views were based on a two-step process of election. Both had been advocated by Bishop White, although at different points in his career. The confusion was compounded in the period before 1840 by the lack of a uniform convention in referring to ecclesiastical election.

For an example of an author who did not distinguish the two views, see *A Catechism of the Thirty-nine Articles of the Protestant Episcopal Church* (Baltimore: James Young, 1846). The anonymous author wrote that Episcopal clergy understood the seventeenth article in a Calvinist, Arminian, or nationalist sense but said nothing of the increasingly popular ecclesiastical view.

69. The illogical alternative would be to talk about God's absolute choice of individuals and a choice of nations dependent on the response of those individuals. Such an arrangement defeated the whole purpose of nationalism—the finding of an alternative for Calvinist views of individual election.

70. William White, *Comparative Views of the Controversy between the Calvinists and the Arminians,* 2 vols. (Philadelphia: M. Thomas, 1817), 2:34.

71. Ibid.

72. Ibid., 2:28–29.

73. Ibid., 2:35.

74. Ibid., 2:34–35.

75. Ibid., 2:515.

76. Ibid.

77. Browne, *Exposition of the Thirty-nine Articles,* 421–26.

78. Samuel Buel, *A Treatise of Dogmatic Theology,* 2 vols. (New York: Thomas Whittaker, 1890), 2:263, 278.

79. George Stanley Faber, *The Primitive Doctrine of Election or an Inquiry into the Ideality and Causation of Scriptural Election As Received and Maintained in the Primitive Church,* 1st American ed. (New York: Charles Henry, 1840), 307–8.

80. Charles Pettit McIlvaine, *Righteousness by Faith, a New Revised Edition of "Oxford Divinity"* (Philadelphia: Protestant Episcopal Book Society, 1862), 239–40.

81. Goodwin, *Syllabus,* 104–11.

3 Baptism and the Covenant

~

WHEN JOHN PRENTISS HENSHAW was baptized, he elected to follow a practice that was infrequent but not unknown among adult candidates for baptism in the Episcopal church. He chose a new name. He was no longer to be John Prentiss Henshaw; he was to be John Prentiss Kewley Henshaw, the additional name chosen in honor of the Reverend John Kewley, who baptized him.[1]

Episcopalians such as Henshaw regarded baptism with a seriousness that many other nineteenth-century Protestants did not share. For them baptism was not simply a sign of inclusion within a covenant relationship between God and the church, nor was it merely a seal of a previous election by God. It was the actual commencement of the covenant relationship, of which forgiveness and life everlasting were the desired results. Although Episcopalians suspected that God might at least occasionally offer these benefits to the unbaptized, they argued that there was no certainty, no sure scriptural promise to that effect. It was better for an individual to enter a relationship with God through the manner prescribed by Jesus Christ than to rely on what they referred to as the "uncovenanted mercies of God."

Episcopalians found little assurance of salvation in the doctrine of predestination; the concept was to be more avoided than proclaimed. The waters of baptism were a solid foundation for assurance, however. Any baptized person need not worry about election. In baptism the possibility of salvation was sure. For a baptized child dying in infancy, salvation was not only a possibility but a certainty.

Candidates for the ordained ministry, following Bishop White's Course of Ecclesiastical Studies, found this understanding of baptism in Bishop John Pearson's *Exposition of the Creed*. They found it as well in Burnet's *Exposition of the Thirty-nine Articles* and Bishop White's own writing.

BISHOP WHITE AND COVENANT THEOLOGY

After his consecration to the episcopate in 1787, William White found himself with an unaccustomed chore. He was to confirm. The office of confirmation—a service that required the visitation of a bishop—had been unknown for the 180 years of Anglicanism in the New World. As long as there had been no bishops in America, there was no confirmation. With the consecration of White and other candidates for the episcopate in the 1780s, however, confirmation had become a practical possibility. Some lay persons and clergy soon came to see confirmation as central to the office of bishop. For them the office of bishop differed from that of priest in only three ways: only bishops enjoyed the ability to confirm, to ordain, and to preside at ecclesiastical meetings.[2]

The American Book of Common Prayer, following its English counterpart, contained a short catechism for the instruction of children. Rubrics instructed parish clergy to prepare the young with this catechism. Those who had mastered the catechism were to be presented to the bishop for confirmation and were thereafter allowed to receive Holy Communion.[3] If presentation to a bishop was a practical impossibility, those who were ready and desirous for confirmation were allowed to receive Holy Communion.[4] This had been the case in colonial America. Clergy had used the catechism to prepare children for confirmation, but the children were admitted to Holy Communion without ever appearing before a bishop.

The creation of an American episcopate gradually began to change the colonial pattern. Although large dioceses and poor transportation prevented the early American bishops from visiting every parish, their presence brought both a new emphasis on confirmation and a renewed interest in catechizing. The bishops did confirm at some parishes. They frequently published their confirmation sermons and lectures on the catechism. Diocesan and national canons repeated the requirement for regular catechizing, a requirement that was found in the English and American prayer books. The General Convention, for example, adopted a canon on catechizing in 1808 and a resolution on the subject in 1817.

Bishop White's own lectures on the catechism were published in 1813. He found, as other clergy had, that a series of lectures provided an opportunity to reflect on the Episcopal church and its theology. Among the issues that occupied his attention was assurance.

White believed that most nineteenth-century Protestants sought assurance of salvation from their own emotional state. He suspected that those who experienced the most violent waves of fear, anxiety, and joy on hearing the Gospel were convinced they were saved. Those who, like White himself, lacked such violent emotions were therefore viewed with suspicion.

White understood that Christians needed a ground for assurance. His interest in the predestination debate convinced him of the dangers of an unanswered anxiety about salvation. Yet he would not trust to anything so volatile as mere human emotions. Some other ground for assurance was needed.

White's commentary on the catechism spelled out just such a means of assurance—a means, moreover, that was in keeping with his own conviction that God's election was to participation in the church. One could be assured of salvation because one had entered into a covenant relationship with God through the sacrament of baptism. This covenant relationship was an absolute guarantee of salvation for an infant. For an adult, the covenant provided the assurance that if one lived with faith, repented of one's sins, and attempted to live according to the Gospel, one would be saved—regardless of the particular fluctuations of the emotions.

The covenant relationship with God was a common theological concept for nineteenth-century Americans, but White had a specific understanding of the place of baptism within the covenant, one that not all Protestants shared. One of the primary authors on whom White relied in gaining this understanding was John Pearson (1613–86). White had placed him at the head of his list of theologians in his 1804 Course of Ecclesiastical Studies.

John Pearson was the grandson of a bishop of London, a promising young classics scholar who graduated with a master's degree from Cambridge in 1639. Ordained in the same year, he entered into his first cure shortly before the start of the British Civil War. He was loyal to the king and church, however, so his promising career was soon in shambles. The member of the royal court to whom he served as chaplain fled to the Continent. Parliament deprived him of his living and his rectory. He moved to London, where he lived a spare life on a small inheritance and the charity of friends.[5]

Pearson lived in obscurity, devoting his time to his studies, until he was invited to preach weekly sermons at a London parish in 1654. The invitation lasted until the Restoration, providing Pearson a pulpit from which to expound a comprehensive picture of the Anglican faith. In 1659 his sermons on the Apostle's Creed were published. After the Restoration Pearson rose rapidly in the church, serving first as the Lady Margaret Professor of Divinity at Cambridge and then in 1673 advancing to become the bishop of Chester.[6] His *Exposition of the Creed* remained his most influential work.

Puritan divines, such as William Ames (1575–1633), had developed a line of covenantal thought in the earlier part of the seventeenth century as a way to soften the harsh lines of the doctrine of Dort and to provide assurance to individual Christians. It was to this covenant theology that Pearson turned.[7]

Ames accepted Dort's premise that God alone predestined the elect. He argued that in practice God's free choice followed a logical pattern that offered some grounds for both assurance and response. God offered a covenant relationship to individuals whom he chose. He did so first to Adam and then to Abraham. Finally God offered the covenant in its fullness through Christ.

God's covenant, like any legal agreement, entailed responsibilities to both parties involved. God offered forgiveness of sins and everlasting life. The individual to whom God offered the covenant in turn had the responsibility of repentance and belief in Christ.[8]

The Puritan covenantal divines recognized that God was not bound to offer the covenant to all humankind. Nonetheless they suggested that, in most circumstances, the persons to whom God offered the covenant were those who had associated with Puritan congregations. God chose to work through ordinary means, they argued, through the mouths of preachers and the celebrations of the sacraments. All those who heard the Puritan preachers' summons to a covenant relationship with God were offered participation.[9]

For the Puritans the advantages of this approach were manifold. The individual Christian who fulfilled the terms of the covenant by belief in Christ could be assured of salvation. Having heard the words of the preacher, he or she would be encouraged to act out the Gospel without despairing about God's election. God became a more loving, less terrible deity. Moreover, as Puritan divines John Preston (1578–1628) and Peter Bulkley (1583–1659) assured their flocks, once God made the offer of the covenant, it could not be withdrawn. A Christian, fulfilling the covenant by belief in Christ, had a legal right to salvation.[10]

Although Puritan theologians devoted considerable attention to covenant themes, they were by no means the only English authors to express interest in them. From the late sixteenth century on, it became increasingly common for authors of works that were intended to assist Anglican clergy in catechizing to include a brief discussion of covenant theology.[11] After the Westminster Assembly of Divines adopted the Westminster catechisms (1647), Presbyterian and Independent Puritans no longer used the Book of Common Prayer's catechism or commentaries on it. In contrast, those members of the episcopal party who favored use of the Book of Common Prayer continued to use older catechetical works.

Members of the episcopal party found the covenant themes in such catechetical works to be appropriate during the interregnum in a way that it had been to Puritans earlier in the century. During the first half of the seventeenth century, the Puritans had been a minority within the Church of England. Often the object of repressive legislation, they had a palpable sense of leaving a larger, less faithful community for a congregation created in response to God's summons. With the Puritan Presbyterians and Independents in power during the interregnum, however, it was the members of the episcopal party who were persecuted. They were forbidden to use the Book of Common Prayer, their clergy were turned out of their cures, and their bishops were dismissed. Their king and archbishop were executed. For Anglicans such as Pearson, the covenant theology provided a logical vehicle for thought. They were now the faithful covenant community in the midst of apostasy.

Puritans had been troubled with an aspect of the covenant thought that ultimately led some to abandon the approach altogether. They understood that God's offer of the covenant to them had included their offspring, in the same way that the offer of the covenant to Abraham had included his offspring. Thus there were two ways of entering the covenant: hearing the covenant preached while an adult or being born to parents who had heard the call. There would be no conflict between the two groups as long as those children of the covenant matured and reached a level of conviction comparable to those who responded to the covenant as adults. Puritans found that this was not always the case, however. By 1662 New England Puritans were forced to deal with adults who not only had not attained the degree of conviction of their parents but also had children of their own.[12]

Some Puritan pastors in New England suggested that they could

rectify the difficulty by preaching on sacramental themes, urging those
who had been baptized to recognize baptism as a sign of inclusion in
the covenant and therefore to respond with faith to God's summons.
They met with no particular success. By the early eighteenth century
many Puritans abandoned this line of preaching.[13]

The Puritans did retain the covenantal approach as a common explanation for baptism, however. Baptism was the rite that sealed the
covenant into which the individual had been called. Nevertheless
preachers most frequently focused their remarks on adult response
rather than on honoring a relationship already begun in baptism.

Pearson was not faced with the same difficulties as were the Puritan
covenantal thinkers. He did not feel the need to defend God's predestination of humankind; Puritans, who were anxious to do so, were
careful to note that baptism did not bring one into the covenant but
only sealed the offer of the covenant that God had already extended
to the elect individual. Pearson also saw no need to describe a covenant community against the faithlessness of the established church. He
was therefore able to emphasize a link between baptism and the covenant at which most Puritans had been able only to hint. God, Pearson
believed, offered a covenant relationship to all who were baptized.
Baptized persons had the assurance that they were included in the covenant community. If they fulfilled the conditions of the covenant by belief
in Christ and repentance, they could be certain of the benefits of relationship. Pearson explained: "It is certain that *forgiveness of sins* was
promised to all who were baptized in the name of Christ; and it cannot be doubted but all persons who did perform all things necessary
to the receiving of the ordinance of baptism, did also receive the benefits
of that ordinance."[14] Pearson reversed the priorities of the Puritans. He
made the norm to be entrance into the covenant through baptism,
which had been the troublesome inconsistency for the Puritans.

Other Anglican theologians soon followed Pearson's lead. Gilbert
Burnet adopted Pearson's approach in his *Exposition of the Thirty-nine
Articles*. For him baptism was the "federal [i.e., pertaining to a con-
tract] admission into Christianity."[15] Bishop Ezekiel Hopkins (1634–
90) reconciled the covenantal approach with a belief in justification by
faith alone in his *Doctrine of the Two Covenants*. Thomas Stackhouse
incorporated the approach in his *Complete Body of Divinity*.

Anglican authors who wrote new works on the prayer book catechism following the Restoration continued to employ covenantal

themes. Thomas Bray (1656–1730) explained baptism as an entrance into the covenant in his popular *Catechetical Lectures*. John Lewis (1675–1747) was the author of another popular work on the catechism, one that would go through twenty-four editions by the end of the seventeenth century. He divided his commentary into five sections: the Christian covenant, the Christian faith, Christian obedience, Christian prayer, and Christian sacraments.[16] The latter four divisions followed logically from the arrangement of material in the text of the catechism. The first did not. There was no explicit reference to the baptismal covenant in the catechism or anywhere else in the Book of Common Prayer.[17] The inclusion of the heading was a testimony to the continuing importance of the covenant theology originally introduced in the Church of England by Puritans.

Bishop White, who had placed Pearson, Burnet, and Stackhouse on the Course of Ecclesiastical Studies, found in the covenant argument precisely the grounds for assurance that he sought. Certainly, he reasoned, the Christian adult must fulfill the provisions of the covenant to be saved, but all baptized persons had the assurance that if they did so, they would be saved. There was no need to rely on a welter of emotions for that assurance.

White followed John Lewis and began his *Lectures on the Catechism* with a section on the Christian covenant. White told the young people who attended his lectures that, because they were baptized, they could be assured of their relationship to God without relying on transient emotions. He contrasted this position with that of other denominations: "But the opinion the most pointedly opposed to the decisions of our Church on the present subject, is that of the persons who suppose all baptized infants to remain under the continuing effects of the sin of Adam and to be the objects of the wrath of God, until relieved from the condition by conversion."[18] The baptized Christian could be assured of inclusion in this covenant.

White believed that the baptized adult must respond to the covenant to receive salvation, and he urged his listeners to do so. He also had a comforting word for the parents of children who died in infancy, as two of his own offspring had done. Since such children had been received into the covenant in baptism, and since they had not reached an age in which they were capable of renouncing the covenant, they could be assured of salvation. Again, in making the point to his listeners, he stressed the contrast to those denominations that followed the Westminster Confession's limitation of salvation to *elect* infants. The Episcopal church

> might declare not her hope, but her certainty concerning baptized infants.
>
> How we differ, in this respect, from some other Christian communions may be seen in their . . . catechisms; in which they make a distinction of "elect infants," who are declared to be included within the promises of salvation.[19]

White was certain that Christians need not fear for the salvation of baptized infants.

Bishop White, suspicious as he was of the dangers of overreliance on emotions, was also anxious to avoid any sacramental view that involved mystery. Nineteenth-century Protestants were highly rationalistic in their approach to religion, and White was no exception.[20] Their God was all powerful but careful to respect their intellects. Nothing that God revealed in Scripture would contradict the knowledge available to humans in nature. God could, of course, interrupt the orderly flow of history but chose instead to operate through ordinary voices and actions of people. Standard religious texts, such as Joseph Butler's (1692–1752) *Analogy of Religion, Natural and Revealed, to the Constitution and Course of Nature* and William Paley's (1743–1805) *View of the Evidences of Christianity,* underscored again and again this rationality of God.

White claimed that all who were baptized entered into a new covenant relationship with God, but he believed that the relationship could be explained in a logical, nonmysterious fashion. In an appendix on baptism in his *Comparative Views,* he explained: "The point to be maintained is, that without any mysterious operation on the mind of the party, baptism, duly administered and received, is a putting into a state of grace or covenant with God."[21] The key to this claim lay in White's modifying phrase "on the mind of the party." As long as the mind of the baptized person was not in some mysterious way overcome, the Christian could comprehend the sacrament.

The covenant metaphor was a legal one. The transaction involved in the rite of baptism was not mysterious. God had proposed a legal contract and specified a manner in which that contract could be accepted. The Christian entered into that contract by submitting to baptism and could even be said to have, White explained, "a covenanted title" to salvation.[22] The orderly course of nature was no more interrupted than it would be by any other judicial transaction. The believer's mind had to remain free in order to fulfill the conditions that the contract required.

The efficacy of the sacrament lay not in any innate power contained in the rite but in the fact that God had designated it as the way of accepting the covenant. Gilbert Burnet made the point by dwelling on a distinction between a mean and a precept.

> Our Saviour has also made baptism as one of the *precepts,* though not one of the *means* necessary to salvation. A *mean* is that which does certainly procure a thing, that it being had, the thing to which it is a certain and necessary *mean* is also had; and without it the thing cannot be had; there being a natural connection between it and the end. Whereas a *precept* is an institution, in which there is no such natural efficiency; but it is positively commanded: so that the neglecting it, is a contempt of the authority that commanded it: and therefore in obeying the *precept* the value or virtue of the action lies only in obedience. This distinction appears very clearly in what our Savior has said both of *Faith* and *Baptism.* "He that believeth, and is baptized, shall be saved; and he that believeth not shall be damned." (Mark XVI.16.)[23]

The particular action—the baptizing of a child—was not in itself significant. It was the obedience that made the act efficacious. Moreover the change wrought by the act was not one that interrupted or contradicted the normal course of the world.[24]

Like the covenant theology itself, this approach to the sacraments originated in the Reformed community; it was the understanding of the sacraments advocated by John Calvin. Members of the Reformed denominations in America had distanced themselves from this position after the Great Awakening, however.[25] For most, baptism became primarily a sign or seal: a sign of the believer's faith for the Baptists, a seal of the elect's inclusion in the covenant for Presbyterians and Congregationalists, and a seal of the conditional covenant into which all were born for the Methodists.[26] Nonetheless for most Protestants it did not objectively alter or initiate a relationship with God.

Burnet's argument about a precept provided White with a middle ground between these Protestant views, in which the sacrament of baptism drew its value from the relationship it signed or sealed, and the objective view of the sacraments held by Roman Catholics. For the latter group the sacraments were in themselves effective; by their administration they imparted grace. White, drawing from Burnet, offered an intermediate alternative: under normal circumstances neither the sacrament itself nor the relationship it certified was sufficient. It was the combination of these elements—a relationship leading to obedience to the injunction to be baptized—that opened the covenant.

White found in the covenant theology a ground for assurance other than emotion: the Christian who accepted the covenant in baptism and responded with faith and repentance had a legal right to salvation. This accorded with his understanding of predestination, namely, that God's election was to and of the church, not to unconditional salvation. Moreover it provided a view of the sacraments free from the charge of mystery.

White advanced the covenant theology both in his *Lectures on the Catechism* and his *Comparative Views*. He placed Pearson, Stackhouse, and Burnet on the Course of Ecclesiastical Studies. The approach was original neither to the bishop nor to the Restoration Anglicans, but White, relying on seventeenth-century Anglicans, gave the argument an emphasis—baptism was the admission to the covenant—that differentiated it from the version advanced by most other Protestants. For Episcopalians the sacrament itself was a stronger ground of assurance. One who was baptized had a legal title to salvation. Both high-church and evangelical Episcopalians would find comfort in that title.

THE BOUNDS OF THE COVENANT

Bishop White's understanding of the baptismal covenant proved to be useful to both parties within his denomination. The covenant provided a valuable source of assurance to evangelical and high-church Episcopalians alike. The groups brought their characteristic emphases to their understanding: evangelicals emphasized the adult faith that was required in the covenant relationship; the high-church Episcopalians emphasized the great benefit of the relationship. The two groups brought an additional question to the interpretation of the covenant as well. How broad was the covenant community to be? Evangelicals suggested that all Protestants were included; high-church Episcopalians limited the covenant community to those baptized in churches with apostolic succession.

Evangelicals and the Covenant

Evangelical Episcopalians accepted the covenantal interpretation of baptism as normative. Most had read Pearson. Lewis's catechism was another pervasive influence. Bishop Griswold, an older evangelical whom the younger evangelicals regarded as a father figure, had also taught that baptism "admitted to participation in the Christian covenant."[27]

John Henshaw, the evangelical who had changed his name when he was baptized, explained the catechism to his congregation in Baltimore along the lines followed by John Lewis and Bishop White. He divided his material into five sections, the first of which dealt with the baptismal covenant. "In baptism," he told the young people of his parish, "the subject of it is brought from the world into the Church—from an uncovenanted into a covenanted state."[28] Bishop Meade of Virginia similarly taught that baptism admitted one to the covenant. Following a legal metaphor also used by Stackhouse, he noted that it was not inconsistent to admit infants to the covenant: "the forgiveness of original sin, and the gift of the Holy Spirit, may be granted to the child on its very birth, or before it, in its previous state, and yet no moral change take place at the time; just as an estate may be left or given to a child, though he cannot use it at the time, and may abuse or lose it afterwards."[29] The child could receive the title to salvation, just as he or she could receive the title to any other inheritance.

The evangelicals were always careful to point out that for the adult, admission to the covenant was not sufficient for salvation. The adult must fulfill the conditions of the covenant to receive its benefits. The individual who did not do so would be lost. White had made the same point, but the evangelicals gave it greater emphasis. Henshaw, for example, warned his parishioners that it would be a gross perversion to believe that the Episcopal church "does not inculcate the necessity of any other change in the sinner than that which is effected by baptism."[30]

The change for which evangelicals looked in the life of the baptized person was the fulfillment of the covenant through repentance and faith. Like White, the evangelicals safeguarded this adult response by stressing that baptism alone was no substitute for it. White argued that baptism made no change in the mind of the baptized person; the evangelicals also argued that there was no moral change in baptism, nothing that made individuals righteous in their own right. It was the righteousness of Christ that justified. William Wilmer explained the doctrine in this way: baptism affected "the *condition* and not the *character* of the recipient. . . . The Church understands baptism as descriptive of a new *state* rather than of a new *nature;* as implying a recovery from a state of guilt, and wrath to a state of pardon and acceptance, rather than as a recovery from a sinful disposition to holiness of heart."[31] The moral change in the believer would come about only as a result of adult repentance and faith, which fulfilled the requirement of the covenant.

With the exception of Reuel Keith, evangelical professors of divinity followed Wilmer in teaching that baptism admitted the Christian to the covenant. Wilmer identified Bishop Pearson as held "in the highest esteem as a divine."[32] Pearson's *Exposition of the Creed,* already designated by White as a text for those preparing for orders, was used at all four evangelical seminaries—Virginia, Kenyon, Philadelphia, and the Episcopal Theological School—for the entire nineteenth century. No other work, in any category, was as popular.

Although evangelicals did not always stress the fact, they defined covenant membership to include other Protestants. Methodists, Baptists, Presbyterians, Congregationalists, and members of other denominations were also baptized and also placed importance on adult Christian life. The evangelicals' high-church coreligionists would view the matter in a very different way.

High-Church Covenant Thought

Several eighteenth-century high-church leaders subscribed to an objective understanding of the sacrament of baptism. This view, shared by Bishop Samuel Seabury of Connecticut, was displaced in the nineteenth century by White's covenantal understanding.

In 1791 Seabury became the first Episcopal bishop to sanction a particular catechism for use in his diocese. He chose a work prepared by Scottish bishop George Innes (d. 1781), a catechism with which Seabury may have become acquainted while in Scotland in 1784 for consecration to the episcopate. Innes organized his material on a plan different from that of Lewis. Instead of dividing the material into five major sections—baptismal covenant, the creed, commandments, Lord's prayer, and the sacraments—he prepared forty-three sections, an approach that allowed him to emphasize the sacraments and the episcopacy.

Innes argued that baptism was valid only if administered by someone commissioned by Christ (i.e., in the apostolic succession).[33] For

Innes, moreover, baptism, which was administered by the parish priest, was subordinated to confirmation, which was administered by the bishop. In baptism Christians received a right to possess the Holy Spirit, but they did not come into full possession until confirmation:

Q. Is not the Holy Ghost given us at our Baptism?
A. In our water-baptism the Holy Ghost purifies and fits us to be a Temple for himself, and in Confirmation he enters in and takes Possession of this Temple.[34]

The gift of the Holy Spirit, first received through the hands of the bishop at confirmation, was then nourished "by private and public Prayer, and the Sacrifice of the Holy Eucharist."[35]

This sacramental view of baptism, specified by Seabury for his diocese, would soon be displaced by a high-church variation of the covenantal view. In 1799—three years after Seabury's death—high-church deputies at the General Convention meeting were already suggesting covenantal arguments. In the first two decades of the nineteenth century two successive bishops of New York—Benjamin Moore and John Henry Hobart—popularized the covenantal view, ensuring it a prominent place in high-church theology.

Bishop Benjamin Moore saw much to admire in Seabury's edition of Innes. The insistence on the necessity of an apostolic ministry for the church attracted him, but he cared little for Innes's sacramentalism. Deciding to prepare an edition of Innes's catechism for his own diocese, Benjamin Moore simply omitted Innes's discussion of confirmation and his extended section on confession.[36] In their place he substituted sections from Lewis's catechism.

Moore's edition of Innes was frequently reprinted and came to be known as the "Old New York Diocesan Catechism."[37] Later high-church Episcopalians would look back nostalgically on Seabury's important role in fashioning high-church theology, but in fact Moore had sidetracked Seabury's understanding of sacramental grace. It was Moore's edition of Innes, not Seabury's, that would be reprinted.

Moore was acquainted with the covenantal argument. He prepared a summary of this understanding of baptism for use by his clergy in arguing against the Baptist practice of postponing baptism until maturity.[38] It was Moore's successor Hobart, however, who most carefully explained the advantages of the covenant theology to high-church Episcopalians. Hobart produced a new catechism for use in his diocese;

it was published by the General Protestant Episcopal Sunday School Union and used in other dioceses as well. He also expounded his understanding of the covenant in sermons, many of which were later collected and published.

Hobart had studied theology with Bishop White. It was unlikely that White could have had a more diligent student. Throughout his ministry Hobart would show a familiarity with the texts to which White introduced him. Hobart had a clear vision of the Anglican tradition with which he hoped to shape and direct the church at large.

Although the basic outlines of Hobart's arguments agreed with White's, the specific conclusions often differed. This was the case with baptism. Relying on Gilbert Burnet's *Exposition of the Thirty-nine Articles* and other texts favored by White, Hobart was able to imply that other denominations were excluded from the covenant.

In his *Exposition of the Thirty-nine Articles* Burnet had suggested that the value of a sacrament lay not in the objective grace it contained but in the obedience involved in its administration. If some important element was purposely excluded, the obedience would be incomplete. Burnet had suggested that a heretical baptism might involve such an omission:

> But after all, the covenant of grace, the terms of salvation and the ground on which we expect it, seem to be things of another nature than all other truths, which, though revealed, are not of themselves the means or conditions of salvation. Wheresoever true baptism is, there it seems the essentials of this covenant are preserved; for, if we look on baptism as a federal admission into Christianity, there can be no baptism where the essence of Christianity is not preserved. As far then as we believe that any society has preserved that, so far are we bound to receive her baptism, and no further.[39]

Burnet himself had argued that episcopal ordination was "regular" but not necessary and therefore that the lack of such ordination did not exclude one from the covenant.[40] Not all authors who wrote commentaries on the catechism that used covenant themes would agree, however. Thomas Bray, for example, had written in his *Catechetical Lectures* that

> it does not appear that God is under any Promise, or Engagement to hear the Prayers, that [those who either take on themselves the min-

istry or receive an ordination to it from those hands] shall put for the People, to convey the Graces of his Holy Spirit, by the Sacraments they shall Administer, or to Ratify the Pardon of those Penitents, whom they shall Absolve; whereas he has assured the Church, with respect to his lawful Ministers, that whatsoever of this Nature they shall do on Earth, shall be Establish[ed] in Heaven.[41]

Bray recognized that the "Sister Churches Beyond-Sea" (the Reformed and Lutheran churches on the Continent) could argue that they had abandoned episcopal ordination out of necessity. Those who were "secure of being within the Pale of a right Constituted Gospel-Church" could make no such claim and therefore should not separate from a church with episcopally ordained clergy.[42]

Unlike Bishop Moore, Hobart relied on the form of the covenantal argument that had been shaped by Bray rather than by Lewis. In his third catechism—the third catechism printed by the General Protestant Episcopal Sunday School Union—Hobart argued that the episcopacy was a necessary part of the Christian covenant. Although he did not draw the obvious consequence of this position for non-episcopal denominations, many of his readers would.

Hobart's response to ecumenism did little to reassure those who hoped that he had only inadvertently excluded other Protestants from the covenant. In 1816 he publicly urged all Episcopal clergy to refrain from participating in the ecumenical American Bible Society, an organization in which his old nemesis John M. Mason was active. Hobart argued that any participation would weaken the principles of the church. In 1822 he repeated the injunction in relation to other ecumenical societies.[43]

Like Hobart, most high-church Episcopalians left their readers to draw their own conclusions about the fate of other Protestants. They did not entirely condemn all other Protestants to perdition, however. Burnet had provided a loophole that allowed high-church Episcopalians to believe that Protestants excluded from the covenant for their disregard of the apostolic ministry might still be saved. For the Puritans who had first advanced the covenant theology, this was unthinkable. Humanity was sinful, and without the benefit of the covenant one could expect only death before God. But Burnet, less interested in the rigors of Dort and Westminster, was more optimistic about the fate of those excluded from the covenant. He argued that although persons outside the federal relationship had no legal title to salvation, theologians should not limit "the extent to which the goodness and mercy of God may go." Those outside the covenant had no "federal right to be saved," but they might be saved by a merciful God nonetheless.[44]

Burnet fashioned the argument to explain the fate of persons who never heard the Gospel and who therefore never rejected it. American high-church Episcopalians broadly hinted that Protestants without episcopal orders belonged in the same category. William Walter and his committee took this approach in the draft of the Articles of Religion they prepared at the 1799 meeting of the General Convention. The eighth article of the draft—a rewritten version of the English eighteenth article on salvation only through Christ—included this addition: "We are not authorized to assert, that men shall not be saved by the name of Jesus Christ to whom His Gospel has not been promulgated. We leave them to the uncovenanted mercies of God." The following article specified recipients of this uncovenanted mercy; it defined the visible church as a body with "the pure work of God . . . preached, the Sacraments duly administered, and the order of the priesthood observed."[45]

Evangelicals believed that Christ had intended and instituted the episcopacy for the church, but they would accept none of the high-church theologians' exclusive claims. William Sparrow at Virginia Seminary protested: "What we contend against is, giving over the pious and good to uncovenanted mercies, which are no mercies at all."[46] Other Protestants were equally aware of the implication of Hobart's doctrine. In the pages of the *Biblical Repository*, a magazine originally published at Andover, the Reverend Ansel Eddy cited Hobart and complained: "This is declared to cut off the soul from all covenanted mercies and the hope of eternal life!"[47]

Perhaps the most telling criticism of the exclusive covenant came from William Augustus Muhlenberg. Like Hobart, he was a product of a theological education with White. Although a leader in introducing ritual innovations in America and one of the very few in the mid-nineteenth century daring to call the Episcopal church catholic, he would never accept the implications of exclusivity. The Episcopal church, he argued pragmatically, had never effectively reached all the elements of the American population. With the loss of British missionary funds and state support following the American Revolution, the real growth of the church had been in the larger cities among the affluent classes. The normative means of finance—pew rent—effectively

consigned persons of modest means to the balconies. Since the Episcopal church (and other churches with apostolic succession) had not
reached all the nation, it would be heretical to limit the saved to their
members.[48]

The evangelicals were as willing as the high-church Episcopalians
to admit, as had Burnet, the possibility of salvation for those who did
not enter the covenant by baptism. What they objected to was consign-
ing whole denominations to an uncovenanted state on the basis of
church polity. Meade, for example, explained that baptism was generally necessary for salvation, but he suggested that there might be exceptions. He made it clear that the exceptions were few and far between,
however: "Any requirement, however comparatively trivial, willfully
intended, and habitually neglected, must prove fatal to the soul."[49]
Those who lived pious and Christian lives must not be consigned to
such a category simply because their denomination did not have an
episcopal form of government.

In addition to linking the question of the episcopacy to the covenantal argument, John Henry Hobart emphasized the great benefit of entrance into the covenant. Daniel Waterland (1643–1740), a master of
Magdalene College, Cambridge, developed the covenant argument in
much the same way. He noted the phrase "state of salvation" in the
Book of Common Prayer's catechism and equated it with participation
in the covenant relationship. To enter the covenant was to change to a
state of salvation: "This *change,* translation, or adoption, carried in it
many Christian blessings and privileges, but all reducible to two, *viz.*
remission of sins (absolute or conditional) and a covenant claim, for
the time being, to eternal happiness."[50] Whether the person baptized
was a child, a faithful adult, a future reprobate, or an open hypocrite,
Waterland thought, the sacrament effected a real change. All the baptized acquired the title to salvation, although manifestly not everyone
made use of it.[51]

Hobart reproduced Waterland's argument in his own preaching. He
explained, for example, the case of the hypocrite:

> Now those adults who come to baptism with faith and repentance,
> actually receive in this ordinance the forgiveness of their sins, the
> favour of God, and a title to the happiness of heaven. But those adults
> who come to baptism without faith and repentance, are disqualified
> from the actual *enjoyment* of these privileges. Still these defects do

not render them incapable of being admitted into the church, and of receiving in baptism a solemn proffer, on the part of God, of all the privileges of this mystical body, and a title to them, on the conditions of repentance and faith. . . . A conditional grant of all the blessings of the Gospel covenant is made to them in baptism, to take effect when they shall truly repent. . . .

The unworthy recipients of baptism are therefore translated by this sacrament into a state of salvation.[52]

A change had taken place, and the person baptized gained a promise of a forgiveness of sins and everlasting life.

Committed to the covenant theology and finding no less objectionable way to explain the "state of salvation" in the prayer book, evangelicals did not deny Hobart's argument. They did try to minimize its force, however. Thus for John K. Henshaw baptism denoted "*only* a change of state or condition."[53] For William Meade it was "*a mere* change of state and conditional title to salvation," and for Charles McIlvaine it was a "*relative* change of state."[54]

Bishop Hobart suggested at the 1826 meeting of the House of Bishops that the liturgy be altered to include an explicit reference to the baptismal covenant. His effort would have been successful had he not pushed for another change as well, a clarification of the meaning of the word *regeneration.*[55] The specific change proposed by Hobart was in the confirmation office. He suggested adding an optional collect at the start of the service that summarized the change that had already taken place in baptism. God, the prayer stated, had given to the baptized person "a title to all the blessings of [the] covenant of grace and mercy."[56] The resolution passed the House of Bishops unanimously on first reading, but it was rejected three years later because of the disagreement over the word *regeneration,* which was also contained in the prayer. It would not be until one hundred fifty years later that the bishops and deputies of the General Convention would incorporate reference to the baptismal covenant in the Book of Common Prayer.[57]

Hobart, although unsuccessful in convincing the General Convention to alter the liturgy, demonstrated the utility of the covenantal argument to high-church Episcopalians. High-church seminary professors adopted the works of Pearson and Daniel Waterland as standard texts for their students. Later in the century William Adams of Nashotah House and Samuel Buel of Seabury and General Seminaries still would patiently lay out Hobart's argument. Baptism in a church with apostolic ministry admitted one to the covenant. Adams argued that omitting the requirement of the apostolic ministry would make "the baptism of infants . . . an absurdity,"[58] for as Buel explained, the form of the church "is manifestly an essential constituent of the Gospel of Christ, not a mere external appendage of the Gospel."[59]

On a popular level Hobart's third catechism and similar efforts by other high-church authors provided vehicles for the instruction of lay persons. Although drawing different conclusions because of their disagreement on the necessity of the episcopacy, high-church Episcopalians found the covenant theology as useful a vehicle for their views as had the evangelicals.

THE TYPOLOGICAL ARGUMENT

Like Presbyterians and Congregationalists, Episcopalians found in the covenant theology a suitable response to the Baptists' rejection of infant baptism. They argued that a single covenant was offered to Adam and Abraham and in Christ. The earlier forms of the covenant were forerunners of the covenant's fulfillment in Christ. To understand the covenant, therefore, one could look back at the earlier instances. In particular the Old Testament rite of circumcision was a type of New Testament baptism. Since infants had been circumcised, infants should be baptized. This typological argument was often coupled with a long recitation of patristic texts to show that infant baptism was the norm in the early church.

Although the argument was commonly advanced by most Reformation divines, the immediate sources for American Episcopalians were English works such as Charles Jerram's *Conversations on Infant Baptism* and William Wall's *History of Infant Baptism*. Bishop Benjamin Moore in New York distributed a summary of the argument in his diocese. Philander Chase purchased a large issue of a pamphlet on the argument for the clergy of the diocese of Illinois.[60] Meade, Henshaw, and a number of other Episcopalians used the typological argument in their own works.[61]

At midcentury Bishop John Henry Hopkins of Vermont took the typological argument and shaped it to serve a different purpose. Hopkins had been elected rector of Trinity Church, Pittsburgh, while still a layman. With Bishop White's approval, he had accepted the call and begun to study for clerical orders. Ordained a deacon in 1823 and a priest in the following year, Hopkins advanced quickly in the church's hierarchy, leaving Pittsburgh to become assistant rector of Trinity Church, Boston (1831), and then being elected bishop of Vermont (1832). In 1865 he became presiding bishop—that is, the bishop who was senior by date of consecration.

At the time Hopkins became presiding bishop, a number of clergy were introducing colored stoles, vested choirs, incense, sanctus bells, and more elaborate ritual into their parishes.[62] A group of clergy wrote to Hopkins to ask his opinion as presiding bishop about the changes. Hopkins represented the same kind of moderate churchmanship as had Bishop White. He sought an answer that would both protect the integrity of his own views and allow the possibility of alternative positions. He found it in the typological argument.

Hopkins found precursors in the Old Testament not only for baptism but for "all ritual worship."[63] He argued further that the Council of Jerusalem (Acts 15) had declared these types to be optional. The Gentile Christian thus had two options: either accept the ritual authorized by the Old Testament while recognizing that it was unnecessary for salvation or forgo ritual worship.

According to Hopkins, the Jewish altar was the type of the Christian holy table, and the vestments of the Jewish priests were the type of the Christian minister's dress. Jewish singing, processions, and incense were the types for similar Christian practices.[64] All these could be either followed or rejected.

One could not create rituals for which no such types existed, however, and Hopkins also presented this negative side of his argument, suggesting that the Old Testament had no types for certain Roman Catholic practices, which were therefore illicit. There was no type for the papacy, for auricular confession with private absolution, or for monastic societies under a vow of obedience to a superior. These were improper inventions of the Roman Catholic church.[65]

Hopkins buttressed his argument with a review of Anglican and Episcopal canon law. He found that these allowed but did not require an advanced ritual. Hopkins's own personal preference was not to adopt such forms of worship. "Personally," he wrote, "I prefer the more simple ceremonial."[66] According to Hopkins, those Episcopalians who advocated use of a more elaborate ceremonial and those who opposed it agreed on the substance of the faith. When disagreeing on the finer points of ritual, they were simply exercising the freedom given to them in Scripture.[67]

Hopkins's argument was a bold attempt to reconcile differences among Episcopalians by appealing to the covenantal argument that all accepted. He allayed the fears of some and quieted the tempers of others. Unfortunately he lacked one component that had helped to make Bishop White a substantial force for stability—longevity. Two years after the publication of his *Law of Ritualism,* he died.

~

Episcopalians of the early and mid-nineteenth century found a source of assurance in baptism that they had not gained from the doctrine of predestination. All baptized persons had the assurance that they could be saved as long as they exercised repentance and faith. John Henshaw and others who altered their names when baptized did so out of the firm belief that in baptism they not only signed or sealed but actually entered a covenantal relationship with God. Baptism was a cornerstone of personal assurance.

NOTES

1. William B. Sprague, *Annals of the American Pulpit: Or Commemorative Notices of Distinguished American Clergymen of Various Denominations from the Early Settlement of the Country to the Close of the Year Eighteen Hundred and Fifty-five with Historical Introductions,* 9 vols. (New York: Robert Carter and Brothers, 1857–69), 5:545. From 1813 until 1816 Kewley was to be the rector of St. George's, New York, a parish that became an important evangelical center. Kewley himself later became a Roman Catholic.

2. Robert W. Prichard, "Early Development of the Diocesan Standing Committee," *Historical Magazine of the Protestant Episcopal Church* 43 (Sept. 1974): 212.

3. In the early church the actions that were later to be separated into confirmation and baptism had been part of a single service of initiation over which the bishop presided. When the church grew too large for the bishop to be present at every rite of initiation, Christians in the western end of the Roman Empire subdivided the service into baptism, over which the parish priest presided, and confirmation, over which the bishop presided. In the thirteenth century bishops, who were angered by parents' increasing tardiness in bringing their children for confirmation, began to require confirmation as a precondition for reception of Holy Communion. The general expectation that bap-

tized persons were to await confirmation before receiving Holy Communion persisted in the Roman Catholic church until 1910 and in the Episcopal church until 1970. For a further discussion, see Geoffrey Lampe, *The Seal of the Spirit: A Study in the Doctrine of Baptism and Confirmation in the New Testament and the Fathers*, 2d ed. (London: SPCK, 1976).

4. Rubrics allowing those who were ready and desirous of confirmation to receive communion had been added to the English Book of Common Prayer in 1662. American prayer books retained the rubric until 1979, when the rites of initiation were thoroughly revised. Elements of the confirmation service were rejoined to baptism, which was then declared to be "full initiation by water and the Holy Spirit into Christ's Body the Church." Thereafter all baptized persons were allowed to receive Holy Communion.

5. *Dictionary of National Biography* (1917–), s.v. "John Pearson," by Francis Sanders.

6. Ibid.

7. Current scholarly interest in Protestant covenant theology dates back to a 1935 essay by historian Perry Miller titled "The Marrow of Puritan Divinity." Although subsequent authors have generally accepted Miller's reconstruction of covenant theology, they have questioned many assertions that Miller made about its origin and use. Contemporary historians have suggested, for example, that Miller overemphasized the degree of Puritan anxiety about salvation, misunderstood the link between performance of covenant responsibilities and salvation, failed to understand the biblical and Continental roots of many covenant ideas, and erred in suggesting that eighteenth-century American theologian Jonathan Edwards abandoned covenant themes. For a detailed discussion of the current state of scholarship on covenant theology, see David D. Hall, "On Common Ground: The Coherence of American Puritan Studies," *William and Mary Quarterly*, 3d ser., 44 (Apr. 1987): 193–229. Hall focuses on American Puritan studies and does not take into account Episcopal use of covenant themes.

8. Perry Miller, "The Marrow of Puritan Divinity," *Errand into the Wilderness*, 48–97 (New York: Harper and Row/Torchbooks, 1957). This theological approach was also referred to as "federal theology."

9. Ibid., 85.

10. Ibid., 63–74.

11. Ian Green's study of English catechetical works revealed that "references to the covenant of grace were rare [in catechetical works] before the 1590's, but so common as to be almost standard by the second quarter of the seventeenth century." See Ian Green, "'For Children in Yeeres and Children in Understanding': The Emergence of the English Catechism under Elizabeth and the Early Stuarts," *Journal of Ecclesiastical History* 37 (July 1986): 404n.

12. Williston Walker, *The Creeds and Platforms of Congregationalism* (Boston: Pilgrim, 1960), 246–50.

13. E. Brooks Holifield, *The Covenant Sealed: The Development of Puritan Sacramental Theology in Old and New England, 1570–1720* (New Haven, Conn.: Yale University Press, 1974), 228–29.

14. John Pearson, *An Exposition of the Creed,* new ed., ed. E. Burton (Oxford: Clarendon, 1890), 649.

15. Gilbert Burnet, *An Exposition of the Thirty-Nine Articles of the Church of England,* new ed. (London: Thomas Tegg, 1827), 180.

16. John Lewis, *Church Catechism Explained,* 27th ed. (New York: reprinted with a few necessary alterations by James Oran, 1800).

17. The word *covenant* appeared in the 1662 prayer book only in direct quotations from Scriptures and in reference to marriage. The 1979 Book of Common Prayer would be the first American prayer book to refer explicitly to the baptismal covenant.
See Green, "'For Children in Yeeres,'" for a discussion of the place of the covenant in catechetical works.

18. William White, *Lectures on the Catechism of the Protestant Episcopal Church* (Philadelphia: Bradford and Inskeep, 1813), 14.

19. Ibid., 13.

20. See E. Brooks Holifield, *The Gentlemen Theologians: American Theology in Southern Culture, 1795–1860* (Durham, N.C.: Duke University Press, 1978), 73–77, for a discussion of the rationality of American Protestants. Holifield examined Christians in the Lutheran, Reformed, Anglican, and Methodist traditions.
Advocates of conversion experience saw no conflict between the rationality of the Christian faith and the need for conversion. They used logical arguments to explain the necessity of conversion and to interpret its significance, just as they used logical arguments to show the importance of Scripture and interpret its meaning.

21. William White, *Comparative Views of the Controversy between the Calvinists and the Arminians,* 2 vols. (Philadelphia: M. Thomas, 1817), 2:283.

22. Ibid., 2:280.

23. Burnet, *Exposition of the Thirty-nine Articles,* 304.

24. For a contrasting view of White's understanding of baptism, see Harvey Hill, "Worship in the Ecclesiology of William White," *Anglican and Episcopal History* 62 (Sept. 1993): 317–42. Hill identified a tension that ran through White's thought, but he may have overstated his case when he suggested that "White seemed to articulate two extreme views of baptism, consistent with either a high, sacramental or a low, voluntaristic view of the church (320)." White did try to balance entrance into the baptismal covenant with adult repentance and faith, leaving it to his evangelical and high-church followers to emphasize either element.

25. Holifield, *Covenant Sealed,* 229.

26. Holifield, *The Gentlemen Theologians,* 115–85.

27. Alexander V. Griswold, *Discourses on the Most Important Doctrines and Duties of the Christian Religion* (Philadelphia: William Stavely, 1830), 223.

28. J. K. Henshaw, *Theology for the People: In a Series of Discourses on the Catechism of the Protestant Episcopal Church* (Baltimore: Daniel Brunner, 1840), 32.

29. William Meade, *Companion to the Font and the Pulpit* (Washington: J. & G. S. Gideon, 1846), 29; Thomas Stackhouse, *A Complete Body of Speculative and Practical Divinity, etc.,* 2d ed., corrected (London: printed for J. Batley at the Dove in Pater-Noster Row and T. Cox at the Lamb under the Royal-Exchange, Cornhill, 1734), 603–4.

30. Henshaw, *Theology,* 35.

31. William H. Wilmer, *The Episcopal Manual: A Summary Explanation of the Doctrine, Discipline, and Worship of the Protestant Episcopal Church, in the United States of America,* new and improved ed., ed. John Coleman (Philadelphia: R. S. George, 1841), 134, 137.

32. Wilmer, *Episcopal Manual,* 106.

33. George Innes, *A Catechism or, the Principles of the Christian Religion Explained in a Familiar and Easy Manner, Adapted to the Lowest Capacities* (Edinburgh; repr. New Haven, Conn.: T. & S. Green, 1791), 9.

34. Ibid., 38.

35. Ibid.

36. [Benjamin Moore], *A Catechism Designed As an Explanation and Enlargement of the Church Catechism Formerly Recommended by the Bishops and Clergy of the Protestant Episcopal Church in the State of New York to Which Are Added the Omitted Parts of the Original Catechism of Bishop Innes as Republished by Bishop Seabury,* ed. William R. Whittingham (Baltimore: Joseph Robinson, 1851), 48–49, 66–80.

37. Bruce E. Steiner, *Samuel Seabury, 1724–1796: A Study in High Church Tradition* (Athens: Ohio University Press, 1971), 246.

38. Advertisement to Alexander Hay, *A Treatise on Baptism* (New York: J. A. Sparks, 1842), vi.

39. Burnet, *Exposition of the Thirty-nine Articles,* 187.

40. Ibid., 188.

41. Thomas Bray, *Catechetical Lectures on the Preliminary Questions and Answers of the Church-Catechism,* in *Readings from the History of the Episcopal Church,* ed. Robert W. Prichard, 28–40 (Wilton, Conn.: Morehouse-Barlow, 1986), 27.

42. Ibid., 27.

43. E. Clowes Chorley, *Men and Movements in the American Episcopal Church* (New York: Scribner's, 1946), 278–80.

44. Burnet, *Exposition of the Thirty-nine Articles,* 180.

45. William Stevens Perry, ed., *Journals of the General Conventions of the Protestant Episcopal Church in the United States, 1785–1835*, 3 vols. (Claremont, N.H.: Claremont Manufacturing, 1874), 1:233.

46. William Sparrow, *Sermons by the Rev. William Sparrow, Late Professor of Systematic Divinity and Evidences of Christianity in the Theological Seminary of the Protestant Episcopal Church in the Diocese of Virginia* (New York: Thomas Whittaker, 1877), 116.

47. Ansel Eddy, "The Prelatical Principles, Anti-Republican and Unevangelical," *The Biblical Repository and Classical Review*, 3d ser., 1 (Apr. 1845): 324.

48. Alvin W. Skardon, *Church Leader in the Cities: William Augustus Muhlenberg* (Philadelphia: University of Pennsylvania Press, 1971), 176. In this work Skardon noted the difficulty of classifying Muhlenberg, who referred to himself as an "evangelical catholic," as either an evangelical or high-church Episcopalian. Allen C. Guelzo has recently argued that Muhlenberg served as a spokesman for the evangelicals in the 1850s; see Guelzo, *For the Union of Evangelical Christendom: The Irony of the Reformed Episcopalians* (University Park: Pennsylvania State University Press, 1994), 59–65.

49. Meade, *Companion*, 17.

50. Daniel Waterland, *The Works of the Rev. Daniel Waterland, D.D.*, 6 vols. (Oxford: Clarendon, 1822), 6:348.

51. Ibid., 6:354–61.

52. John Henry Hobart, *The Posthumous Works of the Late Right Reverend John Henry Hobart, D.D.*, 3 vols. (New York: Swords, Stanford, 1832), 2:483–85.

53. Henshaw, *Theology*, 31 (emphasis added).

54. William Meade, *Old Churches, Ministers and Families of Virginia*, 2 vols. (Philadelphia: J. B. Lippincott, 1910), 2:386; Charles Pettit McIlvaine, *Righteousness by Faith: A New and Revised Edition of "Oxford Divinity"* (Philadelphia: Protestant Episcopal Book Society, 1862), 301 (emphasis added in both quotations).

55. William White, *Memoirs of the Protestant Episcopal Church*, (New York: E. P. Dutton, 1880), 303.

56. Perry, *Journals, 1785–1835*, 2:189.

57. The American Book of Common Prayer (1979) includes a section in the baptismal office titled "The Baptismal Covenant."

58. William Adams, *Mercy to Babes: A Plea for the Christian Baptism of Infants, Addressed to Those Who Doubt and Those Who Deny the Validity of That Practice* (New York: Stanford and Swords, 1847), 180.

59. Samuel Buel, *A Treatise of Dogmatic Theology*, 2 vols. (New York: Thomas Whittaker, 1890), 1:403.

60. William Shelton, preface to Hay, *Baptism*, xi.

61. Meade, *Companion*, 37–38; Henshaw, *Theology*, 524.

62. There was no one-to-one relationship between the church parties and attitudes on ritualism. The identifying mark of the early high-church Episcopalians had been an emphasis on episcopal polity rather than any particular style of worship. Some high-church Episcopalians did favor a greater degree of ritualism, but there were others who were liturgical conservatives. Evangelical Episcopalians, distinguished more by their advocacy of adult renewal than by any liturgical style, also divided over ritualism. See chapter 6 for a discussion of the reconfiguration of church parties at the end of the century.

63. John Henry Hopkins, *The Law of Ritualism Examined in Its Relation to the Word of God, to the Primitive Church, to the Church of England, and to the Protestant Episcopal Church in the United States* (New York: Hurd and Houghton, 1866), 8.

64. Ibid., 52–55.

65. Ibid.

66. Ibid., 76.

67. Ibid., 90.

4 RENEWAL

⌒

WILLIAM MEADE was a younger member of the Washington evangelicals who became the leader of the movement in Virginia when William H. Wilmer died in 1827. Meade wrote a pamphlet in the 1850s entitled *Reasons for Loving the Episcopal Church*. In it he cited the invitation to confession in the Book of Common Prayer's communion service, which, he said, supposed that "the recipients [of communion] . . . have experienced a new birth unto righteousness."[1] For Meade this new birth or renewal was a pillar of adult assurance. In baptism children entered the covenant; in renewal adults satisfied the terms of the covenant.

Other Episcopalians agreed. The doctrine of renewal appeared in the liturgy, the writings of the evangelicals, and the works of the high-church Episcopalians. Bishop White outlined the doctrine in his *Lectures on the Catechism* and appealed to Gilbert Burnet and John Pearson as authorities.

This understanding of renewal enabled Episcopal clergy not only to call their parishioners to fulfill the terms of the baptismal covenant but also to give them a context in which to understand the great landmarks of American Protestantism—the "awakenings" of the eighteenth and nineteenth centuries.

THE LOGIC OF RENEWAL

In his *Lectures on the Catechism* William White chose an explanation for renewal that did not require reference to the believer's emotional state. The logic of his argument allowed him and later Episcopalians to consider the importance of renewal without first judging the validity of the conversion experiences that were so prominent in nineteenth-century Protestantism. Renewal was a central Christian reality; it was necessary for the salvation of adults. It influenced their manner of living and their response to specific moral issues, and it was the goal and end of Christian education of children.

Divine and Human Initiative

When Bishop White referred to renewal, he intentionally used a word with two connotations. Renewal was either a divine or a human action within the covenant relationship. The word had been used first in English in John Wycliffe's fourteenth-century translation of the Bible into English; it appeared in 2 Corinthians 4:16 and Ephesians 4:23.[2] In both passages *renewal* referred to a divine action giving strength to an individual believer. Thomas Cranmer later used the word with this meaning in the Collect for Christmas Day in the first Book of Common Prayer: "Graunte that we beying regenerate, and made thy children by adoption and grace, maye dailye be reneued by thy holy spirit."[3] Renewal was, in its first sense, a granting of divine aid to the individual who already had a relationship with God through baptism.

White described renewal in this sense to the young people of his parish who had been baptized and were preparing for confirmation. The bishop warned that one needed a "right state of affection" that "we have not from nature." He suggested further that this state "is always described in the . . . Scriptures, as operated by a divine agency; the affect of which is 'a renewal after the image of him who created us.'"[4] God restored the divine image by renewing the Christian adult in the covenant relationship.

Those who did not hear White personally or read his *Lectures on the Catechism* could find a similar account of divine renewal in the texts that White chose for his Course of Ecclesiastical Studies. John Pearson, for example, explained renewal by contrasting a second creation with the first:

> It is evident, that a new creature is such a person as truly believeth in Christ, and manifesteth that faith by the exercise of good works; and the new creation is the reforming or bringing man into this new condition, which by nature or his first creation he was not in. And therefore, he which is so created is called a new man, in opposition to the *old man, which is corrupt according to the deceitful lusts:* from whence the Apostle chargeth us to *be renewed in the spirit of our*

mind, and to *put on that new man, which after God is created in righteousness and true holiness;* and which is *renewed in knowledge, after the image of him that created him.*[5]

The individual who was renewed experienced "a real . . . though not substantial" change.[6]

Renewal could be understood from a second perspective: as a human action, a human recommitment to the terms of the baptismal covenant. Such a recommitment could be made at confirmation, for as William H. Wilmer noted, confirmation was "an act which, as it were, renews the baptismal vows."[7] In a more general sense, however, renewal could take place at any point at which an individual resolved to keep the promises of the covenant.

Thus Bishop White could speak of renewal as a voluntary action by the Christian. He concluded his lecture on the baptismal covenant to the young people of his parish with this exhortation: "Finally—addressing myself to all present, I exhort them so to estimate the baptismal privilege, as to be aware of the great danger of a forfeiture; and in this event, the urgent necessity of a renewal."[8] Christians were able to participate in renewal by recommitting themselves to fulfill the conditions of the baptismal covenant.

These conditions were summarized in the prayer book's catechism as two: repentance and faith.

> Question: What is required of a person to be baptized?
> Answer: Repentance, whereby they forsake sin; and Faith, whereby they steadfastly believe the promises God made to them in the Sacrament.[9]

The way to renew the covenant was to repent and to exercise a living faith.

Christians were able to take such an initiative for two reasons: first, if baptized, they had already been admitted into the covenant; second, Episcopalians argued, the original righteousness of the first creation had not been entirely obliterated by the sin of Adam. According to the ninth of the Thirty-nine Articles, humans were "very far gone from original righteousness" but not entirely sinful.[10] As a result, even unbaptized adults could take the initiative toward renewal. In such adults, as Wilmer would point out, "faith and repentance should precede baptism."[11]

Episcopalians were less than precise about the exact relationship of

the human and divine initiative in renewal. They were unclear whether God or the Christian initiated the renewal, just as they had been
unwilling to take a single position on election and free will. The divine
and human actions in covenant renewal were closely related, however, and it was possible for Episcopalians to speak of them together as
one process. Bishop Hobart, who grew up in Bishop White's parish and
may have sat through his catechetical lectures, would speak on both
elements in a single sentence and feel no need to explain: "The exalted
value of the *privileges* of the Christian covenant which are conferred
on us in . . . baptism, forcibly urges us to *secure* them by fulfilling the
conditions on which they are suspended, and thus becoming renewed
by the Holy Ghost."[12] The Christian renewed his or her commitment
to the covenant and was renewed by the Holy Spirit.

Like the high-church Episcopalian Hobart, evangelical Episcopalians
could similarly combine the Christians' commitment to the covenant
and the action of the Holy Ghost. The first article in the March 1821
issue of the evangelical *Washington Theological Repertory* exhorted
parents to attend carefully to their children's Christian education. If they
followed the exhortation, parents could "expect that effectual co-op-
eration of the Divine Spirit which would regenerate, renew, and save"
their adult children.[13]

Together the divine and human aspects of renewal produced a significant change in the individual. White explained that the inward character was transformed, molded "to a likeness of the adorable excellen-
cies of God himself."[14] He agreed with the editors of the *Washington
Theological Repertory* when they suggested "that in all cases where the
change is real, it will be known."[15]

This remolding was known as a change of character, a change of life,
a change of heart, a moral change, or as Bishop Meade called it, "the
great moral change."[16] It always resulted in a commitment to Christian moral behavior. Without this change no adult could be saved. As
Gilbert Burnet said, "our natures must be sanctified and renewed, that
so God may take pleasure in us, when his image is again visible upon
us."[17]

The Content of the Christian Life

White explained in his catechism that the only sure sign of the renewed life was the presence of fruits of the Spirit. "In proportion as
there is a sensibility of this . . . we may discern in these holy influences

the operation of that spirit of grace." The fruits of the Spirit were "goodness and righteousness and truth."[18]

Although White and other Episcopalians were often willing to describe Christian moral behavior only in such general terms, they could also give specific examples of activities that were not becoming to the Christian.[19] In the years before 1830, Episcopal clergy often counseled abstinence from alcohol. After that time they more frequently urged moderation. Another early issue was dueling. Episcopal clergy were vocal opponents of the practice. Walter Addison, the Maryland clergyman with whom Bishop Meade read for orders, was such an active critic of the practice that he served as an officer of the court. He not only rebuked those who sought to settle their differences on the dueling grounds but also arrested them. He even invaded Jefferson's White House in search of suspected duelists.[20]

When Henry Clay (1772–1852), speaker of the House, challenged congressman James Milnor to a duel, Milnor declined by withdrawing from political life and seeking admission to the ordained ministry.[21] In 1808 the bishops and deputies of the General Convention adopted a resolution that forbade Episcopal clergy from conducting funerals of any who gave or accepted a challenge to a duel.[22]

For Episcopalians the world apart from God was sinful from two perspectives: (1) it was an inadequate object for one's ultimate hopes, so that to rely upon it was to rebel against God; and (2) it was sinful in many of the specific activities it enjoined. As Bishop White would explain, although American society was in the main conformable to good morality, "such a degree of laxity will always exist in the state of public morals, as to produce the toleration, if not the sanction of some customs, to which any one who fears God cannot consistently conform."[23] Thus not only a general reliance on the present world and the commission of private sins but also participation in certain socially accepted activities was dangerous to the Christian's soul.

Bishop White personally refrained from dancing and attending the theater. He also regarded "any practice of the world, which involves impiety, or cruelty, or sensuality" as dangerous as well.[24] Episcopalians commonly included remarriage after divorce and games of cruelty to animals in this category. By 1817 the bishops and deputies of the General Convention were on record as opposing all these activities.

The members of the General Convention of 1789, which brought together the New England and middle states groups, began by addressing the morality of the clergy. They adopted two canons on Christian behavior. Canon 12 of 1789 gave the clergy the right to deprive of church membership or to reject from Holy Communion "any persons within this church offend[ing] their brethren by any wickedness of life." For clergy the injunction was more specific. Canon 13 enjoined them not to "resort to taverns or other places most liable to be abused to licentiousness" except "for their honest necessities." They were not to "give themselves to drinking or riot, or to the spending of their time idly." The canon specified that persons guilty of offense could be admonished or suspended from the ordained ministry.[25]

In 1808 the bishops and deputies of the General Convention returned to the question of Christian morality. The meeting was held in Baltimore, and as was often the case, the largest delegation came from the host state. Only two bishops—White and Claggett of Maryland—attended. Provoost and Madison had long since retired from an active ministry; Bishop Jarvis of Connecticut and Assistant Bishop Benjamin Moore of New York apparently were unable to make the trip.

The host delegation introduced the subject of marriage into discussion in the House of Deputies. They had been instructed by their own state convention to suggest adoption of the English marriage canon.[26] The English canon not only specified the church's position on divorce but also detailed consanguinity restrictions.

The House of Deputies referred the question to Bishops White and Claggett, who were meeting in the home of White's friend Joseph Bend. White and Claggett suggested delaying consideration of the full English canon, because of both their small number and the legal questions involved.[27] The deputies responded by adopting a resolution dealing only with divorce. At the same time a resolution on dueling was introduced. Both passed without difficulty. Clergy were forbidden to preside at the funerals of those who gave or accepted challenges to duels or to perform the marriage of any divorced person except the innocent party in a marriage dissolved because of adultery.[28]

In 1817 evangelical Episcopalians, newly revived by the episcopate of Bishop Richard Moore in Virginia and the gathering of evangelical clergy in the Washington, D.C., area, suggested further resolutions detailing Christian life. Francis Scott Key (1779–1843), a deputy from Maryland best known for writing the national anthem, proposed a resolution on "amusements." Key, a lay member from a Georgetown parish who actively supported the evangelical clergy in the Washing-

ton area and who later would take an important role in the founding
of Virginia Seminary, suggested that

> the Clergy of this Church be, and they hereby are, enjoined to rec-
> ommend sobriety of life and conversation to the professing members
> of their respective congregations, and that they be authorized and re-
> quired to state it, as the opinion of this Convention, that conform-
> ing to the vain amusements of the world, frequent horse races, the-
> atres, and public balls, playing cards, or being engaged in any other
> kind of gaming, are inconsistent with Christian sobriety, dangerous
> to the morals of the members of the Church, and peculiarly unbe-
> coming of the character of communicants.[29]

The House of Deputies voted down the resolution as a duplication
of existing provisions, but the House of Bishops took up the subject.
White presided, and Bishops Kemp (Maryland), Hobart (New York),
Griswold (eastern diocese), Richard Moore (Virginia), Croes (New
Jersey), and Dehon (South Carolina) were present. They adopted their
own resolution, which incorporated much of Key's language. They
warned about the theater and all types of gaming. They passed over
public balls in silence but added "amusements involving cruelty to the
brute creation" to the list of censured activities. The resolution was
passed unanimously.[30]

The bishops explained that such amusements involved "licentious
tendencies" and afforded "strong temptations to vice."[31] They distracted from a person's coming to Christ by diverting attention from the
health of one's soul to ephemeral pursuits. Bishop John Stark Ravenscroft (1772–1830) of North Carolina, who gravitated to Hobart's
high-church party after an initial involvement with the Washington
evangelicals, later warned his parishioners of the danger:

> Remember the poor man who said to his soul—*Soul thou hast much
> goods laid up for many years; take thine ease, eat, drink, and be merry.*
> But in the midst of his security God said unto him, *Thou fool, this
> night thy soul shall be required of thee*—and apply it as a solemn
> warning to all who put off coming to CHRIST on the presumption
> that it is time enough yet, or from a love of the company, the amuse-
> ments, the pleasures or the business of the world. You may fancy you
> are happy, my young friend; you may flatter yourself with many years,
> and in present enjoyment drown the claims of your GOD and Sav-

iour upon your souls, but all this must come to an end. And what then. In all this time what preparation is made for death, for judgment, for eternity—where is your pardon, your interest in JESUS CHRIST, and without these how will you face your last enemy?[32]

Ravenscroft believed that amusements distracted the individual, diverting attention from the Last Day and the judgment that all would face. When the rector of Christ Church, Raleigh, criticized his parishioners in 1840 for attendance at balls, Ravenscroft stood beside him.[33]

While he was a parish priest, William Meade warned his young parishioners about dancing. Hearing that some had begun to frequent balls, he wrote:

> Let me beg you ever to keep in mind and solemnly to feel that you are professors of religion, and of a religion which requires much of its disciples. The author of it, the blessed Saviour, whose obedient servants we ought to be, declares that he came to save us from this present evil world, and purify to Himself a peculiar people. He declares that His disciples "are not of this world"—they are not "conformed to the world," but are "renewed in the spirit of their minds," and "not as the world give I unto you," said this same Saviour; but we ask if the gay assemblies of the children of fashion, the dressing, feasting, idle conversation and bodily gestures performed for the pleasure and admiration of men, is of this world or of God? Are they suitable to the character of serious Christians? Do they agree with those feelings of penitence, that confession of guilt, those renunciations of the pomp and vanities of the world, those self-dedications of themselves, their souls and bodies, which they make on every reception of the Holy Sacrament? Is religion a mere name or profession? or is it a reality, a new life?[34]

The danger was great. The renewed Christian might forsake the renewed life for "the pleasure and admiration of men."

Some individual clergymen, particularly among the evangelicals, drew up lists of questions for those who wished to join their congregations. Gregory T. Bedell, the nephew of Bishop Moore of Virginia, prepared such a list at St. Andrew's Church, Philadelphia. In addition to making lengthy inquiries about whether the prospective parishioner had "experienced that change of heart which is so frequently spoken of in Scripture," he asked the individual's "opinions as to . . . theatres, balls, [and] games." Bedell required a satisfactory answer in writing before admitting anyone to the congregation.[35]

Slave ownership was conspicuously absent from such lists. Episcopalians were too badly divided on the issue of slavery to have any standard expectation about the behavior of renewed adults. High-church Episcopalians may have had personal opinions on such matters, but they believed that the church should remain aloof from the political sphere.[36] Evangelicals, many of whom were connected to political leaders by marriage and friendship, had no such hesitation,[37] but much of their strength was in the South. Although many evangelicals in the South supported the efforts of the American Colonization Society to encourage slave owners to return their slaves to Africa, only a few females advocated elimination of slavery altogether.[38] Northern evangelicals were generally opposed to slavery, and the antislavery leaders whom the Episcopal church did provide—John Jay, Charles Pettit McIlvaine, Salmon P. Chase—came from within their ranks.[39] Fearing disagreements with their southern colleagues, however, most of the northerners delayed speaking out on the issue until the 1850s.

By the 1850s the Episcopalians were no longer united in their opposition to amusements. In 1829 the General Convention had softened the canon that had forbidden clergy presence in public drinking houses in favor of a less specific canon that censured "scandalous, disorderly, or immoral conduct."[40] By midcentury many Episcopalians, particularly in high-church dioceses, would no longer describe public drinking or attendance at balls as scandalous. When Edward Higbee wrote a preface to a volume of sermons by Provisional Bishop Wainwright of New York in 1856, he saw no contradiction in noting that Wainwright had lived an active social life. This was allowable, wrote Higbee, because his "studies, tastes and habits were made subservient to a single end, namely, his faithful ministry of the Gospel."[41]

The change was also clear in the writings of Nashotah House divinity professor William Adams. In 1850 he produced the first work of ethics by an Episcopal seminary faculty member. Although the book was subtitled "a treatise upon Moral Philosophy and Practices," there were none of the practical elements that would have been familiar to the members of the General Convention of 1817. Adams said nothing of the theater, gaming, or public drinking houses.[42]

Evangelical dioceses were somewhat slower in abandoning their negative attitudes toward amusements. By midcentury evangelical clergy and laity still introduced anti-amusement resolutions at their diocesan conventions, but they no longer gathered enough support to pass. The diocese of Virginia was typical in this regard. Charles Wesley Andrews, who was married to Bishop Meade's niece, introduced a resolution at the 1837 diocesan convention that would have identified visits to the post office or places of business; travel on steamboats, railroads, and canals; and social visiting as "profanation of the Sabbath. . . . which we are commanded to keep holy." Lacking sufficient support for its passage, Andrews agreed to table the resolution. In 1850 a majority of the Virginia clergy voted for a canon that listed "gaming, attendance on horse-racing and theatrical amusements, witnessing immodest and licentious exhibitions or shows, attending public balls, habitual neglect of public worship, or a denial of the doctrines of the gospel" as offenses for which communicants "ought to be admonished, or repelled from the Lord's table." The canon failed in the lay order by a narrow vote.[43] Clergy increasingly spoke in general terms about the dangers of "excess" and the value of being "temperate and sedate," as did William Sparrow of Virginia Seminary, instead of offering specific guidelines for acceptable behavior.[44] It was still incumbent on the Christian to turn from reliance on the world to a faith in Christ, but increasingly that turning did not entail avoiding specific amusements.[45]

This gradual shift was in part a result of the Episcopalians' success in the growing urban areas of the United States. In the first two decades of the century, the Episcopalians were a small, largely demoralized denomination. By midcentury, although still a tiny percentage of the nation's population, they were making impressive gains in urban areas. The amusements of urban life that had seemed scandalous to the outsiders seemed respectable to rectors of large urban congregations.[46]

There were undoubtedly other causes of this shift as well. By midcentury some other Protestants linked a call for temperance to the abandonment of the use of communion wine, a move about which the liturgically minded Episcopalians were unenthusiastic. Increasing friction between evangelical and high-church Episcopalians made it difficult to gain a majority for resolutions on amusements. A rising concern for social ills created by immigration and industrialization also diverted attention from the leisure activities of the middle and upper classes. Rather than antagonize present or potential parishioners by criticizing fashionable amusements, parish clergy enlisted their aid in assisting the urban poor. Episcopalians were the first Protestants to speak as a denomination on the needs of the industrial workers.[47]

Although this turn from a concern with amusements to a concern for the industrial workers was in one sense a new pattern, it did reflect a consistent response to novelty. What Episcopal clergy distrusted were new vices. The growth of an American theater had been an object of their suspicion in the early part of the century, but by midcentury the theaters' potential for licentiousness was well known, and clergy might safely counsel a course of moderation. In contrast the individual vices and corporate afflictions of the new industrial workers were novel dangers deserving close attention.

Whether they counseled abstinence from new vices or moderation in old ones, however, Episcopalians agreed that the renewed Christian could not accept all social patterns uncritically. To do so was to endanger the renewed life, to risk things eternal out of too great an attachment for things temporal.

Children and Adults

Episcopalians approached the renewed life from one of two paths: as children, baptized in infancy, who gradually took on themselves the promises made for them by their godparents; or as adults who came to renewal only after engagement with the sinful world. Theologically, Episcopalians argued, there was no difference between the two groups; in both cases God saved those who accepted the covenant with repentance and faith. Practically, however, all agreed that there was a great advantage for persons who gradually accepted covenantal responsibility as they matured.

At the time of baptism infants were unable either to promise to follow Christ or to undergo a moral change in their lives. As Bishop White noted, "no considerate person supposes, that in infant baptism, any moral change is wrought on the mind of the infant."[48] At the same time White argued that infants were incapable of sin. Therefore they would remain in the covenant relationship with God until they reached an age at which they forfeited the relationship by sin or took on themselves the conditions of the covenant by repentance and faith.

White argued that no mysterious change took place at the moment when the young person embraced the covenant, much as he had argued that no mysterious change took place in baptism. In each case, White insisted, the experience could be understood from a rational perspective.

According to White the change wrought in renewal involved a simple exercise of the human faculties. The individual chose between two objects of attention: Christ or the sinful attractions of the world. The person who chose to trust in Christ and to repent of sins would be saved. The person who chose to indulge passions in the sinful entertainments of the world would be lost. In either case, White insisted, the faculties exercised were the same; only the objects of attention differed. As White told the catechumens of his parish, "It is here taken for granted, that all the powers of the human constitution, from the highest of the intellect to the ordinary appetites serving the purpose of our preservation, become either good or evil in their operations, according to the objects on which they are exercised."[49]

The choice that confronted the young person reaching maturity could be understood as a contest between the Holy Spirit, which sought to lead the person to Christ, and temptations of the world, to which the human constitution, weakened by the fall, was susceptible. The Holy Spirit directed its attention to the mind; it attempted to bring the individual to recognize the sinful nature of the world and one's susceptibility to it and therefore to repent and to trust in Christ. The world more often appealed to one's appetites: to lust, greed, envy, and pride.

Since the world's temptations were directed to the passions rather than to the mind, one might well succumb to them without recognizing intellectually what had happened. The Spirit, in contrast, appealed to the mind; the decision for Christ would always be a conscious one. It might not be violent or involve a great stirring of the emotions, but it was always a conscious action. "The seat of all religion," argued White, "is in the mind; whatever does not reach the movements of it, being no more than worldly prudence at the best, in itself perhaps commendable, but not uniting us to the Father of our spirits."[50]

Gilbert Burnet, whom White had put on the Course of Ecclesiastical Studies, explained this contest between the Spirit and the world with scientific hypothesis. As a result of Adam's fall, he suggested, the temperature of the human body had been raised, leading the bodily fluids to spill over the wrinkles in the brain, which Burnet took to represent fixed lines of thought. Burnet suggested that God's grace would engrave the truths of religion to a greater depth on the brain, thereby assisting the intellect to resist the inflamed passions.[51] Although this particular hypothesis was not common among nineteenth-century Episcopalians, variations of the idea were. God assisted the human mind in its contest with the human passions. William Adams at Nashotah House used the idea as the central thread of his *Christian Science*. He taught that the Holy Ghost assisted the intellect by declaring to the conscience the truths of religion.[52]

Baptized infants had a distinct advantage over persons who entered the church after maturity. The infants were subject to the beneficial influences of the church before becoming aware of the sins of the world. Thus their minds were strengthened with the truths of religion at the same time as, or even before, the passions were inflamed by the world. If children embraced the covenant on reaching maturity—at what White called the moment of crisis—renewal would come relatively easily. The world did not yet have a strong hold on the passions.

In a manuscript published only after his death, White went so far as to argue that properly educated infants could reach maturity and embrace the covenant without ever having been under the grip of the world. They could, in effect, embrace Christ without the need to reject the world.[53] Even if this theoretical point of conversion was missed, however, the infants raised in the church had a great advantage. They still had the likelihood and possibility of a renewal before the world's effects on the passions were great. Henry Ustick Onderdonk, White's successor as bishop of Pennsylvania, would explain this in his preaching:

> By entering early on the course of holy rectitude, your piety, as it matures, will have more pleasant features, than if you defer it till some later period—even supposing that you do become pious after long obstinacy. True, indeed, in every person unequivocal Christian piety must be founded on a consciousness of depravity; but this will not be so awful and gloomy in those who have committed but few sins, as in those who have perpetrated many. Religion formed in youth has less fear and more love,—that purer love, which hath not yet felt the more horrible sense of danger.[54]

The earlier one repented, the less one had to repent, and therefore the easier it was to change one's mind. Evangelical William H. Wilmer explained to others that he "took hold of the covenant" at the age of seventeen.[55]

Unfortunately most persons baptized in infancy did not embrace the covenant at a young age. "The bulk of those who were baptized in infancy," warned Bishop Hobart, "have neglected their baptismal vows, and forfeited their baptismal privileges."[56] They lost the great advantage they held over those who were baptized in later life. They were in conformity with a sinful world, and they would be damned if they died without a change of life.

The unrenewed adult—baptized or unbaptized—was in need of immediate repentance and faith. There would be for the adult no period of grace, no enjoyment of the benefits of the covenant apart from an exercise of repentance and faith. Since baptism in this circumstance was no longer an appropriate element in the church's spiritual arsenal, Episcopalians would reach the unrenewed adult only by the preached word. The change of mind, if it came, was more difficult than the change in the person who had repented on first reaching maturity.

The unrenewed adult's behavior also contributed to the difficulty of renewal. A relatively pious individual might pass White's moment of crisis and still embrace the covenant in adulthood. That was the case with Elizabeth Seton, a parishioner of John Henry Hobart with high-church sympathies that would eventually lead her to the Roman Catholic church and sainthood. It was not until she reached twenty-eight that she "renewed [the] covenant."[57] In contrast, those who lived dissolute lives as adults would have much greater difficulty. Their conversion, if it came at all, was not only difficult but often almost violent in nature.

Mary Martha Sherwood's *Stories Explanatory of the Church Catechism,* a popular English tract circulated by the Protestant Episcopal Female Tract Society of Baltimore, painted the difference between the youthful change of mind and the renewal of the dissolute adult in striking terms. Mrs. Sherwood's work centered on three characters: Mary Mills, a young girl gradually turning to Christ; Mrs. Browne, a Christian woman who was instructing Mary in the Christian faith; and Mrs. Barnes, a woman who resisted God's grace. Mrs. Barnes hoarded her possessions while seeking to borrow from others. She drank and swore heavily and knowingly passed bad currency. After the death of her son and a particularly hard drinking bout, she finally repented. The experience was a difficult one: "She would often cry, 'Oh! I cannot die. I will not die. I shall go to hell.' And then again would scream, shudder, and roll her eyes, as if something very shocking passed before them."[58] Mrs. Browne told Mary after the experience that she "well knew that no man can enter into the kingdom of Heaven unless his nature be altogether changed; and yet, she had, in general, observed this change to be a slow and gradual work."[59]

Once Christians had accepted the conditions of the covenant, they still might backslide and return to the sinful pursuits of the world; the covenant was always conditional. Renewal was a lifelong experience, and to be saved one had to be renewed continually. Nonetheless Episcopalians would argue that once renewal had commenced, a subsequent return to the renewed life of faith and repentance was more easily accomplished. Gregory Townsend Bedell of St. Andrew's, Philadelphia, compared the repentance of a Christian who had been once renewed to "the repentance of a child who really loves its parent, and loves its duty." In contrast the repentance of the person who had never experienced the change of mind was "the repentance of a rebel, of an ingrate."[60] Just as the baptized infant enjoyed an advantage over the unbaptized, so also the Christian who had momentarily strayed enjoyed an advantage over the person who had never been renewed. Once made, the change of mind was more easily regained.

The longer one postponed the change of mind, the less the likelihood that it would take place. For the person who postponed renewal to the last possible moment—the deathbed—there was an additional problem. Since the necessary sign of the change of mind was a change in one's life, the repentance that came too late to involve a change in behavior was of questionable value for salvation. The person was left in that shadowy condition of those who lived good lives but who had not entered the covenant by baptism, with no right to God's grace and only a slender prospect based on divine mercy.

In one of his sermons Bishop Hobart explained the point at length.

The fear of punishment alone never excites genuine repentance. This evangelical grace must be founded on a lively apprehension of the baseness and ingratitude which sin displays, as a violation of the authority and laws of the greatest and best of Beings. . . . But in a death-bed repentance, the fear of future wrath will generally predominate, and extinguish those ingenuous feelings which excite godly sorrow.

Nor can there be any certainty that those resolutions of penitence, formed amidst the terrors of conscience and the fears of death, and in the absence of all temptation, would not be forgotten or broken, should those terrors and fears be removed, and should temptation again assail the soul. The best, the only evidence of the sincerity of penitent resolutions, is found in the performance of them. The only test of genuine repentance is in amendment of life. Alas! there can be no such evidence, no such test, in a death-bed repentance. . . . [The deathbed penitent] leaves the world, affording to others no certain evidence that his penitence is genuine, conveying no comfortable assurance of it himself—unless it pleases God to grant him the rare and extraordinary manifestation of divine love. How hazardous is a deathbed repentance![61]

Faith and repentance untested by amendment of life were slender threads on which to hang one's hope of salvation.

Hobart's argument echoed a similar warning made by Gilbert Burnet a century and a half before. In his book *Some Passages of the Life and Death of the Right Honourable John Earl of Rochester,* the bishop related his conversations with a once-profligate young nobleman who lay on his deathbed. "The promises of the Gospel did all depend upon a real change of heart and life," Burnet told the earl. Since the dying man could give no evidence of this change in his life, he had little cause for hope. God in his mercy might renew the sinner, but the likelihood was not great.[62]

The Christian who heard the words of Hobart or read those of Burnet stood warned. Postponement of renewal until late in life and engagement in the sins of the world could be fatal to the soul. How much better off were those who entered the covenant in baptism as infants and fulfilled the conditions of the covenant as soon as they matured.

Whether the Christian came to it early or late, renewal, with its attendant change of character and moral life, was necessary for the adult's salvation. Bishop White, the texts of his Course of Ecclesiastical Studies, and the members of the high-church and evangelical parties all taught that necessity.

RENEWAL AND THE GREAT AWAKENING

In 1829 William Rollinson Whittingham (1805–79), an Episcopal priest with high-church sympathies, was invited to preach to a Presbyterian congregation in South Orange, New Jersey. Whittingham must have hesitated to accept the invitation. One of a generation of high-church leaders who had learned their churchmanship from John Henry Hobart, he was well aware of that bishop's unease about worship with other denominations. Nonetheless Whittingham accepted, deciding to use the occasion for an apology for the Episcopal church.

He was so satisfied with the results of his labors that, after election
to the episcopate in Maryland in 1840, he reused the sermon in addressing Methodist meetings. In 1880 the editors of a memorial volume of fifteen Whittingham sermons chose to include the address in
their compilation.

Whittingham stressed a single principle in his apologetic, one that
he felt the Episcopal church shared with both Presbyterians and Methodists: "The *change of heart,* then brethren, we do most explicitly recognize as indispensable to salvation, and we do *not* consider it as effected in baptism."[63] Whittingham designated this change of heart as
"the renewing of the Holy Ghost," and he made it clear to those who
heard him that it could not be included in the change of state that baptism produced.

Whittingham's remarks were a vivid reminder that the doctrine of
renewal espoused by nineteenth-century Episcopalians was not created in a theological vacuum. Episcopalians were a minority among Protestants, and even such staunch high-church party members as Whittingham were well aware of the predominant patterns in American
Protestantism. The Great Awakening of the eighteenth century and the
multiple ripples of revival of the nineteenth century, known collective-
ly as the Second Great Awakening, shaped the face of American Protestantism in a way that was impossible to ignore.

In 1840 American evangelical Protestants observed the centennial
celebration of the Great Awakening. Contributing to that observance,
Joseph Tracy wrote the first history of the awakening. For Tracy the
awakening was a clear-cut conflict between two understandings of
church membership: the view that those who were well-educated in the
doctrines of the church and who did not lead notoriously sinful lives
should be admitted to full participation and the view that limited admission to those who could provide an account of their conversion.[64]

Advocates of either position would have had cause to protest the
simplicity of Tracy's characterization: certainly personal faith was not
unimportant to the Old Light Congregationalists and Presbyterians
whom Tracy characterized as holding the first view, nor was doctrine
unessential to the New Light Congregationalists, Presbyterians, Baptists, and Methodists whom he depicted as holding the latter view. In
terms of emphasis, however, his description was quite accurate. The
Protestants who favored the awakening did emphasize personal faith
over doctrine; the Protestants who were more skeptical about the au-

thenticity of the conversions that accompanied the revival did find comfort in the Westminster Confession and other traditional statements of the Reformed faith.

Both the supporters and the critics of the Great Awakening continued to use covenant arguments. They did bring different emphases to that use, however. Advocates of the awakening, such as Anglican George Whitefield, often paired their discussions of the benefits of the covenant of grace with stern warnings about the fate of those who placed their confidence in the covenant of works.[65] Those who were critical of the awakening were more likely to stress the positive aspects of the covenant relationship.

In the century following the first signs of the awakening, the religious situation remained much the same among Evangelical Protestants. A prorevival element—Methodists, Baptists, new-school Presbyterians, and Congregational New Divinity Men—led an escalating crusade for revivals, which led to the perfection of certain "new-measure" revival techniques intended to produce a maximum response from a congregation in a minimum amount of time. These new measures, of which Presbyterian revivalist Charles Grandison Finney (1792–1875) was the undisputed master, included the anxious bench, a seat placed in the front of the congregation in a highly visible place and reserved for those concerned about their salvation; public testimony by women; and public prayer for alleged sinners by name. A more conservative group— old-school Presbyterians and more conservative Congregationalists— resisted what they saw as too great an emphasis on emotionalism and attempted to foster a more serious, less sensational form of revival.

Bishop White was well aware of American revivalism. He had adopted a doctrine of renewal in part to provide a consistent response to it. Whittingham had drawn on this understanding of renewal in addressing other Protestants, providing from it an Episcopal commentary on the Second Great Awakening.

As White explained renewal, it did not require a specific set of emotional responses. He did not emphasize "evanescent feelings, which have their seat in the animal economy."[66] For him, moral behavior was the only certain test of the renewed life: "here is the test and the only one . . . whereby to distinguish the true faith from the false."[67]

White's intention was to press for a reality inherent in a true conversion. Renewal was such a reality; emotions were an outward manifestation that might or might not attend renewal. They were the effect of other elements, White argued. Even "temperature or the humors of the body" could affect emotional response.[68]

White's careful argument provided a perspective from which Episcopal clergy and laity could explain renewal. A value judgment remained to be made, however. Once Episcopalians had affirmed the nonemotional reality behind revivalism, what were they to say of the revivalistic endeavors of other denominations? Were they ill-advised efforts that happened occasionally to encourage serious renewal, or were they well-founded efforts that at times were accompanied by unfortunate excesses? More important still, were Episcopal clergy to discourage the emotions, or were they simply not to be misled by them? As on so many other issues, evangelical and high-church Episcopalians gave differing answers. Evangelicals generally approved of old-school revivalists and borrowed techniques from them. They warned of false reliance on emotions but suggested that strong emotions often did accompany renewal. High-church Episcopalians implied the opposite: emotions were to be avoided. They could accompany renewal, but more often they did not.

Evangelical Episcopalians and the Second Great Awakening

The editors of the *Washington Theological Repertory* stated in their first issue that a real change of mind "will be known and felt."[69] Although they warned that "strong emotions alone, are by no class of well informed *Christians,* considered as evidence of conversion," they also suggested that "the distinctiveness of the sensations of conviction and alarm, and other strong emotions in the mind of the adult convert . . . *often* are the attendant circumstances, of the new birth."[70]

The modifying phrase "in the mind of the adult convert" was an important one. The editors of the *Repertory* and other evangelical Episcopalians followed White in believing that the central area in the progress of renewal was the mind. Various moods of hope, faith, and condemnation might pass through the believer's mind and in the case of the adult convert often did. This mental process was nevertheless a different matter from a bodily display of emotions. Such a display had strong negative connotations and was often "associated with ignorance, hypocrisy, and self-deception."[71]

Evangelical Episcopalians formed these impressions not only from their observation of the progress of the Second Great Awakening in other denominations but also on the basis of revivals within the Episcopal church. One of the most influential of these took place in St. Michael's Church, Bristol, Rhode Island, in 1812. Alexander Viets Griswold was both the rector of the parish and the newly consecrated bishop. He later reflected that his election as bishop was "the means of awakening [his] own mind to more serious thoughts of duty as a minister of Christ" and may have led him to preach "with more earnest zeal." Following his first administration of confirmation in the parish, Griswold noticed an "increased seriousness." Apparently his words to the confirmed had struck a chord with other parishioners as well. Many began to "express a religious concern respecting their spiritual state." The awakening attracted others to the parish, and soon the size of the parish doubled. In response to many requests he began to preside at regular evening prayer meetings for the further instruction of members of the congregation.[72]

Griswold's revival was an old-style affair. Its hallmarks were seriousness and perseverance. As a preacher he addressed his parishioners' minds, not their emotions. He was critical of any preacher who did otherwise. He believed that preachers should even avoid the use of gestures:

> What is natural, indeed, involuntary and unobserved by the speaker, is certainly proper. But every thing of the kind, which is studied, affected and artificial, has, and is intended to have, the effect of drawing attention to the speaker; and, the more this is done, the less good is effected. This may well account for what is so commonly seen; that preachers, remarkable for a studied gracefulness in their delivery, and much admired as fine speakers, produced but little effect in changing the heart and converting their hearers to the truth of God. A preacher, to do his best and be the most successful, should forget himself, and have in his mind his subject only and a purpose of persuading his hearers to believe what he teaches, and to live accordingly.[73]

The clergyman must persuade the minds of his hearers.

Evangelical preaching at confirmation was not always met by the favorable response that greeted Griswold in 1812. After the Bristol revival, however, evangelical Episcopalians were convinced that confirmation was a particularly appropriate time to press for commitment to the covenant. Later in the century John P. K. Henshaw, who had read for orders with Griswold, offered a definition of revival that made clear the connection between profession of Christ and confirmation:

When we speak of "revival" in the Episcopal Church, we mean a season of more than usual interest in the subject of religion, produced by the special influence of the Holy Spirit giving efficacy to the ordinary means of grace—such as faithful preaching of the word and fervent prayer. The result is that the graces and virtues of the devout are revived and strengthened; an unwonted depth of solemnity and feeling exists in the congregation at large, and within a short time, many sinners are converted from the error of their ways, who "profess the faith of Christ crucified" in Baptism or Confirmation, and, by participating in the Lord's Supper, become united to the communion of the faithful.[74]

Sinners who abandoned their errors could profess faith in Christ crucified in the service of confirmation.

In Virginia the evangelical Bishop Meade required confirmation for membership in the Virginia diocesan convention, the body that set the budget, elected bishops, and otherwise legislated for the church in Virginia. Meade reasoned that confirmed persons, having made a profession of faith before the bishop and the church, would give evidence in their lives of the moral change that resulted from renewal and would not cause scandal to the diocese. Those who had not been confirmed might be less trustworthy. Before the adoption of the requirement, Meade wrote: "We were still distressed and mortified at the occasional appearance of one or more unworthy members, who were a scandal to the Church, the scandal being the greater because of the number of attendants. The frequenters of the race-ground and the card-table, and the lovers of the intoxicating cup sometimes found their way through this unguarded door into the legislative hall."[75] After adoption of this reform Meade proclaimed with satisfaction, "We have never . . . had cause to . . . blush for the scandal cast upon us by unworthy members."[76]

Evangelical Episcopalians believed that confirmation was an effective means for promoting renewal within the parish. The liturgical act of verbally renewing commitment to the baptismal covenant was also the proper setting for personal renewal. Although this renewal did not have a single necessary emotional pattern associated with it, it was always known and felt in some way and often was accompanied by deep religious feelings in the believer's mind.[77]

In addition to using confirmation in this way, evangelical Episcopalians adopted two other means for promoting renewal: the weekly prayer meeting and the clerical association. In both cases they drew on the experience of other Protestants.

Several years before his consecration to the episcopate, Alexander Viets Griswold had begun the practice of lecturing one evening a week on the Christian faith. His rationale had been entirely defensive; other denominations in Bristol were offering lectures, and he feared that many of his parishioners who had taken to attending them would soon convert. After the awakening in his parish in 1812, he apparently changed the format of his evening sessions, adopting a less formal style, meeting in homes of parishioners, and spending more time in prayer. He sat at a small table and read from a Bible and a prayer book. He delivered a biblical sermon and then allowed time for prayer. Stephen H. Tyng, studying with Griswold for orders during 1819 and 1820, noted little difference from the prayer meetings in which he had participated as a secondary school student at Andover. Only the presence of the Book of Common Prayer marked the meeting as different from those of other denominations.[78]

Other Episcopal parishes in New England soon emulated the Bristol prayer meetings.[79] When Griswold's theological students John P. K. Henshaw and Stephen H. Tyng headed south to Maryland and Washington, they carried the practice with them. When the evangelical Virginia Seminary was founded in 1823, one of its prominent features was a regular Thursday evening faculty meeting, a prayer meeting at which members of the faculty presided.[80]

Evangelical Episcopalians in Virginia developed their own version of the frontier camp meeting that had been popularized by the Cane Ridge, Kentucky, revival of 1801. A group of Episcopal clergy would gather at a single location for what they called a "clerical association." They would lead preaching services, visit homes, offer spiritual advice to individuals, raise funds for missionaries, and celebrate the sacraments. The associations were particularly effective in areas in which there was either a shortage of clergy or an absence of a settled Episcopal parish.

Bishop Moore of Virginia encouraged the approach after his consecration. William Meade and the Reverend Benjamin Allen, later rector of St. Paul's, Philadelphia, were particularly active in the endeavor. John Johns, Meade's biographer and his successor as bishop of Virginia, explained the advantages of the association:

A country clergyman with two or three, and sometimes four churches under his care, and officiating in them in rotation on Sunday only,
necessarily labors to great disadvantage. If the weather or any other
cause, interferes with his appointment, then an interval of four, six,
or eight weeks, passes without service in that congregation. When ministrations are so rare, the instructions from the pulpit must be very limited. If on any occasion, its stirring appeals to the heart and conscience,
prove awakening, the impression is apt to disappear, before another
opportunity, or, in the absence of the teacher preferred, the anxious
inquirer seeks counsel of others, and is liable to be led off, and lost to
the Church in which he was roused to consideration. The quarterly
association secured to each parish, in addition to its stated services, a
series of ministrations, conducted daily and for several days in succession, and this provided in some measure precisely what was needed.
The interest manifested by clergy extended to the people. Large congregations assembled. Persons not often seen in religious meetings, were
attracted to these and so brought under the influence of the Gospel,
both during the public administration and during the intervals of service, in personal intercourse with ministers and other Christians.[81]

A series of rousing sermons by a gathering of several clergy was an
effective means of promoting parish renewal.

Although open to the methods by which other Protestants promoted revival, evangelical Episcopalians were also aware of the dangers
such methods posed. They were careful to distinguish what they saw
as a sober, healthy revivalism from the excesses of the new-school revivalism. They accepted in principle the possibility that renewal might
bring strong feelings to the mind of the adult convert, but they denied
that the preacher should seek to cultivate such feelings or that the believer should put any confidence in them.

William H. Wilmer, the clergyman whose early death stripped Virginia evangelicals of an able leader, sounded this note of caution in the
editorial pages of the *Washington Theological Repertory*. As editor he
wrote a series of columns in which he expounded the evangelical theological position. He argued in a column on the Holy Ghost that it was
an error to demand an emotional renewal whose "time, means, and
other circumstances" could be recounted. In addition he said that the
emotion accompanying a change of heart was only "a very equivocal
and subordinate kind of evidence of the change."[82]

Richard Channing Moore, the evangelical bishop whom Wilmer was instrumental in bringing to Virginia, was similarly cautious about the new measures. Moore wrote to William Meade shortly before the latter was elected as his assistant bishop. He made his position on emotionalism clear: "If Christianity is a system founded on truth, the work of grace must be God's work; and I cannot believe that the Almighty stands in need of the cunning craftiness of man to promote his designs."[83] As he later wrote to Meade, anxious benches were a particular target of his odium: "I think it profane to suppose that the aid of the Holy Spirit can be secured in any other way than in the use of the appointed means of grace, and believe that the faithful preaching of the Gospel, preceded by our own services, constituted those means. I am opposed, totally opposed to 'anxious or enquiring benches' as they are called, and think that humble penitents would prefer a private intercourse with their Maker and their own pastor, to an exposure of themselves to public view."[84] As Moore wrote to another priest in his diocese, he would encourage parish prayer meetings, but he "would keep the reins in [his] . . . own hands."[85] The priest should carefully guard against excesses. William Meade agreed with Moore, and he was soon elected his assistant.

In the 1840s the success of new-measure evangelism in the West caused Charles Pettit McIlvaine to warn his clergy in Ohio not to imitate such practices. McIlvaine had begun his ordained ministry at Christ Church, Georgetown, where his preaching had impressed some members of Congress. Senators chose McIlvaine, who was himself the son of a U.S. senator, first as their chaplain and then as professor and chaplain of the U.S. Military Academy at West Point. McIlvaine presided over a revival there, an accomplishment that some feared would sap the zeal of America's future fighting men. Among his converts was Leonidas Polk (1806–64), later both an Episcopal bishop and a Confederate general.

McIlvaine regarded his revival as a serious turn to the Christian faith based on sound preaching of the Gospel. In his address in 1851 he contrasted that serious revival with the more emotional, mechanical new measures. The older approach was a "genuine and most precious work of grace, of great extent. . . . The fruits were manifest, permanent, and are now bearing precious fruit in their turn. Under the Spirit of God, they proceeded from nothing but the application of the *truth*, in the fullness of the Gospel, and in its simplicity, to the conscience and heart, and that accompanied with earnest prayer for the power of God to make it mighty."[86] The new approach was the work of Satan and the invention of men who courted, rather than shunned, excitement:

> Modes and preachers were estimated, not by the truth they taught or promoted, but by the amount of excitement they were capable of producing. Hence, whether a minister preached the Gospel in its fullness—whether he preached *Christ* always, every where, in all his offices and relations to sinners; whether his ministry was calculated to build up a people in the truth as it is in Jesus, and to make them *consistent* Christians, "*steadfast and unmovable*," became, in such places, an almost unconsidered point. Thus it came to pass that the preaching which was most sought and valued, as most productive of the results desired, under the name of "Revivals," was most lamentably deficient in all legitimate title to the name of *Gospel*-preaching. It claimed to be the specially faithful preaching. It was very much the reverse. *Teaching* was very little its work. To operate on the sensibilities was its calling.[87]

McIlvaine cautioned against overzealous revivalism.[88] In doing so he could have counted on the support of his professor of divinity at Kenyon, Thomas Mather Smith. Smith had left the Congregational church precisely because of his inability to stem new-measure revivalism in his parish. The Episcopal church, he felt, could and should prevent such excesses of emotion.[89]

Smith and divinity professors at other evangelical Episcopal seminaries could turn to Leonard Woods's translation of George Christian Knapp's *Lectures on Christian Theology* for a solid exposition of the old evangelical position on emotionalism. Knapp warned against the doctrine of "immediate illumination and conversion"—the idea that the Holy Spirit could operate directly on the believer's heart without the medium of the preached word. God always worked through the revealed doctrines of Christianity; there could be no conversion apart from a correct knowledge of Christianity.[90] Knapp had further explained that actions and not emotions were the sole reliable evidence of conversion: "One may easily deceive himself with regard to his own feelings. And if a certain degree of feelings is insisted upon as necessary, those who do not come up to this standard, while yet they may have faith, will be easily led into mistake, and involved in doubt and distress. Nor can we properly demand, that every one should give the time and hour, when he began to believe. For faith is not always instantaneous, but from the very nature of the human soul, is sometimes gradual."[91] Smith could add his personal experience to this word of warning.

Other evangelical divinity professors concurred both in using Knapp and in tying renewal to the correct preaching of the Gospel. William Sparrow echoed the argument, for example, in "The Right Conduct of Theological Education," an address at Virginia Seminary in 1843. In it he suggested the need to guard against two errors: the belief that knowledge itself was sufficient for faith and the opposing error of suggesting that Christianity was independent of intellectual content. This latter error led only to "wild and ignorant enthusiasm." Knowledge and faith had to be kept together.[92]

John Seeley Stone of the Episcopal Theological School agreed. He described the preaching of the Gospel as that action by which "Christ, through the Spirit," sought both "to illumine the darkened mind, and to renew the wicked heart." When the Holy Spirit acted, it was on "the intelligent mind."[93]

Evangelical Episcopalians were willing to use theological texts written by other Protestants. They were also willing to accept the prevailing Protestant choice of language. For example, Stone, Sparrow, and Smith accepted a number of terms commonly used by evangelical Protestants to refer to the adult Christian's change of mind: *renewal, renovation, a new creation, the new birth, birth from above,* and *regeneration.*[94] Their high-church colleagues were less enthusiastic about this common usage; they objected to the final term in particular. In the Book of Common Prayer the term *regeneration* was applied only to the change of state produced by baptism. High-church Episcopalians insisted that it could be used in no other way. They did offer an alternative term, however: the change of heart could be referred to as "renovation."

The debate over language revealed the heart of the disagreement between high-church and evangelical Episcopalians. Was the church to emphasize its commonality with other Protestants, or was it to emphasize its distinctive nature? Could Episcopalians accept the term *regeneration,* which had been favored by revivalists since the first Great Awakening, or should they reject it?

The debate divided Anglicans on the other side of the Atlantic as well. During the seventeenth and early eighteenth centuries, neither Anglicans nor English Dissenters had been doctrinaire in their use of terms. Archbishop of Canterbury John Tillotson referred to the adult change of mind as "regeneration."[95] The noted Dissenter Philip Doddridge (1702–51) was willing to accept the language of renovation as legitimate.[96] After the evangelical revival of the mid-eighteenth century, however, the lines of debate in England were more carefully drawn. Evangelicals there, as in the United States, pressed for the term *regeneration* as the equivalent of *adult renewal*. Daniel Waterland (1683–1740), in his posthumously published "Regeneration Stated and Explained" (1740), provided what was to be the standard high-church response: *renovation* was the term for the adult change; *regeneration* was to be reserved for the change in baptism only. Waterland's work became the standard nineteenth-century American high-church seminary text on the issue.

Evangelical Episcopalians brought their own value judgment to the doctrine of renewal that William White had so carefully described. Emotion was not a necessary or sufficient proof of renewal; the only such test was the moral life. Nonetheless, they argued, the presence of deep feelings in the *mind* of the believer was not bad. It often accompanied renewal, and Episcopalians could borrow mechanisms such as the prayer meeting and the association from other Protestants, even though those mechanisms had in some cases been accompanied by excess displays of emotion. They moreover could use the language of other evangelical Protestants, including the word *regeneration*.

High-Church Episcopalians and the Second Great Awakening

High-church Episcopalians brought precisely the opposite value judgment to White's understanding of renewal. Emotion, they taught, was almost always a false sign of renewal. Moreover the mechanisms and language of both old-school and new-school revivalist Protestants ought to be avoided.

High-church Episcopalians carried on a running critique of revivalism throughout the nineteenth century. They observed that highly publicized converts often returned to their sinful ways. They cited old-school revivalists' criticisms of new-school revivalism to support their case. G. T. Chapman of Kentucky, a devotee of Bishop Hobart, must have taken considerable delight in quoting Hobart's archenemy, John M. Mason, on the dangers of revivalism:

No one will question the competency of Dr. Mason . . . to form an accurate opinion upon the subject. His language is peculiarly striking, and I cannot resist the inclination to transcribe it. According to him: "Some, in fine, think that religious experience is the sole test of admission into the Church, provided a man can satisfy them of his conversion, (and they are not always hard to be satisfied;) if he can relate a plausible story of his feelings, can talk of his distress and of his comfort, and has learnt to deal in joys and ecstacies, it is enough. . . . It is lamentable, that so large a portion of conversions, which are the fruit of tumultuous meetings, and the theme of Newspaper praise, prove to be of this class. Dark views, gross ignorance, and even flat contradictions in the simplest truths of Christianity, are no obstacle."[97]

According to Mason, then, highly publicized conversion was often unauthentic.

Since they held that there were no necessary emotional signs of renewal, many high-church Episcopalians sought alternative explanations for feelings experienced by converts. Most frequently they suggested that some particular experience or defect in the convert's life produced the emotional reaction. In its barest terms this observation was entirely negative: the more deeply sinful the person, the stronger the emotional response to conversion. Thus Bishop Jonathan Mayhew Wainwright, a grandson and namesake of a Congregational clergyman who had been a fierce critic of the Episcopal church before the Revolution, suggested that emotional conversion was "an extreme case" that was necessary "to overcome . . . actual transgression."[98]

Milo Mahan (1819–70), a professor of ecclesiastical history at General Seminary and an unsuccessful candidate for bishop of New Jersey, modified Wainwright's observation with a more general formula.[99] The emotional pattern associated with renewal was the result not simply of previous sin but of the whole "character of [the] minds" of converts:

Sensible conversion, moral regeneration, change of heart, or any other term of like signification . . . may go before Baptism, or may follow after. It may be sudden, violent and marked, as in the case of St. Paul. It may the result of a series of sharp strokes as in the case of St. Peter. It may be a graded process, a melting of darkness, into light, as in innumerable cases. And so, of the way in which it is brought about.

It may seize one man, as he sits at ease, thinking of anything else. It
may come upon a second, as "another heart" came to King Saul,
while he was walking along the Way previously enjoined him. All this,
in fact, pertains to the inner life of man. It is a matter of consciousness, of feelings, of an experience as variable and as varied, as the
character of men's minds. Such a thing, therefore, cannot be called
a Way-Mark. . . . Conversion must be treated as a thing pertaining
to the *disposition* of the walker, rather than as a mark of the Way he
is to walk in.[100]

According to Mahan, then, the convert's general disposition influenced
the degree of emotional response to renewal.

Like the evangelicals, high-church Episcopalians felt that the office
of confirmation was a particularly appropriate time to press for renewal. High-church confirmation exhortations could be as convincing as
those of their evangelical coreligionists. Bishop Hobart, for example,
did not hesitate to threaten those who did not take confirmation seriously with the fires of hell:

The conduct of too many seems to authorize the conclusion, that this
impressive instruction [the Catechism] was calculated only for children, and designed with the age of childhood to pass away and be
forgotten. Deluded men! who never, or with occasional and languid
supplications, implore that power from on high, which Scripture,
which reason, which experience teach you can alone save you from
the dominion of sin; you will remain in your present state of sinful
security—remain in your *present* state, did I say? Alas! There is a path
which leads to the chambers of hell, and rapid is the descent; there
is a place where the worm dieth not, and the fire is not quenched.
Oh! then, with fervent and reiterated supplications invoke the power of the Holy Ghost to renew and save you.[101]

Without the change of mind wrought by the Holy Ghost, the covenant
would be forfeited, and the title to salvation lost.

George Washington Doane, Hobart's former assistant at Trinity and
later bishop of New Jersey, was equally persuasive:

To each of you, your heavenly Father says, "My son," my daughter, "give Me thine heart." In infancy He took you, as His children,
in your Baptism. He made no objection to your irresponsibility. He
took you, on the word of those who brought you. He received you,

as His own children, by adoption. He nursed your infancy. . . . And
now that you have reached the point of personal responsibility, are
they [parents, pastors, teachers, and angels who have watched over
the person in youth] not hanging with a trembling love, upon your
choice? What worlds would they not give, if worlds were theirs, that
you would say, with Samuel, "Speak, Thy servant heareth." And,
with Mary, choose that better part, which never can be taken from
you. Beloved children, give the Lord your hearts. Come to Him, in
the way, which He appoints, for you. Open your bosoms to take
in Holy Ghost; to sanctify and bless you. Let not the whisper, keep
you back, that you are yet too young. Are you too young to sin?
Are you too young to die? Let not the thoughtless words of your
companions check you. It is you, that must account for your own
souls, to God.[102]

These high-church preachers urged the candidates for confirmation to
give their hearts to God. They warned of the terrible dangers that would
await the heedless.

The desired response to this passionate summons was confirmation.
High-church Episcopalians were suspicious of other avenues by which
Christians might make professions of faith. They were convinced that
confirmation and other prayer book offices provided a sufficient guide
to renewal. William Kip (1811–93), the author of what was to become
the most popular apology for the nineteenth-century church, suggested that the whole Book of Common Prayer bore witness to the importance of renewal:

That the Church requires her children to be renewed, renovated, and
sanctified by the Holy Ghost, as requisite for membership with her,
while militant here, or in glory hereafter, no one can doubt who has
ever read her offices. She everywhere teaches the truth, that "without holiness no man shall see the Lord." She constantly seeks to draw
men away from dependence on their own changing feelings, or the
delusive visions of the imagination. She presents before them tests
of Christian character which are real and tangible, calling them to
self-denial and a holy life. On this principle every page of our Prayer-
book has been framed, and we might prove it from each of her services, or from the general spirit and tenor of her prayers. We content ourselves, however, with merely quoting the collect for
Ash-Wednesday: "Almighty and Everlasting God, who hatest noth-

ing that Thou hast made, and dost forgive the sins of all those who are penitent: *create and make in us new and contrite hearts,* that we, worthily lamenting our sins, and acknowledging our wretchedness, may obtain of Thee, the God of all mercy, perfect remission and forgiveness, through Jesus Christ Our Lord."[103]

In other words, confirmation was the specific office directed toward renewal, but the authors of the prayer book had written every page with an understanding of its importance. Extra–prayer book methods of promoting renewal were unnecessary.

Bishop Hobart set the tone for the high-church clergy by discouraging evangelical clergy from introducing the prayer meeting or the clerical association in his diocese. When James Milnor began prayer meetings at St. George's, Hobart called on him and demanded that he discontinue the practice. A battle of wills followed between the two strong personalities. Milnor was the apparent winner. He refused to end the meetings unless the bishop would personally tell the parishioners to disband. Hobart declined, and the meetings continued.[104]

Hobart met with greater success in resisting the spread of associations to his diocese in 1828. He admonished the clergy to disband the Protestant Episcopal Clerical Association in the city of New York, which had been formed in that year. Grudgingly they did so.[105]

Another high-church critic of the prayer meeting was Samuel Farmar Jarvis (1786–1851), son of the bishop of Connecticut and a professor of biblical learning during the initial efforts to found the General Seminary. In 1820 he moved to St. Paul's Church in Boston. While there, he used the pages of the *Gospel Advocate* to denounce the prayer meeting then being held by Bishop Griswold.[106] He did not manage to end the practice, but he did stir up a strong party rivalry in the diocese that would continue for most of the century.

Bishop White's own response had been less rigid. In 1825 he cautioned his state convention about the danger of prayer meetings.[107] Five years later Stephen H. Tyng began to hold Sunday evening church services in Philadelphia that were modeled after such prayer meetings. High-church Episcopalians in the diocese were critical, but surprisingly White was not. He made no public comment but began to attend the services regularly. The criticism quieted.[108]

High-church party members were also critical of the evangelical willingness to use the term *regeneration* in the popular sense. Hobart

insisted strongly that only one use of the word—as equivalent to baptism—was allowed by patristic texts:

> The ancient writers of the church uniformly apply the term *regen-
> eration* to baptism denoting the change, from a state of nature to a
> state of grace, which takes place in that sacrament. The compilers
> of the liturgy, following in this, as in other respects, the authority of
> the primitive church, employed the term regeneration in the same
> sense; neither they nor the primitive fathers ever apply it to signify a
> change of heart and life, and this return to holiness from a state of
> sin, they denoted by the terms renovation and repentance.[109]

Hobart attempted to give this distinction between renovation and regeneration official status by including it in a new prayer in the confirmation service that he proposed to the General Convention of 1826.
Evangelicals initially supported the proposal, but when it came up for
a required second reading in 1829, they reversed their opinion out of
fear that it would foreclose the possibility of using *regeneration* as a
synonym for change of heart. Without their support the measure failed.
By the 1860s, however, some evangelicals would look back nostalgically on Hobart's proposal, for it made clear that both a baptismal
change of state and an adult change of heart were expected of the believer.[110]

In the period before 1840, both high-church and evangelical Episcopalians admitted in principle the logic of their opponents' terminol-
ogy. Evangelical bishop Griswold maintained, for example, that although *regeneration* properly referred to adult renewal, "there may be
no great impropriety in speaking of the effects of baptism as a birth or
regeneration."[111] Bishop Hobart, for his part, was fair-minded enough
to admit that Anglican notables such as Tillotson had used the termi-
nology with which he disagreed.[112] In addition there were those on each
side who were willing to use either definition of *regeneration* as long
as it was understood. Henry Ustick Onderdonk, the high-church bishop who followed White in Pennsylvania, broke with the strict Hobartian position by citing without comment Tillotson's use of *regeneration*
for *renewal*.[113] On the evangelical side, Bishop Richard Channing
Moore on occasion referred to baptism as "regeneration."[114]

After 1840 party lines on regeneration and renovation would hard-
en considerably. The publication of works by the theologians of the
English Oxford movement that questioned the need for adult renewal

by any name inflamed feelings on all sides. The Hobartian high-church Episcopalians ultimately rallied with the evangelicals in the 1870s to suppress this perceived heresy, but before they did so, considerable hostility arose between them.

~

Despite their disagreements over methods of promoting renewal and value judgments attached to emotions, high-church and evangelical Episcopalians operated from the same set of presuppositions. From White they had learned that renewal was a reality whose only certain test was the moral life. No emotional pattern could guarantee its presence. Whatever external differences might exist between the Episcopalians and the more revivalist denominations, both groups bore witness to the same reality: a renewing presence of the Holy Spirit in the life of individuals who had renewed their commitment to the covenant.

NOTES

1. William Meade, *Reasons for Loving the Episcopal Church* (New York: Thomas Whittaker, n.d.), 40.

2. *Oxford English Dictionary* (1922), s.v. "renew."

3. *The First and Second Prayer Books of Edward VI* (London: Dent/Everyman's Library, 1968), 41.

4. William White, *Lectures on the Catechism of the Protestant Episcopal Church* (Philadelphia: Bradford and Inskeep, 1813), 147.

5. John Pearson, *An Exposition of the Creed*, new. ed., ed. E. Burton (Oxford: Clarendon, 1890), 205.

6. Ibid.

7. William H. Wilmer, *The Episcopal Manual: A Summary Explanation of the Doctrine, Discipline, and Worship of the Protestant Episcopal Church, in the United States of America,* new and improved ed. (Philadelphia: R. S. George, 1841), 153.

8. White, *Lectures*, 23.

9. *The Book of Common Prayer, and Administration of the Sacraments; and Other Rites and Ceremonies of the Church, according to the Use of the Protestant Episcopal Church in the United States of America: together with the Psalter, or Psalms of David* (London: Virtue, 1868), 250.

10. *The Book of Common Prayer and Administration of the Sacraments and Other Rites and Ceremonies of the Church, together with the Psalter or Psalms of David, according to the Use of the Episcopal Church* (New York: Church Hymnal, 1979), 869.

11. Wilmer, *Episcopal Manual,* 38.

12. John Henry Hobart, *The Posthumous Works of the Late Right Reverend John Henry Hobart, D.D.,* 3 vols. (New York: Swords, Stanford, 1832), 2:473.

13. *Washington Theological Repertory* 2 (Mar. 1821): 226.

14. White, *Lectures,* 148.

15. *Washington Theological Repertory* 1 (Aug. 1819): 5.

16. William Meade, *Companion to the Font and Pulpit* (Washington: J. and G. S. Gideon, 1856), 41.

17. Gilbert Burnet, *An Exposition of the Thirty-nine Articles of the Church of England,* new ed. (London: Thomas Tegg, 1827), 127.

18. White, *Lectures,* 148.

19. For an overview of the way in which Episcopalians use canon law to deal with moral issues, see Robert W. Prichard, "Clerical Morality and Moral Discourse," in *A Wholesome Example: Sexual Morality and the Episcopal Church,* 45–64 (Lexington, Ky.: Bristol, 1993).

20. William Meade, *Old Churches, Ministers and Families of Virginia,* 2 vols. (Philadelphia: J. B. Lippincott, 1910), 1:23.

21. Elizabeth Moulton, *St. George's Church, New York* (N.p: n.p., 1964), 20.

22. The provision was later softened to allow the burial of a person who repented of participation in a duel. See William Stevens Perry, ed., *Journals of the General Conventions of the Protestant Episcopal Church in the United States, 1785–1835,* 3 vols. (Claremont, N.H.: Claremont Manufacturing, 1874), 1:357–58, 378–79.

23. White, *Lectures,* 9–10.

24. Ibid., 10; Sydney A. Temple Jr., ed., *The Common Sense Theology of Bishop White* (New York: King's Crown, 1946), 10.

25. Perry, *Journals, 1785–1835,* 1:128. The regulation against resorting to taverns was based on one of the English canons of 1604 that was in turn based on a tradition running back to at least the eighth century. Similar language is found in the *Admonitio Generalis* from Charlemagne's era.

26. Perry, *Journals, 1785–1835,* 1:341.

27. Ibid., 1:355.

28. Ibid., 1:348.

29. Ibid., 1:458.

30. Ibid., 1:494. Robert Bruce Mullin argued in *Episcopal Vision/American Reality: High Church Theology and Social Thought in Evangelical America* (New Haven, Conn.: Yale University Press, 1986), 78–79, that high-church Episcopalians were largely indifferent to "dueling, horse racing, gaming, theatergoing, and public balls" and credited the failure of the deputies' resolution to "the machinations of the Hobartian party." Mullin overlooked Hobart's

vote for the bishops' resolution, however. Criticizing balls had been a favorite practice of evangelicals since George Whitefield. It was not in the final bishop's resolution. See *George Whitefield's Journal*, a new ed. (Edinburgh: Banner of Truth Trust, 1985), 401.

31. Perry, *Journals, 1785–1835*, 1:494.

32. John Stark Ravenscroft, *The Works of the Rt. Rev. John Stark Ravenscroft, D.D., Bishop of the Protestant Episcopal Church in the Diocese of North-Carolina, Containing his Sermons, Charges, and Controversial Tracts; to Which Is Prefixed a Memoir of His Life*, 2 vols. (New York: Protestant Episcopal, 1830), 2:240.

33. Richard Rankin, *Ambivalent Churchmen and Evangelical Churchwomen: The Religion of the Episcopal Elite in North Carolina, 1800–1860* (Columbia: University of South Carolina Press, 1993), 130–31. The parishioners refused to reform their ways, and the rector left.

The account of the conflict in Durham played a pivotal role in Rankin's argument about the gradual displacement of evangelical attitudes in North Carolina. Rankin, building on Robert Bruce Mullin's assertion in *Episcopal Vision* that high-church Episcopalians did not oppose amusements, saw the Durham conflict as the victory of a high-church pro-amusement attitude over an evangelical anti-amusement one. The general portrait that he painted—of a changing attitude in the 1840s that is closely connected with the class status of leading Episcopalians in the state—is on target, but Rankin seems to have overlooked some other factors. He did acknowledge that Ravenscroft was a high-church Episcopalian, but he implied that the rector, George Washington Freeman (1789–1858), was an evangelical, which is by no means clear. Although Freeman left little in the way of writing with which to evaluate his views, he was elected bishop of Arkansas and the Indian Territory in 1844, at a point at which the House of Bishops generally elected high-church missionary bishops for the West and evangelical candidates for foreign missions. Rankin also cited vestry member George Badger as an advocate of dancing without noting Badger's fierce opposition to the high-church innovations of Bishop Ives. The Durham dispute therefore seems to be a counterexample to the point that Rankin wished to make, one in which high-church clergy opposed the amusements in which a mixed congregation of evangelicals and high-church Episcopalians wished to participate. I offer an alternative interpretation in this chapter—i.e., that the dividing line on amusements was chronological rather than a matter of church parties. Episcopalians of both parties warned against amusements prior to 1840 but moved away from specific condemnations after that date.

For details on the fight between Badger and Bishop Ravenscroft, see chapter 6.

34. William Meade, undated letter in John Johns, *A Memoir of the Life of*

the Right Rev. William Meade, D.D., Bishop of the Protestant Episcopal Church in the Diocese of Virginia, 86–93 (Baltimore: Innes, 1867), 87–88.

35. Stephen H. Tyng, biographical sketch to Gregory T. Bedell, *Sermons by the Rev. Gregory T. Bedell, D.D., Rector of St. Andrew's Church, Philadelphia,* 2 vols. (Philadelphia: William Stavely, John C. Pechin, 1835), 1: cv–cvii.

36. Mullin, *Episcopal Vision,* 86–91. Mullin cited Bishop Hobart's opposition to involvement in the political process and pointed out that many high-church clergy did not even vote.

37. Bishop McIlvaine's father had been a U.S. senator. James Milnor had served in the House of Representatives. Salmon P. Chase, the nephew of Bishop Philander Chase, was governor of Ohio, secretary of the Treasury, chief justice of the Supreme Court, and an unsuccessful presidential candidate.

Allen C. Guelzo has suggested that pre–Civil War evangelicals attempted "to cultivate 'republican' Whig attitudes." See Allen C. Guelzo, "Ritual, Romanism and Rebellion: The Disappearance of the Evangelical Episcopalians, 1853–1873," *Anglican and Episcopal History* 62 (Dec. 1993): 563.

38. See Arthur Dickens Thomas Jr., "O That Slavery's Curse Might Cease," *Virginia Seminary Journal* 45 (Dec. 1993): 56–61, for an account of the anti-slavery activities of Ann Randolph Meade Page: Page, an evangelical Episcopalian from Virginia, was Bishop Meade's sister.

39. For a thorough discussion of the attitudes of northern evangelicals on slavery, see Diana Hochstedt Butler, *Standing against the Whirlwind: Evangelical Episcopalians in Nineteenth-Century America* (New York: Oxford University Press, 1995), 146–68. Butler points out that McIlvaine, who served as a special envoy to England during the early years of the war, urged Lincoln to abolish slavery.

40. Perry, *Journals, 1785–1835,* 2:311.

41. Edward Y. Higbee, preface to *A Memorial Volume: Thirty-four Sermons by the Rt. Rev. Jonathan Mayhew Wainwright, D.D., D.C.L., Provisional Bishop of the Diocese of New York* (New York: Thomas Whittaker, 1877), 15.

42. William Adams, *The Elements of Christian Science: A Treatise upon Moral Philosophy and Practice,* 3d ed., rev. (Philadelphia: Richard McCauley, 1870).

43. T. Grayson Dashiell, *A Digest of the Proceedings of the Conventions and Councils in the Diocese of Virginia* (Richmond: Wm. Ellis Jones, 1883), 130, 206.

44. William Sparrow, *Sermons by the Rev. William Sparrow, Late Professor of Systematic Divinity and Evidences of Christianity in the Theological Seminary of the Protestant Episcopal Church in the Diocese of Virginia* (New York: Thomas Whittaker, 1877), 160, 163.

45. Some evangelical Episcopalians would continue the campaign against amusements well into the second half of the century. The campaign had a sym-

bolic value: it was a way to distinguish the renewed adult from one who had not renewed the baptismal covenant.

46. Richard Rankin has suggested an alternative way of understanding the shift in attitudes in the 1830s, at least in the case of North Carolina. He combined Robert Bruce Mullin's assertion in *Episcopal Vision* that high-church Episcopalians were unconcerned about the morality of "amusements" with an interest in gender roles. He suggested that female Episcopalians in early nineteenth-century North Carolina were evangelical opponents of the amusements of the upper class, but that males embraced a high-church version of the faith that both accepted the social mores of the upper class and reenforced patriarchy. Rankin suggested that males had won females over to their point of view by 1840. See Rankin, *Ambivalent Churchmen*, 78–147.

47. Henry F. May, *Protestant Churches and Industrial America* (New York: Harper and Brothers, 1949), 182.

48. White, *Lectures*, 218.

49. Ibid., 218–19.

50. Ibid., 147.

51. Burnet, *Exposition of the Thirty-nine Articles*, 143–44, 154–55.

52. Adams, *Christian Science*, 90.

53. Temple, *Theology of Bishop White*, 88–91.

54. Henry Ustick Onderdonk, *Sermons and Episcopal Charges by the Right Rev. Henry U. Onderdonk*, 2 vols. (Philadelphia: C. Sherman, 1851), 1:140.

55. Philip Slaughter, "Address on the Deceased Professors of the Theological Seminary of Virginia," in *Semi-Centennial Celebration of the Theological Seminary of the Protestant Episcopal Church in the Diocese of Virginia*, 48–75 (Baltimore: printed for the Seminary, 1873), 74.

56. Hobart, *Works*, 2:489.

57. Ellin Kelly and Annabelle Melville, introduction to *Elizabeth Seton: Selected Writings*, Sources of American Spirituality (New York: Paulist, 1987), 63.

58. [Mary Martha] Sherwood, *Stories Explanatory of the Church Catechism*, ed. James Kemp (Baltimore: Protestant Episcopal Female Tract Society of Baltimore, 1823), 262.

59. Ibid., 264.

60. Bedell, *Sermons by the Rev. Gregory T. Bedell*, 1:75.

61. Hobart, *Works*, 3:183.

62. Gilbert Burnet, *Some Passages of the Life and Death of the Right Honourable John Earl of Rochester, Who Died the 26th Day of July, 1680*, 5th ed. (London: printed for Richard Chiswell at the Rose and Crown in St. Paul's Churchyard, 1700), 141.

63. William Rollinson Whittingham, *Fifteen Sermons by William Rollinson Whittingham, Fourth Bishop of Maryland* (New York: D. Appleton, 1880), 160.

64. Joseph Tracy, *The Great Awakening, a History of the Revival of Religion in the Time of Edwards and Whitefield* (Boston: Tappen and Dement, 1842), ix.

65. See, for example, George Whitefield, *Select Sermons of George Whitefield* (Edinburgh: Banner of Truth Trust, 1958), 78, 81–82, 105–8, 116, and 153–55.

In 1935 historian Perry Miller suggested that Jonathan Edwards, who was one of the primary advocates of the Great Awakening, entirely rejected the use of covenant language. More recent historians, such as Conrad Cherry and Harry Stout, have questioned that assertion, pointing to numerous examples of the use of covenant themes in Edwards and other preachers of the Awakening, such as Whitefield. For Miller's essay, see Perry Miller, *Errand into the Wilderness* (New York: Harper and Row, 1965), 48–98. For Cherry and Stout see Conrad Cherry, *The Theology of Jonathan Edwards* (Garden City, N.Y: Doubleday/Anchor, 1966), 107–23, 202–15; and Harry S. Stout, *The New England Soul: Preaching and Religious Culture in Colonial New England* (New York: Oxford University Press, 1986), 10.

66. White, *Lectures*, 148.

67. William White, *Comparative Views of the Controversy between the Calvinists and the Arminians*, 2 vols. (Philadelphia: M. Thomas, 1817), 2:153.

68. White, *Lectures*, 244.

69. *Washington Theological Repertory* 1 (Aug. 1819): 5.

70. Ibid., 2 (Mar. 1821): 229.

71. Ibid.

72. Alexander Griswold quoted in John S. Stone, *Memoir of the Life of the Rt. Rev. Alexander Viets Griswold, D.D., Bishop of the Protestant Episcopal Church in the Eastern Diocese* (Philadelphia: Stavely and McCalla, 1844), 178–79.

73. Alexander Griswold, "Thoughts on Preachers and Preaching," in Stone, *Griswold*, 563–71; quotation on 564.

74. John P. K. Henshaw, *Memoir of the Life of the Rt. Rev. Richard Channing Moore, Bishop of the Protestant Episcopal Church in the Diocese of Virginia* (Philadelphia: William Stavely, 1843), 94.

75. Meade, *Old Churches, Ministers and Families of Virginia*, 1:44–45.

76. Ibid.

77. See Butler, *Standing against the Whirlwind*, 91–94, for Charles Pettit McIlvaine and Stephen Tyng's attitudes toward confirmation.

78. Stone, *Griswold*, 178, 121–22; Charles Rockland Tyng, *Record of the Life and Work of the Rev. Stephen Higginson Tyng, D.D. and History of St. George's Church, New York to the Close of His Rectorship* (New York: E. P. Dutton, 1890), 44.

79. Stone, *Griswold*, 329–30.

80. Joseph Packard, *Recollections of a Long Life* (Washington, D.C.: Byron S. Adams, 1902), 306.

81. Johns, *Meade*, 105–6.

82. *Washington Theological Repertory* 2 (Mar. 1821): 228–29.

83. Richard Channing Moore, letter to William Meade quoted in Henshaw, *Moore*, 97.

84. Richard Channing Moore, letter to Nathaniel Bowen quoted in ibid., 102.

85. Richard Channing Moore, letter on social meetings for prayer quoted in ibid., 83.

86. Charles Pettit McIlvaine, *Spiritual Regeneration with Reference to Present Times: A Charge Delivered to the Clergy of the Diocese of Ohio at the Thirty-fourth Annual Convention of the Same in St. Paul's Church, Cleveland, October 11, 1851* (New York: Harper and Brothers, 1851), 37.

87. Ibid, 37–38.

88. For a more detailed discussion of McIlvaine's attitudes toward new-measure revivalism, see Butler, *Standing against the Whirlwind*, 67–84.

89. McIlvaine's exposition of the dangers of revivalism had a characteristic touch. McIlvaine was a vocal critic of Roman Catholicism and of Oxford movement influence in the Episcopal church. With a certain leap of logic, he explained that new-measure revivalism was but another form of Roman Catholicism. It was another form of formalism, of works righteousness, a system that accounted grace the result of a particular procedure. See McIlvaine, *A Charge*, 39, 44.

90. George Christian Knapp, *Lectures on Christian Theology*, trans. Leonard Woods Jr., 2 vols. (New York: G. & C. & H. Carvill; Andover: Flagg and Gould, 1831–33), 2:443.

91. Ibid., 2:396.

92. William Sparrow, *The Right Conduct of Theological Seminaries, an Address Delivered at the Twenty-first Annual Commencement of the Theological Seminary of the Protestant Episcopal Church in the Diocese of Virginia, July 13, 1843* (Philadelphia: Edward C. Biddle, 1843), 3–4.

93. John Seeley Stone, *The Mysteries Opened or Scriptural Views of Preaching and the Sacraments, As Distinguished from Certain Theories concerning Baptismal Regeneration and the Real Presence* (New York: Harper and Brothers, 1844), 72, 173.

94. Ibid., 19–20.

95. Hobart, *Works*, 2:466.

96. White, *Lectures*, 219–20.

97. G. T. Chapman, *Sermons upon the Ministry, Worship, and Doctrine of the Protestant Episcopal Church and Other Subjects* (Lexington, Ken.: Smith and Palmer, 1828), 205–6.

98. Jonathan Mayhew Wainwright, *A Memorial Volume: Thirty-four Sermons by the Rt. Rev. Jonathan Mayhew Wainwright, D. D., D. C. L., Provisional Bishop of the Diocese of New York* (New York: D. Appleton, 1856), 286.

99. John Henry Hopkins, memoir to Milo Mahan, *The Collected Works of the Late Milo Mahan, D.D.*, 3 vols. (New York: Pott, Young, 1875), 3:xviii–xix.

100. Mahan, *Collected Works*, 3:407–8.

101. Hobart, *Works*, 2:503.

102. George Washington Doane, *The Episcopal Writings of the Rt. Rev. George Washington Doane, D.D., L.L.D., Bishop of New Jersey, Comprising His Charges: Convention, Missionary and Visitation Sermons*, ed. William Croswell Doane, 4 vols. (New York: D. Appleton, 1860), 3:512–13.

103. William Ingraham Kip, *The Double Witness of the Church*, 24th ed., rev. (New York: E. P. Dutton, 1898), 274–75. The first edition was published in 1843.

104. E. Clowes Chorley, *Men and Movements in the American Episcopal Church* (New York: Scribner's, 1946), 53.

105. Ibid., 272–73.

106. Ibid., 133, 270.

107. Ibid., 270–71.

108. Tyng, *Stephen Higginson Tyng*, 93–94.

109. Hobart, *Works*, 2:463.

110. For an example of this nostalgia, see Diana Butler's discussion of Charles Pettit McIlvaine's *Some Thoughts on Baptismal Regeneration* (1861) in *Against the Whirlwind*, 196.

111. Alexander V. Griswold, *Discourses on the Most Important Doctrines and Duties of the Christian Religion* (Philadelphia: William Stavely, 1830), 217.

112. Hobart, *Works*, 2:466.

113. Henry U. Onderdonk, *Sermons*, 1:93.

114. Meade, *Companion*, 145.

5 HEAVEN AND HELL

~

LIKE OTHER CHRISTIANS, Episcopalians envisioned death and resurrection in a manner that accorded with their overall understanding of assurance. Roman Catholics, relying on the authority of the institutional church, taught a doctrine of purgatory that extended the church's influence beyond the grave. New-school Protestants, emphasizing the all-important conversion experience, promised the convert immediate benefits on death. Old-school Protestants, still adhering to Dort and Westminster, relied on a view of perseverance that made judgment a mere formality for the elect. Episcopalians, looking to the baptismal covenant and to adult renewal for assurance, explicated a doctrine of what they called the intermediate state. It ensured that judgment preceded heaven and hell, so that the only sure sign of renewal—the moral life—was also to be the primary criterion for one's status in the life to come.

As in other matters, Bishop White led the way, summarizing the Episcopal tradition in his own writing and giving it a prominent place in his Course of Ecclesiastical Studies. The high-church and evangelical Episcopalians who came after him accepted his vision, but they disagreed about whether to reconcile or accentuate their differences with other Protestants.

THE INTERMEDIATE STATE

Bishop White followed the precedent of the catechist John Lewis and devoted the second discourse of his *Lectures on the Catechism* to a discussion of the Apostles' Creed. He recited the creed line by line, pausing to explain each expression. When he reached the clause describing Christ's descent into hell, White noted that he had come to a portion of the creed on which Christians disagreed. "It gives me pain," he said, "to introduce into these lectures, any matter in which eminent men, equally correct in general theory, have disagreed."[1]

The article over which they disagreed could be best understood, he explained, when set in the context of the Apollinarian controversy of the fourth century. The words were introduced into the creed at that time:

> The occasion for introducing it is said to have been this. At a time of uncommon prevalence of the desire of being "wise above what is written," and especially of inventing curious distinctions concerning the divine and human natures of the Redeemer; a bishop of considerable note in the Church, of the name of Apollinaris, contended, that the human nature consisted not as well of soul as of body, but of the latter only; which was filled by the divinity, supplying the place of the soul. This fancy is contradicted by any fact, which demonstrates the separate existence of the spirit of Jesus during the sleep of his body in the tomb. Such a fact was found, among other places, in his declaration to the thief on the cross—"To day shalt thou be with me in Paradise." Hence the introduction of the clause; over the meaning of which, however, a doubt has hung.[2]

For those unfamiliar with this dispute, White added a footnote to the published form of his lectures. The note detailed a further historical argument and made clear the sources on which White was relying—the familiar mainstays of the Course of Ecclesiastical Studies, "bishop Pearson and bishop Burnet."[3]

From this historical explanation of the origin of the clause in the creed, White turned directly to the issue: "'Hell' may be thought to signify the invisible world, or the state of departed spirits, between death and the resurrection; without reference to the happiness or the misery of the different descriptions of them."[4] No doubt White took many by surprise at this point. In midparagraph and with little warning, he had moved from a historical explanation of the origin of a clause in the Apostles' Creed to a major assertion: the word *hell* in the Apostles' Creed referred to the condition of both good and bad souls between death and resurrection; it did not refer to a place of punishment. Thus the clause in question referred to the passage of Christ's soul after death, and where he had gone, others would follow.

Most other American Protestants would have differed with the

Anglican position that White set forth. For example, the Westminster Confession of Faith had advanced a very different teaching. Even Protestants who did not agree with the Westminster Confession in other matters generally agreed in this. After death souls "immediately return to God who gave them. The souls of the righteous being made perfect in holiness, are received into the highest heavens, where they behold the face of God in light and glory, waiting for the full redemption of their bodies; and the souls of the wicked are cast into hell, where they remain in torments and utter darkness, reserved to the judgment of the great day. Besides these two places for souls separated from their bodies, the Scripture acknowledgeth none."[5] For most Protestants hell could mean only one thing—a place of damnation to which souls of the wicked went immediately on death. The souls of the righteous never passed through such a place; they went directly to heaven.

Episcopalians, Protestants who accepted the Westminster Confession's position on death, and Roman Catholic advocates of the doctrine of purgatory could appeal to Scripture in the matter with some justification. The New Testament contained a number of overlapping ideas about afterlife rather than a single clear image. The biblical authors had emphasized Christ's resurrection and his coming again on the last day rather than the details of the individual Christian's resurrection. Christ's ministry and preaching heralded the breaking in of his kingdom. His death and resurrection began to break forever the power of sin and death over humanity. Soon he would return to the earth and "send out his angels with a loud trumpet call, and they will gather his elect from the four winds, from one end of heaven to the other."[6]

But what would become of individuals between their deaths and Christ's return? The biblical authors seemed to suggest two possibilities: (1) Perhaps the faithful soul slept or otherwise waited in Christ until his return, at which time it would be resurrected and united with a new body. Paul suggested such a chain of events in 1 Thessalonians 4:13–18 and 1 Corinthians 15:51–57. Matthew's great judgment in 25:31–46 implied such a pattern, not only for the faithful, but also for the wicked; both rewards and punishments await Christ's return and the final judgment. (2) Against these texts, two passages in Luke (Luke 23:43, the promise to the thief on the cross; and Luke 16:19–31, the parable of Lazarus and the rich man) implied that rewards and punishments came immediately after death.

Patristic writers sought a way to reconcile these two lines of biblical thought.[7] Their most frequent approach was to combine a belief in
the soul's continuation after death (an idea compatible with the Middle Platonic doctrine of the immortality of the soul) with a belief in an
intermediate place (or places) where the soul waited. As in the first
biblical view, final entrance into heaven or hell awaited the last judgment. As in the second view, life continued immediately after death—
and who could doubt that waiting in an intermediate state would be
joyful for the person who had faith in Christ? Irenaeus, Hippolytus,
and Tertullian all taught something of this sort.[8] It was to these theologians that Anglicans would later turn in support of their intermediate theory.

Patristic authors used two Greek words used in the New Testament
(both of which are translated into English as "hell") to distinguish
the intermediate place(s) of waiting from the place of condemnation
of the last judgment. *Hades,* the word that was translated as "hell"
in the Apostles' Creed, signified the place in which all the dead awaited
the last day. Alternatively it could be contrasted with *Paradise* as the
name of the portion of that waiting place that was occupied by the
souls of evil persons. *Gehenna* (literally the Valley of Hinnon, a place
of child sacrifice outside of Jerusalem; figuratively the hell of fires) was
the hell into which the evil would be cast at the last judgment.

In the later classical period, Augustine of Hippo and Gregory the
Great suggested that souls of the righteous might be cleansed by puri-
fying flames at the last judgment.[9] Western theologians of the eleventh
to the fifteenth century shifted this period of purification from the last
judgment to the period of waiting, thereby developing the doctrine of
purgatory.[10] According to this doctrine, great saints would go directly
to heaven on death, and sinners would go to hell; the basically good,
who were fettered only by venial sins, were sentenced to a preparatory period in purgatory proportioned on the severity of their sins.[11] This
belief, coupled with a penitential fundraising scheme according to
which one could buy indulgences that released loved ones from time
to be served in purgatory, became one of the most unsavory aspects of
the medieval church. It would be an object of protest not only for
Lutheran, Anglican, and Reformed theologians but for reforming elements within the Roman Catholic church as well.[12]

John Calvin and other Reformed theologians reasoned that the best
way to avoid anxieties about purgatory was to deny the existence of

any kind of intermediate life at all. Although Calvin cautioned against inquiring too closely into the state of the dead, he ruled out any possible intermediate place for the soul. For example, Calvin countered the argument that Christ's three days of waiting after the crucifixion were an indication that all who died faced a period of waiting; Calvin argued that the descent into hell in the Apostles' Creed was only a metaphorical expression, descriptive of the degree of Christ's suffering.[13] Later Reformed Christians adopted as an article of faith the doctrine that the soul immediately passed to heaven or hell, retaining consciousness in transit. According to this theory, only reunion with the body would await the last judgment. As I have shown, it was this position that would later appear in the Westminster Confession.

Anglicans handled the issue in a somewhat different manner, gradually modifying the medieval doctrine of purgatory rather than rejecting it outright. In the early 1530s English Protestants such as John Frith (ca. 1503–33) and Hugh Latimer (ca. 1485–1555) assailed the idea that the pope had the power to shorten or lengthen time in purgatory. They also questioned the need for the souls of the godly to suffer at all; they believed that the experience of the godly after death would be of joy. Nonetheless they did not explicitly reject the state of waiting between death and the last judgment. Latimer was even willing to retain the name *purgatory* for that period of waiting.[14] William Tyndale (1494?-1536) laid the groundwork for later Anglican thought on the subject by explaining the biblical and patristic distinction between Hades as a place of waiting and Gehenna as the place of damnation.[15]

After he nationalized the church, Henry VIII accepted some of these Protestant ideas. The final of the Ten Articles of Religion (1536) agreed with Frith and Latimer in rejecting the belief that "through the bishop of Rome's pardons souls might clearly be delivered out of purgatory and all the pains of it." It also opposed the idea "that masses said at *Scala Coeli,* or otherwise, in any place, or before any image, might likewise deliver them from all their pain, and send them straight to heaven." On the other hand, the article also suggested that in the absence of scriptural clarity about "the place where [the dead] be, the name whereof, and kind of pains there," it would be charitable to continue prayers and masses on their behalf.[16] Henry may also have rejected the distinction between Hades and Gehenna, for both the *Institution of a Christian Man* (or *Bishops' Book,* 1537) and *A Necessary Doctrine and Erudition for Any Christian Man* (or *King's*

Book, 1543) explained Christ's descent to hell as a descent to the place of damnation.[17]

Henry's desire to continue prayers for the dead out of a sense of charity was swept aside when his son Edward VI acceded to the throne. The Forty-two Articles (1552), adopted at the end of Edward's reign, rejected the doctrine of purgatory as "a fond thing, vainly feigned, and grounded upon no warrant of scripture, but rather repugnant to the word of God."[18] Some catechetical works published during the same period accorded with the understanding of Latimer and Frith. For example, the catechism written by Thomas Becon (ca. 1511–67), who served as a chaplain to Thomas Cranmer, replaced the medieval image of purgatory as a place of torment with a portrait of waiting in "a sweet, quiet, and holy dormitory, or resting-place."[19]

Thomas Cranmer prepared burial offices for the 1549 and 1552 prayer books that assumed the same period of rest preceding the last judgment. He included in both offices an anthem from Revelation 14 that spoke of the rest of those who die in the Lord. Both offices also included a lesson from 1 Corinthians 15 in which Paul referred to the dead as sleepers who would awaken on the last day. For the 1549 prayer book Cranmer selected for use at the eucharist an additional lesson from 1 Thessalonians 4 that repeated the image of sleep until the last day. The additional lesson was dropped when the office was streamlined and the eucharistic propers were omitted in 1552, but a collect based on it was preserved.[20]

Latimer and Frith's idea of rest for the dead was not accepted by all, however. The Reformed churches' influence on England grew throughout Edward's reign, and some English Protestants accepted the Reformed idea of an immediate postmortem passage to heaven or hell, where the soul would enter into joy or suffering. This increasing Reformed influence may explain the fortieth of the Forty-two Articles (1552), which made it clear that the rest spoken of in the burial office did not mean entire loss of consciousness or death for the soul.[21] The article was not included in the later Thirty-nine Articles.

From the time of Elizabeth's accession in 1558 to the restoration of Charles II in 1660, there were advocates of the positions of both Latimer and the Reformed churches within the Church of England. The question became one of many issues that separated the Puritan and royalist factions within the national church. Puritans ridiculed the state of rest prior to the last judgment as a nonbiblical concept. William Fulke

(1538–89), for example, argued that Christ had not gone to a place of waiting during the three days after his death. This was important, because advocates of the intermediate period argued that Christ led the way that the godly would follow. "For," wrote Fulke, "if [Christ] descended into that hell only, in which were the souls of the faithful, which was a place of rest, of comfort, of joy, and felicity; what triumph was it to overcome such a hell?"[22] Royalists, such as Jeremy Taylor (1613–67), supported the contrary position, arguing for the period of waiting in which the soul slept.[23]

The restoration of the episcopacy and the Book of Common Prayer in 1662, and the subsequent departure of many English Protestants with Reformed ideas, quieted the dispute over the two views of death. Members of the dissenting Presbyterian and Independent churches accepted as an article of faith the consciousness of the soul after death and its immediate rewards and punishments.[24] Those who remained in the Church of England became more insistent on the intermediate period of waiting.

One of the principal authors to restate this view for the Church of England was John Pearson. In his *Exposition of the Creed* he accepted Tyndale's explanation of the patristic distinction between Hades and Gehenna. As Pearson understood it, the souls of both the good and the bad went to a "receptacle, or habitation and mansion," to which Christ's soul had also gone in the three days of his death. This receptacle included within it "two societies of souls": one for the wicked and one for the just. Pearson referred to this receptacle as "Hades," or the "Mansions below the infernal parts." Pearson noted as well that on some occasions the patristic authors used the word *Hades* of only the negative portion of the receptacle.[25]

Pearson stepped gingerly around the question of the degree of consciousness the sleeping souls experienced. Most advocates of the idea of immediate rewards and punishments had joined the dissenting denominations, but some who remained in the Church of England recognized the value of continuous consciousness after death for moral teaching and began to suggest increasing degrees of awareness during the period of rest.[26]

Gilbert Burnet later drew on Pearson's exposition in his commentary on the third articles: "By *Hell* may be meant the invisible place to which departed souls are carried after death: for though the Greek word so rendered does now commonly stand for the place of the damned, and for many ages has been so understood; yet at the time of writing of the New Testament it was among Greek authors used indifferently for the place of all departed souls, whether good or bad; and by it were meant the invisible regions where those spirits were lodged."[27] Like Pearson, Burnet skirted the difficult question of whether the souls of the departed were conscious.

For the uninstructed catechumen, William White's rapid leap in his lectures from the descent of Christ in the Apostle's Creed to a discussion of the status of the dead would have been startling, but for those more acquainted with Anglican theology, the transition would have been expected. Pearson had patiently explained the Anglican position. Burnet and most later Anglican divines had accepted Pearson's exposition as authoritative. Indeed, in the eighteenth century the Connecticut clergyman John Beach (1700–82) had been investigated and admonished by the Society for the Propagation of the Gospel for publishing a pamphlet with heterodox ideas about death; one of his indiscretions was to question the intermediate state.[28]

White could refer to a note in the American Book of Common Prayer in support of the theory of an intermediate state. The bishops and deputies at the General Convention meeting of 1789 adopted an explanatory note after the Apostles' Creed, making it clear that the hell of the creed referred not to Gehenna, the place of the damned, but to Hades (in the sense of the whole intermediate place): "any Churches may omit the words, he descended into hell, or may instead of them, use the words, He went into the place of the departed spirits, which are considered as words of the same meaning in the Creed."[29]

Bishop White and the bishops and deputies at the General Convention meeting of 1789 made a further alteration in the liturgy in 1789. They edited the committal phrase that had been in the burial office in prayer books since 1549:

Book of Common Prayer (1662)	Book of Common Prayer (1789)
. . . we therefore commit *his* body to the ground; earth to earth, ashes to ashes, dust to dust; in sure and certain hope of the Resurrection to eternal life; through our Lord Jesus Christ;	. . . we therefore commit *his* body to the ground; earth to earth, ashes to ashes, dust to dust; looking for the general Resurrection in the last Day, and the Life of the World to come, through our Lord Jesus Christ;

who shall change our vile body,
that it may be like unto his own
glorious body, according to the
mighty working, whereby he is
able to subdue all things to himself.

at whose second coming in glorious Majesty to judge the World,
the Earth and the Sea shall give up
their Dead; and the corruptible
bodies of those who sleep in him
shall be changed, and made like
unto his own glorious body, according to the mighty working,
whereby he is able to subdue all
things to himself.[30]

In his *Memoirs of the Protestant Episcopal Church*, White made no mention of this change in the committal, although he certainly knew who was responsible for it, because it had also been included in the earlier *Proposed Book* on which he and William Smith had cooperated. It is possible that the revision was intended to tilt the American church on the side of soul-sleep in the Anglican debate over the condition of those in the intermediate state. The new wording would not rule out the possibility of consciousness, however, for interpreters could simply understand *sleep* to be a synonym for *death*. In any case there would be relatively little debate about the subject, although theologically precise John Henry Hobart would not be able to resist saying a word about it.[31]

White's primary concern in his lectures was to explain the contrast between Episcopal doctrine and that of the Westminster Confession. He nevertheless was also aware of the degree to which the Episcopal position on intermediate life differed from that of the Roman Catholic church. White's biographer, Bird Wilson, published a series of "cautionary letters to a young lady, by her pastor, in reference to the danger of being drawn into the Communion of the Roman Catholic Church" as a specimen of the bishop's pastoral ministry. Among White's chief concerns in the letters was his fear that the young lady might embrace the Roman Catholic doctrine of purgatory. He stated first what he understood to be the correct doctrine: "The Scriptures speak of an intermediate state, in which the righteous wait for the consummation of bliss in body and soul; and the wicked are suffering from former guilt, anticipating the judgment of the great day. Here is a truth, than which there can be none clearer in Scripture, or in the early fathers."[32] Going beyond Burnet and Pearson to speculate on motives, White suggested that the Roman Catholic church had abandoned this early doctrine to promote the saints to heaven, where they could be the objects of worship:

> But after some hundreds of years from the beginning it was dropped, for the purpose of elevating former saints to a resemblance of those gods and goddesses who had been displaced by the holy genius of Christian doctrine. It is a retrogradation which must be accounted for from the already mentioned propensity, of withdrawing from the notice of the eye which is "in every place, beholding the evil and the good."
>
> There is not put out of view the distinction imagined between two species of worship, of a higher and a lower grade; and expressed by two Greek words, which apply respectively. This was an after-thought, called for to cover an obtrusive species of worship. The Bible knows nothing of any grade of this to be offered to former men and women, however holy may have been their lives, or whatever may now be their condition.[33]

White suggested that the Roman Catholic church had erred in abandoning the ancient doctrine of the intermediate state.

In another private letter White reasoned further that the Reformed Protestant belief in the immediate passage to heaven or hell on death was simply the Roman Catholic doctrine of afterlife amended by removing the period of purgation. For Roman Catholics the souls of the evil went directly to hell on death, and the pure went directly to heaven. The righteous who were hindered with venial sins passed through purgatory to be cleansed before arriving in heaven. The Reformed Christians had simply eliminated the passage through purgatory.[34]

Hobart's *State of the Dead*

In March 1816 Episcopalians in the state of New York gathered to bury Bishop Benjamin Moore. The bishop had served his whole ministry in New York, and he had generously and actively supported the church. He had been elected by the diocese as the assistant bishop when the discouraged Samuel Provoost had withdrawn from an active ministry. At his death Moore presided over the strongest diocese in the Episcopal church, one big enough to attract the notice of Christians of other denominations.

The preacher at the funeral was Moore's successor as bishop of New

York, John Henry Hobart. Never one to miss an opportunity to expli-
cate publicly the doctrines of his denomination, Hobart devoted his
sermon to the question of the intermediate state. "People of the congregation," he began, "the remains of your pastor lie before you. . . .
When we contemplate the venerated corpse, it is natural to inquire,
What had become of the Spirit which so recently inhabited it?"[35]
Hobart went on to provide the answer:

> Admission to heaven, the place of the vast universe of God, where
> the vision of his glory, more immediately displayed, shall constitute
> the eternal felicity of the redeemed, does not take place, according
> to the sacred writings, until the judgment at the great day; when the
> body raised incorruptible and glorious, shall be united to the soul,
> purified and happy. While the soul is separated from the body, and
> absent from that heaven which is to be her eternal abode, she can-
> not have attained the perfection of her bliss.[36]

Hobart thus told the congregation, which included clergy of other
denominations, that the soul of the bishop was not in heaven. Moore's
soul would have to wait for the last day and judgment to enter that
place of joy.

In his sermon Hobart did not speculate on the names of the places
in which the dead await the last day. The simple affirmation that the
souls of the righteous did not go directly to heaven would have sufficed
to point out the difference between the Episcopal church's doctrine and
that of Protestants who accepted the Westminster Confession. Following the funeral, however, Hobart added a more lengthy dissertation on
the subject, further clarifying his denomination's position. The sermon
and dissertation were published together under the title *The State of
the Departed*.

In this expanded work Hobart cataloged authors to explain and defend his remarks; among them were Bishop White, the familiar Burnet
and Pearson, and Bishop Tomline, also of the Course of Ecclesiastical
Studies. Had he chosen to do so, Hobart could also have cited Samuel
Seabury in support of his position. A posthumous collection of Seabury's
writings that had appeared in the year before Hobart's sermon at Bishop Moore's funeral included a sermon on the intermediate state.[37]

Hobart accepted the term *Hades* as denoting the whole receptacle
of the dead, a designation that Pearson had said was one of two patristic uses. Hobart also linked his position to Christ's descent into hell

as stated in the Apostles' Creed: "This *place of the departed* is particularly designated in Scripture. It is the ᾅδησ, Hades or Hell, into which,
agreeably to an article of the Apostles' Creed, our Lord descended in
the interval between his death and his resurrection."[38] Hobart cited the
third of the Thirty-nine Articles in defense of his position: "Also it is
to be believed, that he went down into Hell."[39]

Hobart, following Pearson, rejected Calvin's exegesis of the descent.
It was not metaphorical language for suffering. "There is *nothing,*"
charged Hobart, "in which the Fathers more agree than this, *a real descent of the soul of Christ into the habitation of the souls departed.*"[40]

Hobart did part company with Pearson in one way, however. He
made clear his own position on the wakefulness of the soul in the intermediate state: "The *sleep of the soul* after death, in that sense which
supposes it to be *unconscious,* is a modern invention, unknown to the
ancient popular creed of both Jews and heathens, repugnant to reason,
and contradicted by Scripture. . . . The *soul exists after death in some
place;* and . . . *she exists in a state of consciousness.*"[41] Although Hobart
rejected this one sense of the phrase "sleep of the soul," he could not
reject the phrase altogether, for it played an important part in the Episcopal burial office.[42]

Hobart's major concern, like that of White in his *Lectures,* was to
distinguish the position of the Episcopal church from that of the denominations accepting the Westminster Confession's doctrine on afterlife. Near the end of *The State of the Departed,* however, Hobart turned
to the secondary subject that had also interested White—the distinction between the Episcopal church's position and that of the Roman
Catholic church.

> The papal doctrine is, that those who do not die perfectly pure
> and clean, nor yet under the guilt of unrepented sins, go to purgato-
> ry, where they suffer certain indefinable pains, and the pains of ma-
> terial fire, until God's justice is satisfied, or they are freed from these
> pains by the masses said for their souls. These tenets, it must be ap-
> parent, are in no degree sanctioned by the doctrine advanced in the
> preceding pages, with respect to departed spirits. The eternal desti-
> ny of the individual is unchangeably fixed at death. His condition in
> the place of the departed, is an *unchangeable* condition of happiness
> or misery, until the day of judgment, when this happiness or misery
> is consummated in body and soul.[43]

The Episcopal church's position was, Hobart argued, far from that of the Roman Catholic church. The intermediate period could not alter the soul's condition, for that condition had been set at the time of death.

The visiting clergy of other denominations who attended the funeral were dismayed by Hobart's sermon. Although offering qualified support to Hobart in a personal letter, Bishop White may have shared some of that dismay.[44] White said that he agreed with Hobart's rendering of doctrine, although he omitted any reference to Hobart's comments on the soul's consciousness in the intermediate state. White would not have chosen such an occasion or such a rhetorical cast for his remarks, however. For White the doctrine of the intermediate state was, as has been noted, a "matter in which eminent men, equally correct in general theory, have disagreed."[45] For Hobart it was an important doctrine "expressly revealed in Scripture" that "should be an object of faith.[46] Like the episcopate, it was for Hobart a matter in which the Episcopal church was correct and all others in error. It was a matter to be proclaimed for the greater glory of the church.

Hobart's *State of the Departed* not only attracted the attention of White and the visiting clergy; it also was accepted as authoritative by the generation of high-church Episcopalians who looked to Bishop Hobart for leadership. They used his book and repeated his arguments about the existence of the intermediate state, although, like White, they did not generally call attention to the question of the soul's consciousness.

Bird Wilson introduced the *State of the Departed* as a text at the General Seminary. Samuel Roosevelt Johnson moved it to a reference category in the 1860s, but the text remained in use in that capacity until late in the century.[47] During his long tenure at Nashotah House, William Adams used the text with his students; the book was listed in the first catalog and was still in use as a reference text in the 1890s.[48]

Bishop Pearson's *Exposition of the Creed* was in use at all high-church seminaries during this same period. Bishop Williams's Berkeley Divinity School in Connecticut as a rule did not list textbooks in the annual catalog; it noted only three authors in any category, of which Pearson was one.[49] Near the century's end Samuel Buel remarked to his students at General Seminary that "the different classes of opinion [about Christ's descent to hell] . . . are so well and so clearly stated by Bishop Pearson on the creed, that a special detail of them is here unnecessary."[50]

Henry Onderdonk of Pennsylvania and G. T. Chapman of Kentucky were but two of a multitude of high-church expositors of the intermediate state. In his sermon "Departure of the Soul," Bishop Onderdonk carefully explained the distinction White and Hobart had made clear:

> In the land of the mortals, then, departed souls are not. Neither, though they are said to go upward, are they in heaven, the heaven of perfect bliss; for our Saviour declared after his soul had come from the place of spirits, and his body had risen from the tomb, "touch me not, for I am not yet ascended to my Father,"—and St. Peter declared of David, a thousand years and more after his decease, "David is not ascended into the heavens." Where is the region of departed souls, we know not; sometimes it is described as above, sometimes as under the earth; but it is neither in the heaven of glory, nor on this globe.
>
> That region is called, in the English Bible, both "hell" and "paradise." The former word, according to its old English derivation, means only a covered or hidden place, or the unseen world,—and so it applied to both the unseen world of souls, good and bad, popularly said to be beneath the earth, and to the unseen world of final torment.[51]

Like Hobart, Onderdonk did not doubt that those who disagreed with him were sorely mistaken. Roman Catholics subscribed to a "baseless . . . doctrine." Protestants who believed in immediate passage to heaven were guilty of denying "the reality of the soul."[52]

Chapman dedicated his *Sermons upon the Ministry, Worship, and Doctrines of the Protestant Episcopal Church* to Hobart. Like Hobart and Onderdonk, he did not hesitate to summon other Protestants to see the error of their ways:

> From their youth up, the great body of the people are taught to believe, that immediately after death the departed soul either ascends to heaven or descends to hell; and never had I witnessed more surprise, than when the idea has been opposed, as entirely groundless and untenable. We are at once suspected of consigning the spirits of the dead to a temporary oblivion, or perhaps the purgatory of the catholick is suggested to the mind of the hearer, and he trembles lest the grossness of that fantasy should be attempted to be palmed upon his understanding. But no such thing! We reject both the one and the other. As in every particular to which I have already adverted, here also we build upon the sure foundation of holy oracles, and are only

astonished at the extraordinary facility, with which one of their most obvious intimations is usually overlooked.[53]

Protestants and Catholics alike had failed to see what Episcopalians maintained was a clear biblical teaching: the souls of the dead, both good and bad, would go after death to an intermediate place to await the last day. Bishop White had explained the doctrine in his *Lectures,* and he had placed the text that made the doctrine most clear, Pearson's *Exposition of the Creed,* at the head of the list of authors on divinity in the Course of Ecclesiastical Studies. Hobart had added a polemical bite to the argument, and the Hobartian high-church party had followed suit.

Evangelical Apologetic

The evangelicals, like the high-church Episcopalians, accepted Bishop White's assessment of the Anglican position on the intermediate state. Unlike that of the high-church party, however, their position posed a problem for those who held it. Evangelicals constantly argued that they agreed with other Protestants in the essential matters of faith, yet the Episcopal church was clearly in disagreement on this issue.

In the 1840s Professor Enoch Pond of the Bangor Theological Seminary (Congregational) in Maine depicted this division quite clearly in the pages of the *Biblical Repository.* The exposition must have been particularly stinging to Episcopal evangelicals, because that magazine had ties to a seminary (Andover) that many Episcopal seminary professors had attended. The magazine moreover had served as a forum for Episcopal authors in the past. Although politely omitting the name of his adversaries, Pond began his article by accurately describing the Episcopal position on the intermediate life. He then remarked boldly: "it may be well to state plainly, and at once, that I reject this whole theory of an *intermediate place;* believing, according to most of the Protestant Confessions of Faith, that 'the souls of the righteous at death, being made perfect in holiness, are received into the highest heavens, waiting for the full redemption of their bodies; and that the souls of the wicked are cast into hell, where they remain in torments and utter darkness, reserved to the judgment of the great day.'"[54] Having thus stated the position of "most of the Protestant Confessions of Faith," Pond went on to make a biblical argument for the soul's immediate passage to heaven or hell on death. He characterized the intermediate

place of the Episcopal church as "of heathen, and not Christian origin," and "of dangerous influence," for "could it be received by Christians, it would be followed in a few years, I have no doubt, with prayers
for the dead, and with the doctrine of a future probation and restoration—perhaps, with all the superstitions of purgatory."[55]

Faced with such direct opposition, Episcopal evangelicals could
hardly deny a difference between their church's position and that of the
Reformed creeds, but they did try to minimize that difference. They
avoided discussing the consciousness or sleep of the souls of the dead.
They then followed two strategies: they stressed that their own particular perspective on the matter was not—contrary to Bishop Hobart—
a necessary doctrine of faith, and they stressed the similarity of the
seemingly conflicting position to that of the Reformed churches.

In 1838, after the *Episcopal Recorder* (Philadelphia) carried a story
on the subject, Bishop Griswold, then seventy-two and perhaps thinking of his own demise, responded with his own views on the subject.
"That there *will* be an intermediate state between death and the final
judgment, seems, from the Scriptures, to be more than probable: but
we may well doubt whether that state be so clearly revealed as that it
should become an *article of faith,* NECESSARY TO BAPTISM."[56]
Griswold felt that the Episcopal church was correct and biblical in its
position, but the danger of disagreement was not so great as to endanger one's salvation.

John P. K. Henshaw attempted to minimize the differences in his
Theology for the People. He stressed that one's condition at death was
fixed according to either the Anglican or the Reformed theory. Episcopalians might have posited another location after death, but that did
not obviate the essential truth: salvation was for the renewed Christian, and damnation was the fate of the person who died unrenewed.
"What will the condition of *our souls* be during the interval between
the death and resurrection of our bodies? . . . 'Where does the soul go
at its departure from the body?' Most persons will answer to heaven,
or to hell; and this is true in a certain sense. The state of the soul is then
fixed—according to its moral character, and the deeds done in the body,
either in happiness or misery throughout eternity."[57] Henshaw went on
to explain the intermediate period in Hades, but his emphasis was on
that which all Protestants would accept—the fixed state of the soul on
death: "there is no device, or work, or faith in the grace, whither we
go. There is no purifier from guilt but the blood of Jesus; no cleanser

from pollution but the grace of the holy Spirit. As the soul leaves this world,—in a state of guilt or a state of pardon—so will it go to the judgment seat: as it leaves this world, renewed or unrenewed, so will it continue throughout the ages of its eternal existence."[58] This was a truth on which evangelical Christians of all denominations could agree.

Despite the difference in emphasis, however, evangelicals accepted the same outline of the Anglican position as high-church Episcopalians did. Scriptures and the early Christian authors taught the doctrine of an intermediate state. To believe it was to understand the truth, but a merciful God would not make recognition of such an abstruse matter necessary for salvation.

Even such evangelical polemicists as Charles Wesley Andrews would repeat the standard Episcopal position on the issue. Andrews, who was married to Bishop Meade's niece, was the rector of St. Andrew's Church, Shepherdstown, West Virginia, and the author of a stream of anti-high-church tracts on the question of baptismal regeneration. In his edition of Joshua Dixon's *Christian Doctrine,* however, he added an extended note with which no high-church Episcopalian would have disagreed. Andrews noted the difference between the place of the dead and the place of damnation. His remarks ended with an allusion to the liturgy that was similar to Bishop White's: "The explanation of the Scriptures is a sufficient explanation of the Creed, though the sense intended to be conveyed by it in our own Church is sufficiently set forth by the rubric immediately preceding, which says that this Article may either be omitted or the words *He went into the place of the departed spirits* used instead, which, it says, are held to be of the same import."[59] Evangelicals may have expressed their convictions in less strident tones than did the high-church party, but their understanding of the intermediate state was the same.

The evangelical seminaries did not use Hobart's *State of the Departed* as a text, but they did use Bishop Pearson for the whole of the century. When divinity professor Daniel Goodwin of Philadelphia Divinity School published his *Christian Eschatology* in 1885, the Anglican position still remained clear: "The place of all departed spirits, both good and bad, may be called Sheol or Hades, in the larger use of the word."[60] He noted, as had Pearson, that patristic authors also referred to Hades in a second sense, as only the negative portion of the place of the departed.[61]

Thus evangelicals and high-church Episcopalians alike taught the doctrine of an intermediate state as both biblical and representative of the patristic authors. In doing so they followed the lead of Bishop White, who had explained the church's position in his *Lectures* and who had given a prominent place in his Course of Ecclesiastical Studies to the leading expositor of the intermediate state in Anglican theology, John Pearson.

THE DAY OF JUDGMENT

Among the texts that Bishop White placed on an appendix to his Course of Ecclesiastical Studies were four works by a single author, William Sherlock (1641–1707), a seventeenth-century dean of St. Paul's Cathedral in London. All four concerned death and the afterlife.

In his *Practical Discourse concerning a Future Judgment* Sherlock did for the doctrine of final judgment what Pearson did for the intermediate state: he examined carefully the presuppositions and implications of the Reformed view and then declared the Anglican position. He summarized the Reformed view as one in which the individual's sentence was executed immediately on death: "The received opinion is, that when any man dies, he is immediately called to Judgment, and receives his final Sentence, which is immediately executed on him, that a bad man is sentenced to Hell, and sent immediately thither; that a good man is received into Heaven, and enjoys the Beatifick Vision from the time of his going out of this Body."[62] To Sherlock this immediate sentence seemed to conflict with the final judgment that he found in Scripture: "And the Truth is, if all Men have a final sentence passed on them as soon as they go into the other World, it is very unaccountable why Christ, at the last Day, shall come with such a terrible Pomp and Solemnity to judge and condemn those who are judged, condemned, and executed already, as much as ever they can be."[63] If a last judgment was to have any integrity, Sherlock reasoned, judgment could not take place immediately on death. "The sum is this," he wrote, "that mankind shall not be finally judged till Christ comes to judge the World."[64] Sherlock's argument assumed the validity of Pearson's intermediate state. For the soul to wait for a final judgment, an intermediate state was needed in which to wait.

In his *Lectures* White agreed with Sherlock, just as he had agreed with Pearson. White asserted that final rewards would come only after the return of Christ for the final judgment and that any view to the contrary was "not scriptural."[65] Bishop White's adherence to Sherlock's position on final judgment was no doubt an attempt to be faithful to his own heritage. White found a doctrine explicitly taught by the Anglican divines to whom he turned that he could not in good conscience reject. White may also have recognized the degree to which such ideas complemented his opinion on adult renewal.

White and other Episcopalians stressed the importance of adult renewal for salvation. There was only one sure test of this renewal: the moral life. Renewed Christians would be identifiable as faithful because of the way they lived. Sherlock's emphasis on a final judgment based on works dovetailed with the emphasis on renewal, for the sign of renewal on earth (the moral life) would be the criterion used at the final judgment. It was not the dying profession of faith that could send the Christian to heaven; it was the renewed life.

The evangelical and high-church Episcopalians who came after White accepted his opinion on the priority of final judgment. John P. K. Henshaw was representative of the evangelicals when he wrote not of a personal sentence on death but of *"the day of judgment,* to be preceded by the resurrection of the dead, when all shall stand before the bar of God to be judged according to deeds done in the body."[66] This was the time when significant judgment would take place. Bishop Henry U. Onderdonk, a Hobartian high-churchman, agreed, warning that "He who brought down from heaven the offer of pardon, will bring down, at His second advent, the commission of the second death for those who have cast that offer from them."[67] Christ would give final rewards and punishments not on the death of the individual but at the great last judgment. Until that day the souls of the dead would wait in the intermediate place.

Episcopalians often echoed Pearson in describing the details of the final judgment. Pearson had explained the last day in these terms:

When those which are to be judged are brought before the judgment seat of Christ, all their actions shall appear: he *will bring to light the hidden things of darkness, and will make manifest the counsels of the hearts:* he will *bring every good work into judgment, with every secret thing, whether it be good, or whether it be evil.* To this end, in the vision of Daniel, when *the judgment was set, the books were opened;* and in that of St. John, *the books were opened; and the dead were judged out of those things that were written in the books according to their works.*[68]

The actions of an individual were "the fundamental and essential consideration for . . . judgment."[69]

In emphasizing a last judgment based on works, Episcopalians appeared at times to be adopting an understanding of salvation that left little room for faith. Indeed, authors at times indicated that a stricter standard of judgment would be applied to the actions of Christians than to the actions of non-Christians. Bishop Henshaw, for example, expressed a typical conviction when he wrote: "The sentence of men will be equitably proportioned to the degree of light and amount of privileges which they have enjoyed. The sins of the wicked heathen will have a less degree of culpability attached to them than those of the wicked Jews, who had Moses and the prophets in addition to the light of nature."[70] Samuel Buel at General Seminary agreed: "By the grace which they have received, as right use or misuse is attested by their good or evil lives, will all men be judged and according to their works be recompensed in the eternal judgment."[71] Those with the greatest degree of light and grace—that is, those who knew most about Christ—would be expected to have a higher standard of conduct.

It will be recalled as well that Episcopalians left at least the charitable supposition that God in his mercy might find a place in the everlasting for those who out of ignorance of the Gospel did not have faith in Christ yet had lived good lives.[72]

Despite its initial appearance, the Episcopal emphasis on works at the last judgment did not go so far as to leave the final reckoning only as a tally of external actions. Works came first, but they were not the sole standard for judgment. After all, as the Reformers noted and the Thirty-nine Articles declared, if judgment were only on actions, all persons would fall short of righteousness. As Henshaw put it: "We are not to suppose that the righteous will receive eternal life as the *reward* of their good deeds. No. All of them feel that they are but unprofitable servants; and that they could by no possibility be acquitted and saved but for the free grace of God through the Redemption that is in Christ Jesus. Even those who closed a life of piety and self-denial with a *martyr's* death, are represented as having 'washed their robes, and made them white, in the blood of the Lamb.'"[73] No one would gain everlasting life if forced to rely on individual merit.

There were two ways to reconcile this reliance on God's grace and the judgment of works: one could first note that faith justified and then follow with the explanation that faith inevitably entailed works, so that the justified person would be one whose life gave evidence of good works; or one could first stress the judgment on works and then explain that those works were related to a faith in Christ. Episcopalians followed the first course when speaking of the present life. In speaking of the last day, however, they invariably followed the second. Only after strongly noting that judgment was on works could the Episcopalians disentangle the complex relationship with faith.

William Sherlock, the dean of St. Paul's, offered perhaps the clearest explanation of these views about the last judgment. After detailing at length the actions and thoughts for which an individual would be judged, he turned to the role of faith. Because of belief in the Gospel, he said, the Christian was not judged strictly for works. Because of the atoning love of Christ, "No Man shall be condemned for such sins as he heartily repented of and reformed: And this is to be judged by Grace, as well as by our works."[74] Christians did not have to prove their own righteousness by works to be admitted into God's kingdom at the last day. Because of Christ's atonement, no Christians would be punished for sins of which they had heartily repented. The judgment based on works was tempered by grace.

The person who was renewed in the present life—who lived with repentance and faith—would be renewed unto everlasting life at the last day. There was no need to fear judgment. Although every person, from the greatest to the worst, would fall short of an objective standard of judgment, Christ would acquit each renewed person.

Variations of this theme were advanced by most Episcopal authors. Works were a standard of judgment not in and of themselves but as a measure of the renewed life. "The works of the righteous will be evidential of their interest in the merits of Christ," wrote John P. K. Henshaw.[75] Seminary professor Daniel Goodwin at Philadelphia Divinity School agreed: "The judgment *according to works* does not conflict with 'justification by faith only,' for faith is the very principle of all good works in the Christian sense, and the faith that justifies is itself justified, proved, by works." Further, he noted, this approach had the advantage of subverting any Roman Catholic notion of purgatory, for "the final judgment is expressly declared according to 'the things done *in the body*.' It will have no reference, therefore, to any probation of purgatory in the disembodied state."[76]

Nothing that Episcopalians said about judgment was novel to other Protestants. Given the biblical image of a judgment by works in

Matthew 24 and Revelation 20, it would have been difficult to deny
that judgment was based at least in part on works. The difference was
one of emphasis. Episcopalians stressed the last judgment and the role
of works within it; Protestants following the Westminster Confession
emphasized immediate rewards on death and the role of faith in final
judgment. Congregationalists at Andover Seminary, for example, omitted any mention of the last judgment in their statement of faith, while
at the same time they were explicit about immediate rewards and punishments.[77]

The emphasis on works at the last judgment moreover accorded with
the Episcopalians' insistence on the intermediate state. The two concepts reinforced one another and provided a link to the doctrine of
renewal. The intermediate state allowed postponing the separation of
the good and evil souls until the last judgment. The need for Christ's
reckoning at the last judgment provided a rationale for the wait in the
intermediate state. Taken together the two concepts meant that the only
sign of renewal in the present world, good works, would be the sign
used by Christ at the last judgment to separate the renewed for salvation and the unrenewed for damnation.

THE APPROACH OF THE LAST DAYS

Bishop White had also included a work by Thomas Newton (1704–
82) in the Course of Ecclesiastical Studies. Newton, the bishop of Bristol, was the author of *Dissertations on the Prophecies Which Have
Remarkably Been Fulfilled and at This Time Are Fulfilling in the World,*
which was a lengthy catalog of prophetic passages from Scripture with
suggested interpretations.

Although Newton attempted to deal with the whole range of biblical prophecy, he concentrated on prophecies concerning Christ's second coming and the end of time. He was particularly interested in predictions of the coming end in passages from Daniel and Revelation.

The author of Revelation gave the church an image of the last days
that went considerably beyond the eschatological passages in the Gos-
pels and Paul. To Christ's return the author added both an elaborate
succession of signs and a millennium, a special thousand-year reign of
Christ and the martyrs that was to precede the general resurrection and
judgment.

The author purposely used ambiguous signs, both to encourage

Christians under persecution and to veil the true meaning from those for whom it was not intended. Over the centuries Christians, particularly in times of persecution and hardship, found solace in Revelation's vision. Their difficulties would soon be at an end; the reign of Christ was near.

Joseph Mede (1586–1638), a seventeenth-century Anglican scholar who spent his life as a fellow of Christ's College, Cambridge, provided the definitive interpretation of Revelation for the post-Reformation Church of England. His *Clavis Apocalyptica* (1627) systematized the promises of Revelation in a manageable pattern. At midcentury the work was translated from Latin into English by order of Parliament.[78]

Mede's work temporarily fell out of favor among Anglicans in the final decades of the seventeenth century, in large measure because the Dissenters were strongly attracted to him. By the time Bishop Newton wrote in the eighteenth century, however, Mede was again in favor. Mede had, Newton explained, "exerted more learning and sagacity in explaining the prophecies . . . than any writer in any age."[79] This wisdom was particularly evident, Newton suggested, in relation to "the true idea of Antichrist."

Among the signs of the coming end in Revelation was the rise, the temporary success, and the final defeat of a force opposed to Christ. Called the Antichrist in 1 and 2 John, this force was represented by two beasts in Revelation. During the Reformation Protestants frequently associated the Antichrist with the Pope and the Roman Catholic church.

Mede relied on Revelation 11:1–4, which predicted that the temple of God would be trampled underfoot for 1,260 days, and on the Protestant tradition regarding the Antichrist to provide a timetable for Christ's victory. Christ's return would take place 1,260 years after the papacy rose to primacy, an event that Mede had fixed as occurring in 456. The world therefore would come to an end around 1716.[80] Newton, writing after that date, rejected Mede's conclusion but not his method of argument. Mede, it seemed, had erred in fixing the height of the papacy at too early a date. The reign of papal power did not begin until 727: "If then the beginning of the 1260 years of the reign of Antichrist is to be dated from the year 727, their end will fall near the year 2000 after Christ; and at the end of the 6000th year of the world, according to a very early tradition of Jews and Christians, and even of Heathens, great changes and revelations are expected both in the natural and in the moral world; and 'there remaineth, according to the

words of the apostle, (Heb. iv. 9) a sabbatism or holy rest to the people of God.'"[81] The world would come to an end at the comfortably
distant year 2000. Newton's date was still safely in the future when
Bishop White designated this work for the Course of Ecclesiastical
Studies.

White himself was interested in the subject, and he eventually wrote
his own critique of Newton. In this work, which was never published,
White parted company with Newton in only one regard. He suggested that the interpretation would be more comprehensive if it took in
account the history of the Eastern Orthodox churches. For example,
Newton regarded a child mentioned in the twelfth chapter of Revelation as an image of the Christ.[82] In contrast White suggested that the
child "was the Christian monarchy begun in Constantine."[83] Apart
from this disagreement, however, White took no issue with Newton.
The end time was still safely distant.

Occasionally Episcopalians found Newton's work on prophecy to
be a useful apologetic weapon to use again Roman Catholics. John
Henry Hobart recommended that Elizabeth Seton read the book when
he became worried that she was growing too fond of Roman Catholicism.[84] Not all Episcopalians agreed with this approach, however.
When Bishop John Henry Hopkins of Vermont produced a book on
eschatology near the end of his life, he titled it *The Pope Not Antichrist*.

Although Hopkins dropped Newton's identification of the papacy
with the Antichrist, he did not drop Newton's chronology. He still
expected the world to end in about the year 2000. Hopkins provided
his readers with only the second of Newton's two rationales for the date,
however: "How far we are still removed from that sublime consummation, no man can tell. For myself, I confess that I have more respect
for the old tradition adopted by the Fathers in the Primitive Church,
than I am able to feel for any modern theory. Six thousand years were
then believed to have been allotted from the Fall of Adam to the restoration of the world under the Lord Jesus Christ. If the ordinary chronology be correct, we should not be one hundred and twenty-nine years
from the period of His second coming."[85] Hopkins justified his dating
by appealing to Newton's concept of a sabbatism.

Baptist lay preacher William Miller (1782–1849) aroused interest
in America in the second coming of Christ by his repeated predictions
that the end would come in 1843.[86] He did not convince many Episcopalians, however. His date was too early. Newton, whose work had

been given official status by Bishop White in the Course of Ecclesiastical Studies, had not spoken of such a rapid end.

Miller's date had a certain attraction for many Protestants. Those who believed in immediate rewards and punishments may have suspected that the doctrine emphasized the individual judgment on death more than it did the final judgment on Christ's return. Did they not teach that the immediate judgment on death was the final, irrevocable sentence and that the final judgment involved only the receipt of a new body? One way to avoid such questions of emphasis was to adopt a date for Christ's return that would precede the death of many then living.

Episcopalians lacked such an incentive, however. The doctrine of the intermediate state preserved an emphasis on Christ's final judgment. For Episcopalians, Miller's predictions offered no special consolation.

As in many other matters, high-church and evangelical Episcopalians chose to emphasize different aspects of their church's doctrine. High-church Episcopalians emphasized the fact that other Protestants erred in their predictions of the date of Christ's return. Evangelicals argued that Episcopalians, too, believed in the day of his coming.

The two parties' reactions to the millennial hopes of the 1840s typified this difference. High churchman G. T. Chapman remarked as the forties drew near: "Every now and then we hear of the dawn of the millennium. Confident calculations are made, predicting its arrival within some ten, twenty, or thirty years. But though attempted to be sustained by the prophecies of Daniel and John, they are, in my estimation entirely preposterous and visionary: Nothing actually exists to indicate so rapid a result."[87] Any prediction of such an imminent end was simply premature. The Protestants who made such predictions were wrong. As Newton had argued, the date was to be much later. Sherlock had also explained in *Future Judgment* that certain prophecies in Scripture, such as the one about the conversion of the Jews, had not yet taken place and that therefore the end was not "likely to be yet."[88] Chapman followed Sherlock in noting the absence of a universal acceptance of the Christ, which might herald an end.[89]

William Kip, the bishop of California, wrote his *Double Witness of the Church* in the early 1840s. It was a time, he commented in a preface, of "strange excitement among the different denominations throughout our land," an excitement that was an "injurious influence."[90] High-church Episcopalians emphasized the error of other Protestants.

In contrast Evangelicals spoke of the common belief in a future coming of Christ instead of calling attention to the difference in dating the event. John P. K. Henshaw, writing in 1842, sought to differentiate a long-held doctrine from Miller's excitement-provoking claims:

> If then, the doctrine of Christ's second coming to establish his kingdom and judge the world be recognized in the services and instructions of the Reformed Church—if it was held by many of the Fathers in the first four centuries—and above all, if it may be fairly deduced from the writings of the Prophets in the Old Testament and of the Apostles in the New, we cannot be deterred from embracing it by any allegation of its novelty, made by those who are misled by the popular theory and have never entered upon a calm and thorough investigation of the subject.[91]

It would be an error, Henshaw suggested, to reject the doctrine of Christ's second advent out of disdain for the popular excitement on the issue.

On at least one occasion a popular evangelical preacher refused to discuss the second coming because of an atmosphere that prevented the calm and thorough study recommended by Henshaw. Stephen Tyng was the preacher:

> It was at the time when there was much excitement among "Millerites" in expectation of the second coming of the Lord. He [Tyng] had been lecturing, at his usual Wednesday evening services, upon the Book of Daniel, as during the previous year he had lectured on Isaiah, and had reached in course the ninth chapter. It has been said that he would on that particular evening give his views of the "Seventy Weeks" and "the time and half a time."
>
> The lecture-room was crowded to its utmost capacity and still people were coming in much curiosity and excitement. This state of affairs was reported by one of the vestry, and immediately Dr. Tyng declared that he would not satisfy the crowd. He went into the desk and conducted a short service, but instead of interpreting prophecy, preached a pointed gospel sermon. . . . His rebuke was, do not concern yourselves with what is no business of yours; do not inquire how many will be saved or when the Lord will come.[92]

With emotions running high, it would have been impossible to discuss a serious issue carefully. Evangelicals nevertheless believed that the discussion was needed; one could not simply point out the errors of other Protestants who predicted too rapid an end.

The 1840s passed without the predicted end. A round of revivals at the end of the following decade led to some continued speculation about an imminent return,[93] but not until the 1870s would Americans again express a heightened interest in the subject. John Nelson Darby (1800–1882), a former priest of the Church of Ireland who joined the Plymouth Brethren, advocated an understanding of the end time known as dispensationalism. God, he said, had dealt with people through a series of dispensations. At the conclusion of the final dispensation, Christ himself would return and inaugurate the kingdom.[94] This view had two advantages: it allowed a pattern to history, apart from the discernment of the immediate signs of the end, and it had obvious parallels to the prevalent covenant theology.

Interest in dispensationalism in the United States was sufficient to spark a series of interdenominational prophecy meetings.[95] Episcopalians reacted to such meetings much as they had in the 1840s: evangelicals were interested in the discussions with other Protestants, whereas high-church Episcopalians stayed away.

Stephen H. Tyng Jr. (1839–98), the son of the noted evangelical rector of St. George's, New York, quarreled with his high-church bishop, Horatio Potter (1802–87), over whether to take part in these interdenominational meetings. Once tried and admonished by Potter for preaching in a Methodist church, Tyng had offered his New York City Holy Trinity parish as a site for a major prophetic conference.[96] Potter, who may have been frustrated with his inability to quiet the priest, took no move to discipline him.

In their reaction to predictions of the second advent, the high-church and evangelical Episcopalians who followed after Bishop White repeated a familiar pattern. High-church Episcopalians emphasized the differences between their understanding and that of other denominations; the end was not to be soon. Newton had predicted its coming in the safely distant year 2000, and Sherlock had pointed out the absence of certain events that would spell its arrival. Nonetheless these authors, placed by Bishop White on the Course of Ecclesiastical Studies, could be read with another emphasis. For evangelicals they pointed to the common reality in which all Protestants believed: the certain coming of Christ on a final day. As long as others were willing to consider the subject seriously, they were more than glad to participate.[97]

~

In their understanding of the intermediate state, final judgment, and the return of Christ, Episcopalians shared a vision that complemented their view of renewal. Good works, which were the only sure sign of renewal in this life, were to be the identifying mark of the renewed at the final judgment. Episcopalians rejected both an early return of Christ that distracted from the renewed life and immediate rewards and punishments that overshadowed the final judgment on works. The adult could accept the conditions of the baptismal covenant and be assured of salvation only through a renewal that issued in good works.

NOTES

1. William White, *Lectures on the Catechism of the Protestant Episcopal Church* (Philadelphia: Bradford and Inskeep, 1813), 31.
2. Ibid., 31–32.
3. Ibid., 32n.
4. Ibid., 32.
5. Westminster Assembly of Divines, *A Harmony of the Westminster Presbyterian Standards*, ed. James Benjamin Green (Richmond: John Knox, 1951), 226.
6. Matthew 24:31 (NRSV).
7. The author of Revelation had already attempted to reconcile the two approaches by differentiating two groups. The first, the martyrs, went directly to heaven on death, where their souls were kept under the altar (Rev. 6:9–11). On the last day they would be raised separately, exempted from judgment, and allowed to enjoy a special thousand-year reign with Christ (Rev. 20:4–6). The second group was composed of the remainder of humanity. They waited outside heaven in some unspecified condition until the second resurrection, when they would be judged (Rev. 20:11–15). Thus elements of both patterns were incorporated. The martyrs had the immediate reward—at least in the sense of entering heaven—on death, as in Luke. The remainder of humanity followed the expectation pattern of Paul and Matthew.
   This approach proved to be too elaborate for the patristic authors. Most avoided the millennium and the double resurrections of Revelation, attempting their own synthesis of the biblical approaches.
8. Irenaeus, *Against Heresies*, 5.31.1; Tertullian, *A Treatise on the Soul*, 55–57; Hippolytus, *Against Plato, on the Cause of the Universe*; all three in *Ante-Nicene Fathers*, ed. Alexander Roberts and James Donaldson, 10 vols. (New York: Scribner's, 1926), 1:560, 3:231–34, and 4:221–23, respectively.

9. Milton McG. Gatch, "Some Theological Reflections on Death from the
Early Church through the Reformation," in *Perspectives on Death,* ed. Liston
O. Mills, 99–136 (Nashville: Abingdon, 1969), 110.

10. Geoffrey Rowell, *Hell and the Victorians: A Study of the Nineteenth-
century Theological Controversies concerning Eternal Punishment and the
Future Life* (Oxford: Clarendon, 1974), 23.

11. See Thomas Aquinas, *Summa Theologiae,* Supplement 3.69.2.

12. This purgatorial-penitential system had developed slowly, in part as a
result of the crusades. During the first crusade (1096) Pope Urban II had declared that those who fought for the church would be excused from the normal discipline imposed for the correction of venial sins. Later popes extended
the permission to those who hired others to go in their place or otherwise
contributed to the church. In 1476 Pope Sextus IV expanded the indulgence
in another way; the church claimed jurisdiction to shorten not only temporal
discipline but also time in purgatory.

13. John Calvin, *Institutes of the Christian Religion,* Library of Christian
Classics, vols. 20 and 21 (Philadelphia: Westminster, 1967), 21:996–98.

14. Hugh Latimer, "Articles Untruly, Unjustly, Falsely, Uncharitably Imputed to Me, by Dr. Powell of Salisbury," in *Sermons and Remains of Hugh
Latimer,* ed. George Elwes Corrie, Parker Society, 225–39 (Cambridge: Cambridge University Press, 1845), 236–39 (Latimer's work was a defense of a
series of sermons he preached in 1533); John Frith, *A Disputation of Purgatory,* in *The Works of John Frith,* ed. N. T. Wright, Courtenay Library of Reformation Classics, vol. 7, 81–203 (Appleford, England: Courtenay, 1978), 193.
Frith wrote his *Disputation* in 1531 as a response to works on purgatory by
Thomas More, John Fisher, and John Rastell. Frith may have believed that only
the righteous waited in Hades for the last day.

Norman T. Burns has suggested that the attitudes of Latimer and Frith were
similar to those of Martin Luther; see his *Christian Mortalism from Tyndale
to Milton* (Cambridge: Harvard University Press, 1972), 23, 30–32. Burns
focused his study on the soul's consciousness after death without taking into
account the parallel discussion on the intermediate state.

15. William Tyndale, "An Exposition upon Certain Words and Phrases of
the New Testament," in *Doctrinal Treatises and Introductions to Different
Portions of the Holy Scriptures,* ed. Henry Walter, Parker Society, 531–32
(Cambridge: Cambridge University Press, 1848), 531.

16. Charles Hardwick, *A History of the Articles of Religions* (Philadelphia:
Herman Hooker, 1852), 234–35.

17. Thomas Cranmer, *Miscellaneous Writings and Letters of Thomas Cranmer,* ed. John Edmund Cox, Parker Society (Cambridge: Cambridge University Press, 1846), 89–90; idem, *The King's Book or a Necessary Doctrine and
Erudition for Any Christian,* ed. T. A. Lacey (London: SPCK, 1932), 22.

18. Hardwick, *History,* 280 (spelling modernized).

19. Thomas Becon, *The Catechism of Thomas Becon,* in *The Catechism of Thomas Becon, S.T.P. Chaplain to Archbishop Cranmer, Prebendary of Canterbury, &c. with Other Pieces Written by Him in the Reign of King Edward the Sixth,* ed. John Ayre, Parker Society (Cambridge: Cambridge University Press, 1844), 33.

20. *The First and Second Prayer Books of Edward VI* (London: Dent, 1968), 269–77, 424–27.

21. The fortieth of Edward's articles read: "They which say, that the souls of such as depart hence do sleep, being without all sense, feeling, or perceiving, until the day of judgment, or affirm that the souls die with the bodies and at the last day shall be raised up with the same, do utterly dissent from the right belief declared to us in holy Scripture" (spelling modernized). See Hardwick, *History,* 304.

22. William Fulke, *A Defence of the Sincere and True Translation of the Holy Scriptures into the English Tongue against the Cavils of Gregory Martin,* ed. Charles Henry Hartshorne, Parker Society (Cambridge: Cambridge University Press, 1843), 302.

23. For a discussion of Taylor's ideas, see William M. Spellman, "Almost Final Things: Jeremy Taylor and the Dilemma of the Anglican View of the Dead Awaiting Resurrection," *Anglican and Episcopal History* 63 (Mar. 1994): 35–50. Spellman devoted little attention to patristic or early sixteenth-century Anglican ideas on death and as a result may incorrectly have seen Taylor as an innovator.

24. The thirty-second chapter of the Westminster Confession (1646) read: "The bodies of men, after death, return to dust, and see corruption; but their souls (which neither die nor sleep), having an immortal subsistence, immediately return to God who gave them. The souls of the righteous, being made perfect in holiness, are received into the highest heavens, where they behold the face of God in light and glory, waiting for the full redemption of their bodies: and the souls of the wicked are cast into hell, where they remain in torments and utter darkness, reserved to the judgment of the great day. Besides these two places for souls separated from the bodies, the Scripture acknowledgeth none." See John Leith, ed., *Creeds of the Churches: A Reader in Christian Doctrine from the Bible to the Present,* 3d ed. (Atlanta: John Knox, 1982), 228.

25. John Pearson, *An Exposition of the Creed,* new ed., ed. E. Burton (Oxford: Clarendon, 1890), 421–22, 429.

26. For a discussion of sixteenth-century Anglican attitudes on the intermediate state, see Philip C. Almond, *Heaven and Hell in Enlightenment England* (Cambridge: Cambridge University Press, 1994), 72–80.

27. Gilbert Burnet, *An Exposition of the Thirty-nine Articles of the Church*

of England, new ed. (London: Thomas Tegg, 1827), 57. A footnote at this point in the nineteenth-century text directs the reader to "Bishop Pearson on the Creed."

28. Marc Mappen, "Anglican Heresy in 18th Century Connecticut: The Disciplining of John Beach," *Historical Magazine of the Protestant Episcopal Church* 48 (Dec. 1979): 465–72.

29. *Book of Common Prayer* (London: J. S. Virtue, 1868), 10.

30. Paul V. Marshall, *The Anglican Liturgy in America: Prayer Book Parallels, Public Services of the Church Arranged for Comparative Study,* 2 vols. (New York: Church Hymnal, 1989), 1:552–53.

31. The 1789 additions were dropped from the American prayer book in 1979.

32. William White, "Cautionary Letters to a Young Lady, by Her Pastor, in Reference to the Danger of Being Drawn into the Communion of the Roman Catholic Church," in Bird Wilson, *Memoir of the Life of the Right Reverend William White, D.D., Bishop of the Protestant Episcopal Church in the State of Pennsylvania,* 419–28 (Philadelphia: James Kay, Jun., and Brother, 1839), 423.

33. Ibid.

34. Ibid., 396. A more recent interpreter joined Bishop White in this estimation of the Reformed position; see Gatch, "Reflections," 127–33.

35. John Henry Hobart, *The State of the Departed,* 4th ed. (New York: Stanford and Swords, 1846), 5.

36. Ibid., 8.

37. Samuel Seabury, *Discourses on Several Subjects,* 2 vols. (Hudson: William E. Norman, 1815), 1:194–201.

38. Hobart, *State of the Departed,* 54.

39. Ibid.

40. Ibid., 62.

41. Ibid., 48.

42. Michael Wheeler has suggested a reason for nineteenth-century Anglicans' concern about the soul's wakefulness in death. He suggested that wakefulness was a precondition for progress, which nineteenth-century Christians accepted as a given of any theological system. See his *Death and the Future Life in Victorian Literature and Theology* (Cambridge: Cambridge University Press, 1990), 77–79.

43. Hobart, *State of the Departed,* 124–25

44. Wilson, *White,* 396–97.

45. White, *Lectures,* 31.

46. Hobart, *State of the Departed,* 127.

47. *Catalogue of the Officers and Students and of the Alumni of General Theological Seminary* (1834–35 to 1878–79).

48. *Catalogue of the Officers and Students of the Nashotah Theological Seminary Situated on Nashotah Lakes, Waukesha Co., Wisconsin* (1855–56 to 1890–91).

49. *Catalogue of the Berkeley Divinity School, Middletown, Conn.* (1856–57 to 1897–98).

50. Samuel Buel, *A Treatise of Dogmatic Theology,* 2 vols. (New York: Thomas Whittaker, 1890), 2:415.

51. Henry Ustick Onderdonk, *Sermons and Episcopal Charges by the Right Rev. Henry U. Onderdonk,* 2 vols. (Philadelphia: C. Sherman, 1851), 1:319.

52. Ibid., 1:320–21.

53. G. T. Chapman, *Sermons upon the Ministry, Worship, and Doctrines of the Protestant Episcopal Church and Other Subjects* (Lexington, Ken.: Smith and Palmer, 1828), 209–10.

54. Enoch Pond, "The Intermediate Place," *American Biblical Repository,* 2d ser., 5 (Apr. 1841): 464.

55. Ibid., 478.

56. Alexander Griswold, "Descended into Hell," in John S. Stone, *Memoir of the Life of the Rt. Rev. Alexander Viets Griswold, D.D., Bishop of the Protestant Episcopal Church in the Eastern Diocese,* 571–73 (Philadelphia: Stavely and McCalla, 1844), 572.

57. J. P. K. Henshaw, *Theology for the People: In a Series of Discourses on the Catechism of the Protestant Episcopal Church* (Baltimore: Daniel Brunner, 1840), 139–40.

58. Ibid., 140.

59. C. W. Andrews, note to Joshua Dixon, *Christian Doctrine Studied in the Order of the Protestant Episcopal Church Catechism* (Philadelphia: Leighton, 1871), 43.

60. Daniel R. Goodwin, *Christian Eschatology or Doctrine of the Last Things* (Philadelphia: McCalla and Stavely, 1885), 10.

61. Ibid.

62. William Sherlock, *A Practical Discourse concerning a Future Judgment,* 11th ed. (London: Printed for J. Walthoe, A. Bettsworth et al., 1739), 144.

63. Ibid., 149–50.

64. Ibid., 152.

65. White, *Lectures,* 34–35.

66. Henshaw, *Theology,* 139.

67. Onderdonk, *Sermons,* 1:118.

68. Pearson, *Creed,* 532.

69. Ibid.

70. Henshaw, *Theology,* 173

71. Buel, *Dogmatics,* 2:481

72. See Burnet, *Exposition of the Thirty-nine Articles,* 180.

73. Henshaw, *Theology*, 173.

74. Sherlock, *Future Judgment*, 326.

75. Henshaw, *Theology*, 173.

76. Goodwin, *Eschatology*, 25–27.

77. Edward A. Park, *The Associate Creed of Andover Theological Seminary* (Boston: Franklin, 1883), 20–22.

78. James West Davidson, *The Logic of Millennial Thought: Eighteenth-Century New England* (New Haven, Conn.: Yale University Press, 1977), 43.

79. Thomas Newton, *Dissertations on the Prophecies Which Have Remarkably Been Fulfilled and at This Time Are Fulfilling in the World* (London: J. F. Dove; repr., Philadelphia: J. Woodward, 1832), 415.

80. Ibid., 615–16.

81. Ibid., 617.

82. Ibid., 532.

83. William White, "Doubts in Reference to Certain Passages in ye Apocalypse," Archives of Christ Church, Philadelphia, ser. 2—Rectors, White Manuscript, 86:10.

84. Elizabeth Seton, *Elizabeth Seton: Selected Writings,* ed. Ellin Kelly and Annabelle Melville, Sources of American Spirituality (New York: Paulist, 1987), 25.

85. John Henry Hopkins, *A Candid Examination of the Question Whether the Pope of Rome Is the Great Antichrist of Scripture* (New York: Hurd and Houghton, 1868), 130.

86. After the failure of the expected end, Miller's followers would establish the Seventh-day Adventist church.

87. G. T. Chapman, *Sermons to Presbyterians of All Sects, Supplementary to Sermons upon the Ministry, Worship, and Doctrine of the Protestant Episcopal Church* (Hartford: F. J. Huntington, 1836), 336–37.

88. Sherlock, *Future Judgment*, 202–3.

89. Chapman, *Presbyterians*, 337.

90. William Ingraham Kip, *The Double Witness of the Church,* 24th ed., rev. (New York: E. P. Dutton, 1898), 3.

91. J. P. K. Henshaw, *An Inquiry into the Meaning of the Prophecies Relating to the Second Advent of Our Lord Jesus Christ: in a Course of Lectures, Delivered in St. Peter's Church, Baltimore* (Baltimore: Daniel Brunner, 1842), 215.

92. Charles Rockland Tyng, *Record of the Life and Work of the Rev. Stephen Higginson Tyng, D.D., and History of St. George's Church, New York to the Close of His Rectorship* (New York: E. P. Dutton, 1890), 123.

93. Bishop McIlvaine of Ohio wrote in his personal journal in 1860 about the possibility of Christ's return in 1866. McIlvaine's speculation, which ran counter to Sherlock's dating, was not published. See Diana Hochstedt Butler,

Standing against the Whirlwind: Evangelical Episcopalians in Nineteenth-Century America (New York: Oxford University Press, 1995), 162.

94. Robert T. Handy, *A History of the Churches in the United States and Canada,* Oxford History of the Christian Church, ed. Henry Chadwick and Owen Chadwick (New York: Oxford University Press, 1977), 290–91.

95. Ernest R. Sandeen, *The Roots of Fundamentalism* (Chicago: University of Chicago Press, 1970), 132–60.

96. Tyng, *Stephen Higginson Tyng,* 468–78; Sandeen, *Fundamentalism,* 148.

97. Ernest Sandeen, in *Fundamentalism,* 149, has noted that a higher percentage of those Episcopalians who would later join the Reformed Episcopal church—a breakaway evangelical group formed in 1873—participated in ecumenical millennial groups. He has suggested that this millennial interest might be a heretofore neglected cause of the Reformed Episcopal church's schism. The suggestion is correct only in a limited sense. Millenarianism was one of a series of issues at stake in the central conflict between high-church and evangelical Episcopalians: were Episcopalians Protestants who shared the basic evangelical truth with other denominations, or did they have a special claim to legitimacy? Evangelicals, seeing themselves as part of a wider circle of believers, associated with other Protestants in millenarian and other ecumenical societies and cast their theology in such a way as not to exclude other Protestants from the covenant. High-church Episcopalians, convinced of their special place, criticized the millennial ideas of evangelical Protestants, but that was only one of a host of charges against them, the most important of which was the Protestant lack of apostolic priesthood.

The Reformed Episcopalians would draw their members from the ranks of the evangelicals. Their statements of faith did not stress the millennium; the relationship of apostolic ministry and the covenant and the proper use of the word *regeneration* would be central concerns.

6 The End of an Era

~

THE THEOLOGICAL CONSENSUS that Bishop White had helped to inaugurate at the start of the nineteenth century collapsed before the century came to a close. Coming to prominence was a new generation of both evangelical and high-church Episcopalians who no longer shared the convictions that had prevailed in the church since the opening of the century.

This change did not come overnight, of course; in large measure it was due to an Oxford theology introduced in the 1840s that directly challenged the two pillars of assurance that White had erected. High-church Hobartians and the evangelicals, whose movement had initially taken shape in the Washington area, had accepted White's notion that the Christian was assured by baptism and the experience of renewal. Oxford theologians redefined the benefits of baptism and denied the validity of adult renewal.

American Episcopalians attracted by the Oxford theology in the years before the Civil War recognized the differences between their view and the existing Episcopal consensus. A significant number found those differences so great that they left the Episcopal church for the Roman Catholic church.

In the years following the Civil War the strength of White's legacy waned. Oxford sympathizers now remained within the church, demanding acceptance for their views. In 1871 the aging members of the House of Bishops managed a last defense of the old consensus, but the spirit within the House of Deputies at that same convention was more indicative of the future. By 1880 the Episcopal church would be well on the way to a broad theological pluralism that Bishop White would hardly have recognized.

Nonetheless White's role in the church had been an extremely valuable one. His leadership came at a time when the denomination was young and its future uncertain. He had forged a consensus on assurance that had served the church well and had been followed by three-quarters of a century of sustained growth. Indeed, the ideas that the Oxford adherents espoused in the 1870s were based on the presupposition of a stable and continuing church, something that White had helped to erect.

NEW FACES IN THE CHURCH

After the Civil War the complexion of both the high-church and the evangelical parties began to change markedly. Among the high-church Episcopalians the long shadow of John Henry Hobart ceased to captivate the interest and loyalty of an increasing number of younger clergy and lay persons. Hobart had died in 1830, and loyal supporters and former assistants at Trinity Church gave continuity and direction to the high-church movement in the 1840s and 1850s. During the Civil War, however, high-church Episcopalians, even in Hobart's own Trinity Church in New York, were unable to preserve Hobart's vision of a church that was silent on matters of politics.[1] In the 1870s Hobart's influence continued to be felt in the House of Bishops, but in the House of Deputies—which lacked the bishops' seniority system—and in the church at large the high-church movement was decreasingly Hobartian.

A vocal group of high-church Episcopalians who identified themselves as the "advanced party," or the "ritualists," looked to the English Oxford movement and to the pre-Reformation tradition of the Church of England for their theological orientation.[2] As William Adams, the Hobartian high-church professor of divinity at Nashotah House, and his fellow faculty members would complain:

> The text books of the high churchmen are the divines of the 16th and 17th centuries: Pearson, Bull, Hooker, Andrewes &c., and the Fathers of the Church.
>
> The text books of the ritualists are the writings of Pusey, Newman, Keble, R. I. Wilberforce, the volume of Gerard Cobb, entitled the "Kiss of Peace, or England and Rome at One," &c., Mohler's "Symbolik," and other scholastic divines and ritualists of the Middle Ages, translations and synopses of which, issue every now and then from the press of this party.[3]

The advanced party no longer looked to the sixteenth- and seventeenth-century divines to whom Hobart had turned. For the advanced party, Pearson had been eclipsed by the Oxford divines.

James De Koven was the acknowledged leader of the advanced party. He was born in Middletown, Connecticut, in the year following Bishop Hobart's death. His father was of German extraction, and his mother was one of the New England Winthrops. De Koven graduated from Columbia College in 1851 and enrolled in the General Seminary. In 1854 Bishop Williams of Connecticut ordained him deacon. Interested from his youth in teaching, De Koven declined several parish positions and went to Nashotah House Seminary in Wisconsin, where he accepted the chair in ecclesiastical history. He apparently felt uncomfortable with William Adams and the other established members of the faculty and began looking for another institution in which to teach. He participated in the attempt to organize St. John's Hall, a preparatory institution for the seminary, but the school closed after one year. Dr. Park of Racine College, a church school founded in 1852 in the Wisconsin town of the same name, generously offered to accept both the students and faculty of the defunct St. John's. De Koven accepted the invitation.[4]

Appointed warden at Racine College, De Koven was able to develop his own ideas, unfettered by the presence of Adams. In particular he introduced the reading of texts by the Oxford divines (something not done at that time in any Episcopal seminary), private auricular confession, and eucharistic adoration. He became recognized as a leading spokesman for those who favored such practices, a group that included Dr. John Henry Hopkins (1820–91), the son of the bishop of the same name; Arthur Ritchie (1849–1921); and Ferdinand C. Ewer (1826–83). In 1868 De Koven was elected a deputy to the General Convention, a position to which he was reelected until the end of his life.

De Koven was an able and skillful spokesperson for the advanced party. Unlike those attracted to the Oxford movement at its first notice in the United States in the 1840s, he would not leave the Episcopal church. He unblushingly stood for what he believed to be Catholic ideas proper to Anglicanism. For him, William Adams of Nashotah House was a Protestant.[5] It was a charge that only an advanced high churchman would level against the professor of divinity at a leading high-church seminary. In 1877 De Koven even suggested to the General Convention that the word *Protestant* be removed from the title of the Protestant Episcopal Church. De Koven's motion received only two votes in addition to his own.[6] De Koven's churchmanship was far removed from that of Hobart.

Among the evangelicals, too, there was a passing of the old order. Of the first generation of evangelicals, Wilmer, Meade, and Henshaw were all gone. Charles Pettit McIlvaine, surviving along with Stephen Tyng and Bishop John Johns in Virginia, was the apparent leader of the movement.[7] These senior members of the evangelical party sensed a serious change in mood among their younger colleagues. For more than fifty years the evangelicals had coexisted with high-church Episcopalians, expounding the evangelical character of the liturgy and doctrine of the Episcopal church. They had believed that the Episcopal church, although not necessary to salvation, was the best and most biblical of churches. Now among their number they found those who were ready to concede to the high-church Episcopalians the interpretation of the standards of the Episcopal church and to go elsewhere.

The most prominent of these restless evangelicals was George David Cummins.[8] Born in Smyrna, Delaware, in 1822, he attended Dickinson College while a revival was sweeping the institution. His mother, widowed in his youth, had remarried a Methodist minister. Cummins had a conversion experience in the college revival and soon determined to follow in his stepfather's footsteps. He was licensed to preach in the Methodist churches in Maryland and did so for several years. By 1845 he had decided to seek orders in the Episcopal church. Leaving Maryland and its high-church bishop, he went to Delaware to request ordination from Bishop Alfred Lee (1807–87). Lee complied.[9]

Cummins proved to be a popular priest. He served in a succession of evangelical parishes in Virginia, Maryland, New York, and Illinois. In 1865 he was elected a deputy to the General Convention from Chicago. The following year he was elected to be the assistant bishop of the diocese of Kentucky.

The transition from rector to assistant bishop was not an easy one for Cummins. During his twenty years of priesthood, he had risen rapidly in prestige and importance. As an assistant bishop his status was less certain. The diocesan bishop, Benjamin Bosworth Smith (1794–1884), was twenty-eight years his senior. Smith, who had been consecrated a bishop by William White, had served for thirty-four years without an assistant bishop, and he was slow to relinquish authority to Cummins.

To Cummins, the relationship with Smith symbolized the state of the church as a whole. Like many other evangelicals, Cummins felt the Episcopal church was at a critical moment. The advanced high-church Episcopalians were not only rejecting the church's Reformation heritage but also questioning the liturgy's integrity. Cummins saw the need for decisive action, but Smith, a moderate of an evangelical bent who had no hunger for controversy at that point in his life, did nothing to meet the danger. To the contrary, Smith mildly rebuked Cummins for holding services in a Presbyterian church building. Bishop Smith moved to New Jersey in 1872, but two consecutive diocesan conventions refused to make Cummins the ecclesiastical authority of the diocese, despite private assurances by Smith that he would resign. Cummins's sense of alarm increased.[10]

Cummins looked to other evangelicals for support. He began to advance the hypothetical case of an evangelical who could no longer remain in the Episcopal church without immediate remedial action. As he wrote to Gregory Thurston Bedell (1817–92), the assistant bishop to McIlvaine, the church had a responsibility to such a hypothetical individual. *"Has the Church no duty to fulfil toward the man whom I have described?* Has she no voice of sympathy or of kindness with which to respond to their cry for relief? Is she to remain, silent, stern, cold, and deaf to the conscientious prayer of these her faithful sons? Is she not wise enough, strong enough, tender enough to throw out her arms about them and say, we will not drive you beyond our fold."[11] For Bishop Cummins the church's responsibility to such an individual was clear.

Bishop Cummins and James De Koven were on the opposite ends of the theological spectrum in the Episcopal church of the 1870s, but in one way they were alike. Neither would accept as adequate the theology that Bishop White had advanced and that high-church and evangelical Episcopalians had espoused for most of the century. The synthesis had become old and confining: for De Koven it obscured the deeper heritage of the Catholic church; for Cummins it provided insufficient defenses for the evangelical truth.

THE ROOTS OF CHANGE

The new mood in the church during the 1870s grew from the Episcopalians' experience with the Oxford movement in the 1840s and 1850s. Evangelicals had responded in horror when reports of the English movement reached the United States. High-church Episcopalians had applauded the movement for its spirited defense of the episcopacy and the church's Catholic heritage, but they had been slow to accept the theological innovations of the Oxford divines. Those who did so sensed that their convictions were inappropriate for the Episcopal church of the 1840s and 1850s and left for the Roman Catholic church.

Those who departed nevertheless left their mark on the church they abandoned. They both fostered a deep suspicion between high-church Episcopalians and evangelicals and drew attention to the Catholic ideas that would be accepted by the advanced high-church group in the generation after the Civil War.

The Oxford Storm

In the 1830s a small group of high-church Anglicans centered at Oriel College, Oxford, waged an intense polemical war against what they saw as heresy and error in the Church of England. Their two major targets were significant ones: the long-standing alliance in Parliament between the high-church party and the Tories and the church's theological rationalism. The first target was one in which the Americans could express interest but in whose outcome they had little at stake. The second challenge struck at the heart of the theological consensus among high-church and evangelical Episcopalians.

The Political Complaint   On July 14, 1833, John Keble (1792–1866) of Oriel College preached a sermon titled "National Apostasy," in which he denounced the British Parliament's elimination of ten episcopal sees in the Church of Ireland. Keble and his colleagues Richard Hurrell Froude (1803–36), John Henry Newman (1801–90), and Edward Bouverie Pusey (1800–1882) rejected a longstanding church-state political alliance and called on Anglicans to assert their independence as a spiritual body, even from the traditionally favorable Tories. Keble and his colleagues unfolded their vision of a Catholic Church of England in a series of ninety pamphlets titled *Tracts for the Times* (1833–41). They soon attracted a committed circle of followers, who were sometimes referred to as "tractarians."

Although their call to arms aroused wide sympathy, particularly among the junior clergy, it did little to end what these individuals saw as state interference in the church's domain. In 1841 Parliament accepted a scheme proposed by Frederick William IV of Prussia and joined the Lutheran church in establishing a bishopric in Jerusalem. The see was to be jointly supported by Prussia and Britain, and it was to be staffed by clergy who subscribed either to the Augsburg Confession or the Thirty-nine Articles. Britain and Prussia were to alternate in appointing the bishop.

Some tractarians believed that the scheme had beneficial aspects; it would be a way to extend the influence of the Church of England and the institution of the episcopacy to a portion of Lutheranism. To John Henry Newman, however, the proposal seemed to be an even worse violation of the church than the elimination of the Irish sees had been. He saw Parliament creating a hybrid, semiheretical church. He lost his faith in the integrity of the Church of England as a spiritual institution and began a gradual withdrawal that culminated in a profession to Rome in 1845. Pusey and Keble, in contrast, chose to remain in the church but to turn their efforts away from the church-state issue and concentrate on the people's spiritual needs.[12]

Critique of Rationalism: The Denial of Renewal   More serious for the Americans who followed reports of the Oxford movement was the its explicit challenge to the comfortable rationalism of the nineteenth-century church. Like their fellow nineteenth-century Protestants, Anglicans and Episcopalians envisioned a God who, although able to do so, rarely trespassed the normal bounds of nature. In contrast the Oxford divines painted a picture of a God who operated in ways that defied logical comprehension. Rather than enter into legal relationships with Christians and grant them salvation on the performance of their prescribed duties, the God of the Oxford divines infused a sacramental grace that could not be easily confined to logical categories.

This Oxford critique threatened American Episcopalians' understanding of baptism. The Americans had viewed the sacrament as a divine legal transaction, a transfer from one judicial category to another. Adult renewal was at stake as well. Pusey argued in tract 67 that a correct understanding of baptism made adult renewal unnecessary. Those who held, as American Episcopalians had, that both baptismal regeneration and adult renewal were necessary were only "imagining that they hold Baptismal Regeneration" but "in fact using it as a screen to hide from themselves the necessity of the complete change of mind and disposition necessary to *them*."[13] A proper understanding of baptismal regeneration made such a change unnecessary. Indeed for the

Oxford divines a change of heart was only an indication of previous infidelity:

> Those miracles of God's mercy, whereby He from time to time *awakens* souls from their lethargy, to see the reality of things unseen, and the extent of their own wanderings from the right way, no more indicate that they had no life imparted to them before, than a man awakening from an unnatural slumber would that he had been physically dead. These analogies go but a little way; but the very terms "quickened," "awakened," "roused," and the like, wherewith men naturally designate the powerful interposition of God's Holy Spirit upon the hearts of men hitherto careless, convey the notion that the life was there before, although in torpor; the gift there, although not stirred up, the powers implanted, although suffered to lie idle.[14]

Pusey's understanding of baptism went beyond the belief that the sacrament involved only a change of state. On the contrary, it was the moment in which life was imparted, a gift given, and powers implanted.

Pusey's handling of eighteenth-century divine Daniel Waterland was one indication of his departure from the position of earlier high-church Anglicans. Waterland's explanation of the change of state in baptism was a standard work for most high-church theologians. In the United States it was used as a textbook at General and Nashotah Seminaries for most of the nineteenth century. For Pusey, however, Waterland's explanation of baptism as a change of state or relation, as an entrance into a covenant relationship with God in which salvation was granted to those who had faith and repentance, was inadequate. The true meaning of baptism could not be "bound down to any mere *outward* change of state" advocated by Waterland.[15]

Christopher Bethell, the Anglican bishop of Bangor, was one of many to detect this change in the tractarians' orientation. He came to Waterland's defense:

> I still think that the statement which I have borrowed from that eminent Divine [Daniel Waterland] who speaks of Regeneration as a change not "of *outward* but of *spiritual* state, circumstances, and relations," supplies a softer and truer account of the grace conferred in Baptism, than any definition or representation of this grace which may seem to identify it with conversion, repentance, faith, or any of those Christian virtues or holy habits which are the fruits and evi-

dence of the Spirit's influence. . . . It would appear too, from some
passages of the Professor's [Pusey] Treatise, that he himself has no
strong objections to the notion of such a change being effected in the
souls of infants by regenerating grace of Baptism. But to my mind,
such statements as these seem to depend rather on imagination and
hypothesis, than on Scriptural authority or just reasoning.[16]

Bethell argued that it was the individual's condition and circumstance,
rather than character, that was altered in baptism.

Pusey disagreed. He believed that others such as Bethell and Waterland denied the change in character in baptism because of the mystery
involved. They wanted to make of the gift of God's grace an adult intellectual experience. To tie God's grace to a particular human age or
a particular human state of mind would be an error, however. No human conception of adult renewal could compare with the grace mysteriously imparted in baptism:

> No change of heart, then, or of the affections, no repentance, how-
> ever radical, no faith, no life, no love, come up to the idea of this
> "birth from above;" it takes them all in, and comprehends them all,
> but is itself more than all; it is not only the creation of a new heart,
> new affections, new desires, and *as it were* a new birth, but it is an
> *actual* birth from above or from GOD, a gift coming down from GOD,
> and given to faith, through Baptism; yet not the work of faith, but
> the operation *of* "water and the HOLY SPIRIT," the HOLY SPIRIT giv-
> ing us a new life, in the fountain opened by Him, and we being born
> therein *of* Him, even as our Blessed and Incarnate Lord was, accord-
> ing to the flesh, born *of* it in the Virgin's womb. Faith and repentance
> are the conditions on which God gives it; water, sanctified by our
> LORD's Baptism, the womb of our new birth; love, good works, in-
> creasing faith, renovated affections, heavenly aspirations, conquest
> over the flesh, its fruits in those who persevere; but it itself is the gift
> of GOD, a gift incomprehensible, and not to be confounded with or
> restrained to any of its fruits (as a change of heart, or conversion)
> but illimitable and incomprehensible, as that great mystery from
> which it flows, the incarnation of our REDEEMER, the Ever-blessed SON
> of GOD.[17]

Baptism was the source of an actual change of life in the Christian; it
was "the washing of regeneration and renewal by the Holy Ghost."[18]

The Oxford divines had thus ruled out the possibility of a separate adult renewal. Baptism could no longer be understood as a legal transaction in which the external circumstance—call it spiritual or not—changed without any change in the believer's internal character. There was a mysterious "infusion" of renewed life into the baptized infant or adult.[19]

The Oxford divines had questioned the rationality of baptism when they rejected this separate adult renewal. By advocating a separate renewing of the covenant relationship by the person old enough to understand what God was asking, Anglicans had been able to depict a God who dealt on a rational, almost legalistic basis with creation. God never asked more than could be performed and never violated the intellect or the volition of human beings. Now the Oxford divines were threatening all this. They contended that the requirement of human understanding was but another form of works-righteousness. Those who believed in adult renewal tied God's grace to the human work of intellectual assent.[20]

Oxford divines replaced this rational and legal image of God's dealing with humanity with an understanding of mystery grounded in the doctrine of the incarnation. Robert Isaac Wilberforce, the son of anti-slavery activist William Wilberforce, developed the Oxford position in detail in his *Doctrine of Holy Baptism*. By becoming incarnate, Christ had united his divine nature with sinful human nature, thereby re-creating humanity. All who were baptized were renewed in the image of Christ. Renewal was not a human intellectual act; it was a sacramental participation in the incarnation of Christ.[21]

The American Response

Initial Word of the Oxford Movement   Nineteenth-century Episcopalians remained in close touch with their English coreligionists. Episcopal bishops, priests, and laypersons with sufficient funds visited England; those who lacked the resources to visit were able to follow events in the English church through accounts published in the church press. The news of the Oxford movement and the publication of *Tracts for the Times* reached the United States rather quickly, therefore. By 1839 the tracts were the subject of sufficient public interest to warrant plans by a New York publisher for an American edition.[22]

High-church Episcopalians generally applauded the early reports from England. Without carefully examining the issues involved, they accepted *Tracts for the Times* as a vindication of their own emphasis on the importance of the episcopacy and the Catholic tradition in the church. Bishop Onderdonk of New York, Bishop Doane of New Jersey, and Dr. Samuel Seabury, who was the editor of *Churchman* magazine, all commended the tracts in some way.[23]

The general interest in *Tracts for the Times* did not extend to the high-church divinity professors, however. Insulated by the fixed Course of Ecclesiastical Studies, they did not introduce the Oxford divines to their students—nor would they. On the all-important subject of baptism, Daniel Waterland remained the high-church seminary standard.

Evangelical Episcopalians reacted negatively to the first reports of the Oxford movement. Whether they perceived in the movement a new threat to the doctrine of renewal or simply regarded it as another in the long series of high-church polemics in favor of the episcopacy, they regarded the Oxford divines with intense suspicion. One after another, evangelical bishops denounced the Oxford movement to their diocesan conventions. Evangelical editors warned their readers, and evangelical seminaries cautioned their students. For Bishop Meade the presence of a copy of *Tracts for the Times* on the bookshelf of Episcopal High School teacher Milo Mahan was evidence enough for him to suggest that the teacher leave Alexandria, Virginia, and teach elsewhere. Meade did not want the students of the Virginia Seminary's secondary school exposed to such dangers.[24]

McIlvaine's Critique   In 1841 Charles Pettit McIlvaine of Ohio published his *Oxford Divinity,* the first thorough analysis of the Oxford movement by an American evangelical. McIlvaine went beyond the occasional denunciations of the Oxford divines that had been written with little firsthand knowledge of the movement. He studied the English authors and tried to provide his readers with a careful description of the arguments and implications of their work.

McIlvaine grasped the real force of the Oxford critique. It was a direct challenge to adult renewal. He quoted Pusey, who had characterized "'*a large portion*' of the clergy of the Church of England as holding 'that Justification is not the gift of God through his sacraments, but the result of a certain frame of mind, of a going forth of themselves and resting upon their Saviour.'"[25] McIlvaine freely admitted that he was among those to whom the criticism applied.[26]

McIlvaine reasoned that the way to counter this criticism was to insist on renewal's ambiguous nature. Episcopalians had long argued that renewal involved two different agents. The individual renewed the commitment to the covenant made in baptism, and God renewed the character of the individual. McIlvaine could acquit the evangelicals of the charge of rationalism by stressing this double aspect of renewal. The frame of mind of the believer did not justify. The decision to renew one's commitment to the covenant was only the means by which the baptized Christian accepted justifying grace.

Having answered his accusers, McIlvaine proceeded to examine the Oxford view of justification. He suggested that the Oxford concept of justification through baptismal regeneration differed from that of most American Protestants.

> The justification of a sinner must be in one of two ways. It must be either by *a personal change in man's moral nature,* or by *a relative change in his state,* as regards the sentence of the law of God. The former justification is opposed to unholiness; the latter, to condemnation; the one takes away the indwelling moral pollution; the other, imputation of judicial guilt. If we understand Justification, in the first sense, as expressing the making a man righteous *"by an infusion of righteousness"* . . . we make it identical with *Sanctification.* It is as gradual as the progress of personal holiness, and never complete till we are perfected in heaven. . . . But if we take Justification in the latter sense, as indicating a relative change, it is then a term of law, used judicially, and expresses the act of God, as the Judge, the accused acquitting, accounting him righteous; so that he becomes the man "unto whom the Lord imputeth no sin."[27]

Most American Protestants understood justification in the latter sense, as a judicial declaration by which Christ's righteousness was applied to the sinner. The Oxford view, McIlvaine suggested, was based on a very different premise: the sinner was justified by being made morally righteous. God did not so much forgive as remove the need for forgiveness. Adult renewal was therefore unnecessary.

Evangelicals were convinced that McIlvaine had struck at the heart of the matter. The great Oxford heresy was to advocate a moral change effected by the sacrament. The doctrine confused the biblical teaching of justification by faith. It undermined the importance of adult renewal.

McIlvaine's work would be adopted as a text at both Kenyon and Philadelphia seminaries. His central complaint became the rallying cry for evangelicals rejecting the Oxford movement. There was no moral change in the sacrament of baptism.

John Seeley Stone, an evangelical stalwart who later became the professor of divinity at the Episcopal Theological School, followed up McIlvaine's work with his own *Mysteries Opened* (1844). He buttressed McIlvaine's charge of a moral change in baptism with an investigation of the understanding of original sin shared by the Oxford divines. Citing Newman, Stone detected "a notion of what at first constituted *original righteousness,* and of what still constitutes *original sin.* ... *Original righteousness* consisted, not in 'actual inherent holiness' (the image of God), but in a 'supernatural clothing' over and above nature. ... Consequently, original sin consists, not in the loss of 'actual inherent holiness,' or the image of God, but in the deprivation or forfeiture of the supernatural clothing, this extra endowment of Divinity."[28] The consequence of this view of original sin—a view that Stone argued was without scriptural support—was the denial that any measure of repentance, faith, and obedience could be accounted spiritual renewal. Regeneration, for the Oxford divines, could be understood only as an infusion of external grace brought about by the sacraments. Such an infusion made Christians "partakers of the incarnation." For Stone's readers, it was sufficient to dismiss any such suggestion as "miraculous."[29]

Stone recognized that the Oxford divines spoke of a grace imparted in baptism that would mature later in life, but he did not see such a suggestion as measurably changing the situation. The growth in grace would still be miraculous, bearing no relation to actual human conditions. It was not the work of "a renewed human mind" but a question of the seed or germ of grace's "own unfolding self, the fuller expanding of that mysterious Divine embryo."[30]

The evangelical position was thus clear. The Oxford divines were to be condemned, because they postulated a moral change in baptism that precluded any need for adult renewal. Even when the Oxford theologians spoke of the maturing of grace in human life, evangelicals charged, it was not a renewing of the human mind but an unfolding of the mysterious, infused grace. The Episcopal church needed to repudiate such heresy.

Defections to Rome   The initial evangelical cries of complaint received little sympathy from high-church Episcopalians. The high-church press dismissed McIlvaine's *Oxford Divinity* as misguided. The General Convention of 1844 refused to condemn the Oxford movement.[31] Nonetheless the high-church Episcopalians soon began to have their own reservations about the Oxford movement. They were particularly concerned about the number of Episcopalians who followed the example of John Henry Newman and joined the Roman Catholic church. The ranks of converts to Rome swelled between 1835 and 1852 to include twenty-nine Episcopal clergy and a number of candidates for orders who had not yet been ordained.[32]

Although the news of the departures was distressing to Episcopalians, it was at the same time an indication of a certain strength. Support for the consensus about baptismal regeneration and adult renewal was strong enough that those who wished to reject it felt themselves to be outsiders in the denomination and left it. Unlike the advanced party of a generation later, the supporters of the Oxford movement in the 1840s and 1850s acknowledged, if only in a negative sense, the theological consensus among high-church and evangelical Episcopalians.

The most publicized clerical defection to Rome would be that of Levi Silliman Ives. He had been one of the young men who surrounded Bishop Hobart during the bishop's tenure in New York. Although he had not served with Hobart as an assistant at Trinity Church, Ives had studied for orders under the bishop, who ordained him as a deacon. In 1825 he married the bishop's daughter.[33] After serving in several parishes in the dioceses of Pennsylvania and New York, Ives was elected the bishop of North Carolina. He followed the high-church bishop John Stark Ravenscroft, a vocal ally of Hobart. Ives's early episcopate was characterized by a Hobartian emphasis on the importance of apostolic orders and the inadvisability of mixed worship with Protestants.[34]

Toward the later 1840s, however, Ives began to move beyond the Hobartian position, especially in regard to the question of private confession and absolution. Although optional private confession had continued in some corners of the Anglican Communion since the time of the Reformation, it was a limited practice in England in the first third of the nineteenth century, and it had never enjoyed any wide popularity in the United States. The English Oxford divines were vocal advocates of the practice, and they had succeeded in reviving interest in England.[35]

During the summer of 1848 Ives fell seriously ill. Convalescing at the Hobart summer home in New Jersey, he apparently had confessed privately to John Murray Forbes (1807–85), the rector of St. Luke's Church in New York City. Forbes was an advocate of Oxford theology; he would leave the Episcopal church for Rome the following year but would return to the Episcopal fold in 1859. Ives recovered from his illness and began to speak out publicly in favor of private confession.[36]

Returning to his diocese, he delivered a series of sermons in 1848 and 1849 defending private confession and the Oxford position on baptismal regeneration. Ives rejected as a "pernicious error" the view that there should be "any sudden and marvelous changes in men's hearts," and he argued that baptism was "the root of regeneration" in which "a new life is communicated."[37] As Pusey had done, he assailed the evangelical position as a rational faith in one's own intellect: "What is likely to be depth and accuracy of a self-examination, conducted under the Protestant notion, that no matter what may be the stains of sin, or the stubbornness of evil habit, all may be suddenly cancelled by a mere act of the mind called faith? What our concern and effort to be freed from sin, and imbued with righteousness, under the notion that righteousness of Christ, *imputed to us,* is the only garment which we need, to hide the nakedness of our souls?"[38] McIlvaine's argument to the contrary notwithstanding, the imputed righteousness of Christ was not enough. One needed a new life, communicated in baptism and preserved by private confession. Each individual Christian must mentally recall "every fact" of sinfulness that stained the new life and confess it privately to a priest.[39]

Ives also attracted attention for educational reforms in his diocese. In the mid-1830s a priest from Virginia named Adam Empie was hired to manage a diocesan seminary. The diocesan convention was hesitant to support the school, which went bankrupt in 1842. Its assets were sold to a women's seminary.[40] To avoid sending theological students to far-off General Seminary or to the closer Virginia Seminary, where they would be exposed to evangelical theology, Bishop Ives established a second diocesan theological seminary at Valle Crucis, North Carolina, in 1845. The school was patterned along the lines of Nashotah House, a school that Ives's brother-in-law had helped to establish. The school was to be a self-supporting institution at which resident clergy and students would engage in study, physical labor, and missionary work. By 1846 Ives proudly reported to his convention that seven candidates for orders were in residence.[41]

The school was intended to serve as an academy for young men as well as a seminary, but the experiment was unsuccessful. The young men were unwilling to accept the regimen of work and study. Ives was undaunted, however. He decided that the school would become a self-supporting monastic community, with Ives himself as the general of the order. A Roman Catholic devotional manual was adapted for use at the community.[42]

In 1849 George E. Badger, a vestryman of Christ Church, Raleigh, and a senator from North Carolina, called the bishop to task in a pamphlet titled *An Examination of the Doctrine Declared and the Powers Claimed by the Right Reverend Bishop Ives*. Badger used the work to analyze Bishop Ives's statements on confession. Although noting that the bishop had been purposely foggy on the issue, Badger suggested that Ives's comments were capable of only two interpretations:

> 1. that private particular confession of mortal sins to a priest, with priestly absolution thereupon, where it may be had, is necessary to the remission of such sins. . . [or]
> 2. that priestly absolution, where it may be had, is necessary—that as the condition on which absolution may have effect, a particular confession of all *mortal sins* is necessary, and that, either as necessary means, or a useful and valuable aid, such confession *of all mortal sins* ought, *in some cases,* to be made to a priest.[43]

For Badger either position—the necessity or advisability of private confession—was contrary to the doctrine of the Episcopal church. Most Episcopalians in the diocese agreed.

While the evangelicals rallied around Badger, few of Ives's fellow high-church Episcopalians came to the bishop's defense. Moderate bishop John Henry Hopkins of Vermont maintained in his *Law of Ritualism* that private confession was a nonscriptural novelty.[44] High-church bishop William Rollinson Whittingham of Maryland printed an edition of the Seabury-Innes Catechism plainly showing that the portions of the original catechism pertaining to private confession had been removed in all subsequent American editions of the catechism.[45]

Ives capitulated. In 1849 he told his diocesan convention that he would conform all worship at Valle Crucis to the Book of Common Prayer and that he would dissolve the monastic order. In 1851 he renounced private confession. The following year he traveled to Europe with his wife, renounced his see, and made a profession of faith to Rome.[46] The Episcopal church had afforded no comfort for his Oxford sympathies.

Ives's experience was that of one man, yet it was indicative of the state of the church as a whole in the 1840s and 1850s. Despite an initial nod of approval from several bishops, the American high-church leaders were unwilling to accept the new theological departures of the Oxford movement. As long as the debate stayed on the familiar grounds of episcopacy and Anglican exclusivism, the Americans supported the Oxford movement; beyond these familiar issues, they had little sympathy. When Bishop Ives began to introduce real changes in his diocese with his advocacy of private confession, his fellow high-church Episcopalians left him to the mercy of evangelical critics. After his defection to Rome, they wrote him off as suffering from mental illness.[47]

Confusion and Stalemate in the Church   High-church and evangelical Episcopalians reached a theological impasse in the two decades before the Civil War. In their constructive theological endeavors—each group's attempts to explain the Christian faith to the parishioners under its care—they continued to teach much as they had before 1840. Yet they deeply distrusted each other. Evangelicals began to suspect that high-church theories on the episcopacy necessarily led to Oxford sacramental views; high-church Episcopalians perceived the evangelicals as attacking doctrines they had held since the time of Hobart.

This mutual suspicion lead to an intensification of the squabbles over churchmanship from earlier in the century. Evangelicals pressed for an investigation of the General Seminary and for the trial of several high-church bishops. High-church Episcopalians outmaneuvered the evangelicals in the House of Bishops, electing their own candidates and rejecting qualified evangelicals.

Perhaps the best example of the evangelical side of the impasse was Bishop Meade's vacillations with regard to the memory of Bishop Hobart. In one respect Hobart was to be revered as one who had clearly subscribed to a theory of baptismal regeneration that did not involve infused grace. Nevertheless Hobart had also been the leading spokesman of the church party that was least willing to see the dangers in the innovations of the Oxford movement. In his *Companion to the Font and Pulpit* (1846) Meade conveyed a complimentary tone. Hobart's commentary on the catechism was "generally received by the Church as expressing her views." Meade also commended Hobart's liturgical proposals to the General Convention of 1826. Meade expressed approval of the changes, which were defeated in 1829 because of evangelical opposition to the use of the word *regeneration*; the changes specified that baptismal regeneration involved a change of state rather than the reception of infused grace.[48] Other evangelicals shared Meade's nostalgia for Hobart's theology. In 1869 Bishop Cummins suggested two means of keeping the more restless evangelicals within the church. The first was to allow optional use of the word *regeneration* in the prayer book; the second was to "formally declare in some mode, as proposed by Bishop Hobart, and unanimously adopted by both Houses of General Convention in 1826, that regeneration in baptism is . . . designed to indicate a sacramental and ecclesiastical change, a change of state and not of character."[49]

Although his *Companion* commended Hobart's liturgical proposal, Meade criticized the bishop on other fronts. In the 1820s he had inquired about publications of the Protestant Episcopal Sunday School and Tract society, with a particular interest in Hobart. At the time he was convinced of the propriety of Hobart's catechism, but in the 1840s he feared the tract society was becoming dominated by those with Oxford views. Meade wrote a sixty-page review of the society's publications, which still included Hobart's catechism, and found them to be unsound. In 1848 he joined with other evangelicals to charter a separate tract organization, the Protestant Episcopal Society for the Promotion of Evangelical Knowledge.[50]

High-church Episcopalians were hardly more consistent. William Rollinson Whittingham, the secretary of the tract society at the time of Meade's protest, engaged in a long debate with the editor of the *Southern Churchman,* an evangelical periodical published at Virginia Seminary. Rather than stress the common ground of both church parties, Whittingham turned to the Anglican reformers to demonstrate that *regeneration* was a term properly tied to baptism.[51] Whittingham's argument was not a new one. What was noteworthy about his approach was that while he was arguing with the evangelicals over the use of the term *regeneration,* he also was preaching to Methodists that the Episcopal church believed in "the change of heart . . . as indispensable to salvation."[52] If he had delivered that message to the evangelicals in his own church, or if Bishop Meade had been able to share his reliance on Hobart with high-church coreligionists, the tensions of the 1840s and 1850s might have subsided. It was not to be. Distrust and mutual suspicion ran too high.

Evangelical and high-church bishops became increasingly antagonistic. The evangelicals pressed for trials of three high-church leaders, allegedly guilty of immorality. There was some theological consistency to the evangelical behavior; feeling the Oxford challenge to the integrity of adult renewal, they did not want any member in the House of Bishops whose renewed character was in question. Nonetheless the issue soon became one of pure partisanship.

The first two trials in the House of Bishops took place as a result of charges leveled against the Onderdonk brothers in 1844. Bishop Henry Ustick Onderdonk of Pennsylvania was accused of intemperance; his brother, Benjamin Tredwell Onderdonk of New York, of sexually harassing women in his diocese, including the wives of clergy. Henry admitted the charges against him to be true. He offered his resignation to his diocesan convention, hoping it would be refused. When the convention accepted the resignation, he appealed to the House of Bishops. Benjamin flatly denied the charges against him, despite the statements of numerous witnesses.

Henry's resignation was handled quietly, with high-church and evangelical bishops agreeing to suspend him from the ministry. Benjamin's denial of guilt, however, polarized the House of Bishops. Evangelicals voted for his removal; most high-church bishops voted for acquittal. The evidence against the bishop was fairly convincing, however, and a few high-church bishops voted with the evangelicals, producing the majority needed for a guilty verdict. The unrepentant Onderdonk characterized the action against him as an evangelical plot led by Bishop Meade.[53]

A third fight followed. G. W. Doane of New Jersey had supported two church schools in his diocese, St. Mary's Hall and Burlington College. When the schools ran into financial difficulties, Doane had borrowed against the diocese's endowment fund with little hope of repayment. In 1849 lay delegates in his diocese began to demand an accounting of the diocesan funds. Doane put off the matter with promises and parliamentary maneuvering until 1852, when an aggrieved layman appealed to the evangelical bishops. Bishops Meade, McIlvaine, and George Burgess (1809–66) of Maine agreed to press the matter. They entered a formal presentment, the canonical action to convene a trial.

Doane took countermeasures. He convened multiple meetings of his own diocesan convention to deal with the issue and requested delays in the trial date. He eventually was able to negotiate an agreement whereby he admitted guilt on the condition that he would be neither condemned nor suspended by the bishops. He was thus able to escape the fate of the Onderdonks.[54]

The evangelical victories in the House of Bishops were short-lived. New York and Pennsylvania elected bishops with sentiments similar to those of the suspended Onderdonks. Indeed, the high-church Episcopalians made gains in the House of Bishops. Bishops of established dioceses were chosen by the conventions of their dioceses, but bishops of new missionary dioceses were elected by the House of Bishops. In 1859 the high-church bishops succeeded in electing their candidate for the Southwest while blocking an evangelical nominee for the Northwest. Evangelicals, traditionally more successful fundraisers for missionary activities, formed their own missionary society in response.[55]

At the General Convention meeting of 1844, in which the conduct of the Onderdonk brothers came under scrutiny, high-church and evangelical Episcopalians also fought on the orthodoxy of the General Seminary. The charter of the seminary designated the House of Bishops as the board of visitors. When several students left the Episcopal church for Rome, and when rumors of innovative liturgical practices circulated, evangelicals pushed for a visitation of the school. The House of Bishops agreed.

At stake was the chair of systematic divinity at the General Seminary and the successor to the aging Bird Wilson. Wilson, of course, was above suspicion. The evangelicals' real concern was with his heir apparent, John David Ogilby. In Episcopal seminaries the professor of ecclesiastical history or polity was often considered the logical successor to the professor of systematic divinity. Such men as James May (Virginia and Philadelphia), J. J. McElhinney (Kenyon and Virginia), William Sparrow (Kenyon and Virginia), and Milo Mahan (General) all taught polity or history prior to their appointment to chairs in systematic divinity. Ogilby's theological views were thus of vital interest to the evangelical bishops.

Ogilby had come to the General Seminary in 1840 to fill the chair vacated by William Rollinson Whittingham's election to the episcopate in Maryland. In 1841 Ogilby openly questioned the validity of lay baptism. He rebaptized several General Seminary students and published a defense of the action. His rationale was purely Hobartian. Baptism admitted one into a covenant relationship, and "no one can sign and seal a Covenant, but the parties contracting, or those whom they empower to act in their name and behalf."[56] He said nothing of infused grace. Although this rationale was Hobartian, the manner in which he approached the issue certainly was not. Hobart confined his doubts about the validity of lay baptism to personal correspondence with Bishop White. Ogilby not only published his opinions on the subject but quoted and rejected Bishop White's position.[57]

A committee of the House of Bishops addressed a series of forty-three questions to the entire faculty. The questions were prepared to indicate the presence of three errors: Oxford or Roman Catholic theology, Calvinism, and "German . . . Rationalism." All members of the faculty were exonerated except Ogilby. He admitted use of John Henry Newman's *History of Arianism*—the only text by an Oxford divine in use at the institution. Moreover he would not condemn the Roman Catholic church as heretical "in the strictest sense."[58]

Bishop McIlvaine prepared an additional list of twenty-four questions for Ogilby. This time Ogilby took care to buttress his answers with standard divines. He quoted from the Homilies. He cited Gilbert Burnet's *Exposition of the Thirty-nine Articles* a half-dozen times. Apparently convinced that they had done all they were able, the bishops asked no further questions. The evangelicals had made their point, however. Ogilby avoided censure, but a sufficient suspicion had been raised to eliminate him from consideration as Bird Wilson's successor as professor of systematic divinity. Ogilby left the General Seminary in 1849, pleading ill health. Wilson, responding to repeated requests from the Board of Trustees, remained in the chair of systematic divinity until 1850, when he retired at the age of seventy-three. He was replaced by the relatively tame Samuel Roosevelt Johnson (1802–73), a graduate from the seminary's second class (1823) whose most important published work would be a defense of the atonement from the Arian and Socinian heresies.[59]

The interrogation of the General Seminary faculty, the trials of the high-church bishops, and the competition for the election of missionary bishops were all signs of the mutual distrust among high-church and evangelical Episcopalians. In one sense the church had not changed since the 1820s; the constructive theological efforts of the Episcopalians remained largely intact. Fervent supporters of the sacramental theories of Oxford found no place in the church and left it. From another perspective, however, matters were quite different. Suspicion reigned. Evangelicals feared that high-church Episcopalians secretly harbored

Oxford sympathies. High-church advocates felt that evangelicals were challenging longstanding Hobartian ideas.

Unsuccessful Moderates   There was no one with the stature of William White to bridge the gulf between the feuding high-church and evangelical Episcopalians in the 1840s and 1850s. Nonethless two men, both former theology students of White, tried to do so. William Augustus Muhlenberg and John Henry Hopkins nobly sought to moderate the growing debate in the church. A third person, James Craik (1806–86), tried a different tactic, suggesting a theological paradigm that he believed would incorporate the insights of both evangelicals and high-church Episcopalians. All three were unsuccessful in bringing peace to the denomination.

Muhlenberg's approach was organizational.[60] He presented a memorial (resolution) to the House of Bishops suggesting that the Episcopal church offer apostolic succession to "other bodies of [Protestant] Christians," thereby removing the basis for high-church opposition to ecumenical cooperation. Episcopal canons did not provide for the consecration of bishops for other denominations, however, so Muhlenberg called for the opening of "a wider door . . . for admission to the Gospel ministry than that through which . . . candidates for holy orders are now obliged to enter." He suggested that once an "American [i.e., non-Roman] Catholic Episcopate" had been created, the Protestant denominations that had accepted apostolic succession might affiliate with the Episcopal church in "some ecclesiastical system, broader and more comprehensive than that which [Episcopal bishops] now administer, surrounding and including the Protestant Episcopal Church as it now is, leaving that Church untouched, identical with that Church in all its great principles, yet providing for as much freedom in opinion, discipline and worship as is compatible with the essential faith and order to the Gospel."[61] Unfortunately the memorial became more a lightning rod for complaints than a means of reconciliation. Evangelicals wrote to the committee appointed to consider the memorial, attacking high-church views on regeneration. High-church Episcopalians rejected any relaxation of discipline that would encourage evangelical revivalism. Virtually all complained about the partisanship of seminary graduates.[62]

Hopkins's approach was theological, but it was hardly more successful. In 1849 he chose to address his diocesan convention on an explosive, unresolved English ecclesiastical case. Bishop Henry Phillpotts

(1778–1869) had refused to admit George Cornelius Gorham (1787–1857) to a parish to which he had been appointed. Phillpotts, who held an Oxford view of regeneration, contended that Gorham's evangelical view was incorrect. When Hopkins addressed his convention, Gorham had lost in the lower church courts, but he had appealed to the Judicial Committee of the Privy Council.[63]

Hopkins told his diocesan convention that three different views of baptism were involved: the Hobartian position, the evangelical position, and the Oxford position. Only the first two views were legitimate in the Episcopal church: "The term regeneration, therefore, appears to be interpreted in a two-fold sense by our divines. In its higher and spiritual sense, it is used to signify a moral and internal change. . . . Besides this higher and spiritual sense, however, we have also seen that the word regeneration is used in a lower, symbolical and sacramental signification; from which it could follow, that a man may be called regenerate in one sense, while he is unregenerate in another."[64] The third sense, that of the Oxford movement, was not legitimate, for it confounded the baptismal change of state with adult renewal (renovation): "The . . . opinion, held by some, extends the benefits of infant regeneration, in all cases where the Sacrament is rightly administered, to a complete spiritual renovation of nature . . . [so] that the future aim of the Christian life is chiefly directed to the maintenance or recovery of baptismal purity. This notion, to my mind, seems quite untenable."[65] For Hopkins, Bishop Phillpotts's position was wrong and Mr. Gorham's was an acceptable alternative. The judicial committee would later exonerate Gorham.

Hopkins's two senses of *regeneration* were accepted by some Episcopalians as a means of compromise, but maintaining a higher and lower sense of the term was too subtle an approach to satisfy the more determined advocates of either construction. Twenty years later evangelical Charles Wesley Andrews, who was married to Bishop Meade's niece, ridiculed the whole approach by listing seven different intended meanings of *regeneration*.[66]

Hopkins already was among the older bishops in 1850. In the 1860s he was briefly the most senior (by date of consecration) prelate and therefore served as the presiding bishop. During the latter decade James Craik served as president of the House of Deputies. Craik sought to establish something of a centrist position during the 1850s, both by criticizing what he saw as extremes and by offering a new theological paradigm for the church.

Craik was the grandson of George Washington's doctor.[67] Although the Craik family home was located across the street from the Virginia Seminary, Craik never received a formal theological education. He had a good mind, however. He was trained in law and read extensively in theology. After entering the ordained ministry in Virginia, he spent most of his career as the rector of Christ Church, Louisville. He soon became an important leader in both the diocese of Kentucky and the national church. He was an early supporter of George David Cummins and probably was instrumental in bringing him to Kentucky as assistant bishop.[68]

Craik learned of the incarnational theology of F. D. Maurice (1805–72) by reading the works of English theological essayist Richard Holt Hutton (1826–97).[69] Maurice was an English theologian initially attracted to the Oxford movement by its emphasis on the incarnation. He soon had reservations, however. Pusey's understanding of baptism tied the incarnation exclusively to sacramental channels; it left no room for the presence of God in all creation.[70] Maurice felt, moreover, that Newman's idea of development in church was too rigid; it little resembled the real change that characterized a living creature.[71]

Maurice reasoned that both the high-church and the evangelical understandings of regeneration were too narrow. The evangelicals correctly understood the necessity of "personal faith as the condition of Christian fellowship in the Church," and the high-church Anglicans understood the importance of "the idea of catholicism," but both chose a self-defeating exclusivism. The evangelicals, bound by the idea of a spiritual renewal of a few, were effectively prevented from preaching to the many in the church. The high-church Anglicans, bound by the continued effort to keep pure the grace given in baptism, were self-centered and unable to reach out to others.[72]

Writing in contrast to these partial understandings, Maurice talked of the presence of the incarnate Lord who regenerated all human life; not only the individual adult who had repentance and faith, not only the recipient of the sacraments, but all human life had been made new in Christ. "Christ came into the world to regenerate all human society, all forms of life—all civil order, all domestic relationship."[73] Thus God was present to each of his creatures, even before the graces of baptism or adult renewal, although his presence in these events was also real and important.

Craik found in this English incarnationalism an answer to the split between the evangelical and high-church parties in the United States.

He reasoned that if both evangelicals and high-church Episcopalians would realize that the incarnation's renewal of human life began at a point prior to baptism or adult renewal, they could end their dispute.

Craik used the analogy of the birth of a child. Birth presupposed conception. The new birth of the child in baptism presupposed the previous conception of what Craik called the divine life. Nonetheless both the actual birth and the adult experience of repentance and faith were needed for the individual to be saved.[74]

Craik hoped that he could provide an alternative to the continuing debate over baptismal regeneration and adult renewal by locating the divine life's beginning before either of the two events. He circulated pamphlets on the subject in the 1850s and expanded them in book form in 1869. He impressed some with his reasoning, and eventually his work received some acceptance at Episcopal seminaries.[75] Nevertheless his efforts at mediation were no more successful in the pre–Civil War period than were those of Hopkins and Muhlenberg.

As the 1850s drew to a close, the high-church Episcopalians and evangelicals were still at loggerheads. Despite the labors of those such as Hopkins, Muhlenberg, and Craik, who tried to reassert the obvious affinities of the high-church Episcopalians and evangelicals, the relationship between the two parties was at its nadir. The presence of a few Oxford adherents had badly inflamed the sensibilities of the evangelicals and the high-church Episcopalians alike. In their constructive teaching both sides continued to assert the baptismal change of state and adult renewal. Neither the high-church nor the evangelical divinity professors markedly changed their course materials from the texts in use before 1840. Catechetical lectures, parish sermons, and episcopal charges continued to outline theology in much the way that White, Hobart, and Wilmer had done. In their relationship with one another, however, high-church and evangelical Episcopalians took an increasingly polemical stance, seriously questioning one another's loyalty to the church's traditional theological position.

THE LAST DEFENSE OF THE OLD ORTHODOXY

The Civil War provided only a temporary distraction from the debate. No sooner had it ended than the participants began again to pursue the dispute. Works published in the 1840s and the 1850s, including McIlvaine's *Oxford Divinity* and Stone's *Mysteries,* were reissued.

The debate was not simply a repetition of the 1840s debate, however. The leaders of both parties sensed that they must reach some agreement to avert disaster. They were no longer sure of their followers' loyalties. Charles Pettit McIlvaine, the acknowledged senior leader of the evangelical party, feared that the more restless evangelicals were on the point of deserting the denomination; continued debate would guarantee their departure. William Rollinson Whittingham, an acknowledged spokesman for the senior members of the high-church party, shared some of the same fears; he could no longer be certain of the orthodoxy of his fellow high-church Episcopalians. Had they, he began to wonder, abandoned the Hobartian position, as the evangelicals had alleged?

At the General Convention meeting of 1871 McIlvaine and Whittingham would compromise on a resolution that condemned what McIlvaine had alleged to be the greatest error of the Oxford movement. It would be a monument more to the past than to the future, however. It was accepted neither by the restless evangelicals nor by the advanced high-church party. The age of theological consensus that White had helped to usher in was rapidly being replaced by a pluralism that obviated the need for an explicit theological consensus among Episcopalians.

The Evangelical Plea for Leniency

The evangelicals who came to the convention in 1871 pleaded for the church to recognize in some measure the appropriateness of their convictions. Back in 1857 William Meade's contribution to the *Memorial Papers* had suggested making the word *regeneration* optional in the baptismal service.[76] He argued that the Oxford advocacy of a moral infusion in baptism had so confused the proper doctrine of baptismal regeneration that it was best to avoid use of the word altogether. After the war evangelicals took up Meade's suggestion as a compromise capable of easing tensions in the church. Some restless evangelicals did not wait for the General Convention to act; they took matters into their own hands and began to omit the word from the service.

In June 1869 the high-church bishop Henry John Whitehouse (1803–74) of Illinois learned of an evangelical priest in his diocese who had made this alteration in the baptismal liturgy. He brought the clergyman, Charles E. Cheney of Christ Church, Chicago, to trial. The news spread rapidly among evangelicals in the church.[77]

Bishop McIlvaine attempted to the defuse the situation in two ways. He wrote an open letter, published in the evangelical *Standard of the Cross,* to a clergyman thinking of leaving the church. McIlvaine's assistant bishop, Gregory T. Bedell, wrote to the leading evangelicals to gain their approval of McIlvaine's letter.[78] McIlvaine's second strategy involved a formal petition to alter the liturgy. He presided as senior bishop at a special meeting of the House of Bishops for the election of a missionary bishop for Arkansas and the Indian Territory in 1870. Afterward he met with eight evangelical bishops to draft a plea to the General Convention; the other bishops were Alfred Lee, John Johns, John Payne (a Virginia-born missionary bishop to Liberia), Gregory Thurston Bedell, Henry W. Lee (first bishop of Iowa), William Bacon Stevens (assistant bishop of Pennsylvania), Thomas H. Vail (bishop of Kansas), and Ozi Whitaker (bishop of Nevada). Their plea expressed "the conviction that, if alternate phrases or some equivalent modification in the office for the ministration of baptism of infants were allowed . . . a measure of relief would be afforded of great importance to the peace and unity of the Church."[79]

The immediate response to the proposition was hardly encouraging. Horatio Potter (1802–87), bishop of New York, returned from his diocesan visitation to find a copy of the nine bishops' proposition and immediately issued a pastoral letter to his diocese calling the document "capricious" and "unenlightened." He charged that the bishops who issued it were breathing "threats, and denunciations, and vehement accusations."[80] He made his own opinion on the matter clear: the church should teach what Christians should believe, not make allowance for their errors.[81]

Bishops Alfred Lee and Vail answered for the nine in the following year.[82] The evangelical effort proved to be useless to Cheney in Chicago, however. On February 7, 1871, the ecclesiastical court there suspended the priest from the exercise of his ministry.[83]

In Ohio, where both the bishop and the assistant bishop had been among the nine, the faculty of the theological school at Kenyon College sided with Cheney. Sherlock Bronson, J. J. McElhinney, who was the dean and professor of divinity, and Morris Tyng of the evangelical Tyng family all wrote in defense of the suspended priest.[84]

The bishops and deputies of the thirtieth General Convention assembled in Baltimore in October 1871 to face a difficult task. The delicate balance between evangelicals and high-church Episcopalians, seriously strained since 1840, was in danger of being destroyed altogether. Eleven bishops (Cummins and Francis M. Whittle, who had been consecrated bishop coadjutor for Virginia in 1868, later signed the statement) and a theological seminary demanded revision of the Book of Common Prayer. For many evangelicals the Oxford divines had so compromised the Episcopal church's theology that even the prayer book was no longer acceptable.

The House of Bishops Defends the Old Orthodoxy

When the General Convention assembled in Baltimore, evangelicals were quick to push for the desired change in the liturgy. The word *regeneration* would have to be removed from the baptismal service or made optional. Hugh Sheffey, the speaker of the Virginia House of Delegates and an active lay Episcopal evangelical, rose to suggest this alteration to the House of Deputies.[85] The evangelicals lacked numbers to pass the resolution, however, and Sheffy's resolution was not acted on.

Within the House of Bishops plans for a solution of a different kind were afoot. High-churchman Whittingham introduced into the record a resolution with which McIlvaine and the other evangelicals could heartily agree: "We, the subscribers, Bishops of the Protestant Episcopal Church in the United States, being asked, in order to the quieting of the consciences of Sundry members of the said Church, to declare our conviction as to the meaning of the word 'regenerate' in the Offices for the Ministration of Baptism of Infants, do declare that in our opinion that the word 'regenerate' is not there so used as to determine that a moral change in the subject of baptism is wrought in the Sacrament."[86] When Bishop Johns of Virginia asked McIlvaine about the nearly unanimous acceptance of the resolution, McIlvaine smiled and called it, "the best thing yet."[87] For twenty years he had characterized the doctrine of infused moral change in baptism as the greatest Oxford threat to American orthodoxy. Now, at long last, the House of Bishops had repudiated the error.

The bishops were not content with laying to rest the old Oxford threat to the baptismal convent. They went on to adopt a regulation dealing with the rising ritualism of the advanced party. By a vote of twenty-two to fifteen, they approved a proposed canon specifying that the bishops had the authority to settle "any question which shall at any time concern ritual."[88]

The old order had been defended. The bishops had repudiated both those restless evangelicals who omitted the word *regeneration* from the baptismal liturgy without authorization from the General Convention and those advanced high-church Episcopalians who believed that a moral change took place in the person baptized. A theological formula, much in keeping with Bishop Hobart's proposal to the General Convention of 1826, was accepted by all but one bishop as a statement of the Episcopal church's baptismal theology.

Both evangelical and high-church Episcopalians returned to their dioceses to reassert their church's theological stance. In Ohio Bishop McIlvaine scheduled a special meeting of the board of trustees of the theological seminary at Kenyon College. The trustees chastised the faculty for supporting Cheney of Chicago in his rejection of baptismal regeneration. All three faculty members resigned. Bronson and Tyng went to parishes. McElhinney moved to Virginia Seminary, but systematic divinity no longer would be his major responsibility. McIlvaine was willing to defend the accord reached in the House of Bishops even at the cost of devastating his seminary. In the fall of 1873, the year McIlvaine died, the school had neither faculty nor students.[89]

President of the House of Deputies James Craik fought on two fronts. On the one hand, he engaged in a fierce political struggle with Assistant Bishop Cummins, whom he suspected of attempting to flood Kentucky with evangelical clergy.[90] On the other hand, he followed up the bishops' action on baptism by debating James De Koven on the latter's eucharistic theology. The faculty at Nashotah House rallied to block De Koven's election as bishop of Wisconsin.[91]

Advanced high-churchman John Henry Hopkins Jr. later complained that an "alliance . . . ominous of mischief" had been formed between the "high and Dry" (i.e., high-church Hobartians) and the evangelicals. Hopkins detected the alliance's birth as having taken place at the convention of 1868. He suggested that the object of the alliance was suppression of ritualism.[92] Hopkins's description was correct. High-church and evangelical bishops had united to defend the old order against both the advanced high-church theology of baptism and the more restless evangelicals' accusation that only a change in the Book of Common Prayer could preserve the integrity of Episcopal theology.

Winds of Change

The bishops' statement on moral change and baptism was drafted in such a way as not to require the House of Deputies' consent. The

proposed canon on ritual required the lower house's approval, however. The deputies did not give it.[93]

The House of Deputies in 1871 had far less sense of tradition and
continuity than did the House of Bishops. James De Koven of Wisconsin
proved to be a convincing floor leader for the advanced high-church
party. The deputies met less frequently than the bishops did, and their
membership was based on election rather than hierarchical status, so
that they lacked many of the personal ties that united the bishops.

The bishops had defended the old orthodoxy for the moment, but
the deputies were more reflective of the coming generation. Theirs
would be a more pluralistic heritage. The seminaries would continue
to teach many of the old ideas, in part because of the longevity of the
divinity professors. Even the seminaries would exhibit a difference,
however. Already in the 1870s the seminary catalogs contained a new
notation in their book lists. The old recitation method of study, involving the memorization of a handful of books, was replaced by the lecture system, accompanied by large reference lists. Burnet and Pearson,
once the most distinctive expositors of American Anglicanism, soon
were buried among long columns of reference authors.

Bishop Cummins, the deposed priest Cheney, and a relatively small
group of restless evangelicals formed the Reformed Episcopal church
soon after McIlvaine died.[94] Their statement of faith adopted in 1873
condemned the "erroneous and strange" doctrine "that Regeneration
is inseparably connected with Baptism." They approved a revision of
the Book of Common Prayer removing the word *regeneration* from the
baptismal office.[95] Departing, they claimed to be more loyal to the tradition of Bishop William White than were those who remained behind.

Whatever the justice of their claim of loyalty, they were correct in
one matter. An age had come to an end in the church. No longer would
Episcopalians share a single vision of the assured Christian, the one
hammered out by Bishop White and perpetuated by the seminaries and
the Course of Ecclesiastical Studies. White had understood the Christian as assured by a baptism that guaranteed inclusion within the covenant and by an adult renewal manifested in the moral life. He had
sought a doctrine of predestination that would not pose a threat to
individual confidence, and he had taught that on the day of judgment
the sober, renewed Christian would be acquitted.

Within fifteen years of the General Convention meeting of 1871, the
House of Bishops would adopt a resolution that White would not have

recognized as the work of his own church. The bishops' Chicago Quadrilateral (1886) specified only four essentials of the Christian faith: belief in the Scriptures, the Nicene Creed, the two sacraments, and the episcopate.[96] Gone was the definition of baptism as a change of state. There was no mention of adult renewal or of the intermediate state.

The consensus was gone, but it had played a vitally important role in the history of the church. In 1801 the denomination had been a bold experiment with an uncertain future. Never before had a former colonial branch of the Anglican church attempted self-government and independence from England. The church lacked any Episcopal colleges or seminaries, as well as the continued state support that the Congregationalists enjoyed in New England. Many Americans who recalled the Anglican chaplains to the British troops during the Revolution remained hostile to the denomination. Bishop White's leadership had provided the church with a badly needed theological identity, ample enough to embrace the major segments of the church and distinctive enough to locate the denomination among other Protestant bodies.

By late in the century the situation had changed. Episcopalians could claim a common past and a proven liturgical tradition. They had colleges and seminaries, and they could look back on a century of sustained growth. The consensus that had proved a needed buttress to a young church seemed too confining. It had served its purpose and its day had passed.

NOTES

1. Robert Bruce Mullin, *Episcopal Vision/American Reality: High Church Theology and Social Thought in Evangelical America* (New Haven, Conn.: Yale University Press, 1986), 202–11.

2. The name *ritualist* can be somewhat misleading. Members of the advanced high-church party did advocate the introduction of such traditional Roman Catholic ritual practices as the Adoration of the Blessed Sacrament. They were not the only advocates of a more ritual worship, however. William Augustus Muhlenberg, who was not a member of the advanced party, had been among the first to introduce such practices as weekly celebrations of the Eucharist and vested choirs. While not calling attention to the fact, evangelical clergy also gradually introduced more ritual elements into their worship.

3. Lewis A. Kemper, William Adams, John H. Edgar, Robert N. Parke, John Wilkinson, and Marison Byllesby, "Principles, Not Men," appendix to James De Koven, *A Theological Defense for the Rev. James De Koven to the Coun-*

cil Held at Milwaukee, February 10th and 12th, 1874, 48–51 (Racine, Wisc.:
Advocate Steam Printing House and Book Bindery, 1874), 49.

   4. William C. Pope, *Life of the Reverend James De Koven, Sometime Warden of Racine College* (New York: James Pott, 1899), 9–24.

   5. William Adams, *Three Letters upon the Confessional to James De Koven,
D.D., with the Resolution of the Faculty of Nashotah House and A Speech
upon Eucharistic Adoration Read before a Special Council Held in Milwaukee, February 11, 12 and 13, 1874 for the Election of a Bishop in the Diocese
of Wisconsin* (Milwaukee: Burdick and Armitage, 1874), 131.

   6. Pope, *De Koven,* 83.

   7. For an excellent study of Bishop McIlvaine, see Diana Hochstedt Butler, *Standing against the Whirlwind: Evangelical Episcopalians in Nineteenth-
Century America* (New York: Oxford University Press, 1995).

   8. Diana Butler suggested alternative language for the distinction that I have
drawn here between evangelicals (who remained in the Episcopal church) and
restless evangelicals (who felt they could not in conscience remain a part of
it). She referred to the first group as *moderate* evangelicals and to the second
as *radical* evangelicals. See *Standing against the Whirlwind,* 224–26.

   For a more detailed study of Cummins, see Allen C. Guelzo, *For the Union
of Evangelical Christendom: The Irony of the Reformed Episcopalians* (University Park: Pennsylvania State University Press, 1994).

   9. A. M. Cummins, *Memoir of George David Cummins, D.D., First Bishop
of the Reformed Episcopal Church* (New York: Dodd, Mead, 1878), 13–36.

   10. Ibid., 404–6.

   11. Ibid., 334.

   12. Desmund Bowen, *The Idea of the Victorian Church: A Study in the
Church of England, 1833–1889* (Montreal: McGill University Press, 1968),
67–83.

   13. Members of the University of Oxford, *Tracts for the Times,* 6 vols.
(London, 1840–42; repr., New York: AMS, 1969), 2: tract 67, p. 8.

   14. Ibid., 28.

   15. Ibid., 42.

   16. Christopher Bethell, *A General View of the Doctrine of Regeneration
in Baptism,* 4th ed., rev. (London: Francis and John Rivington, 1845), xxix–
xxx.

   17. *Tracts for the Times,* 2: tract 67, pp. 47–48.

   18. Ibid., 62.

   19. Ibid., 63.

   20. Ibid., 4: tract 82, pp. xiv, xxi.

   21. Robert Isaac Wilberforce, *The Doctrine of Holy Baptism with Remarks
on the Rev. W. Goode's "Effects of Infant Baptism"* (London: John Murray,
1849), 24.

22. E. Clowes Chorley, *Men and Movements in the American Episcopal Church* (New York: Scribner's, 1946), 197.

23. Ibid, 124–200.

24. John Henry Hopkins [Jr.], memoir to Milo Mahan, *The Collected Works of the Late Milo Mahan D.D.*, 3 vols. (New York: Pott, Young, 1875), 1:vi.

25. Charles Pettit McIlvaine, *Righteousness by Faith, a New and Revised Edition of "Oxford Divinity"* (Philadelphia: Protestant Episcopal Book Society, 1862), 54.

26. Ibid., 56.

27. Ibid., 67.

28. John Seeley Stone, *The Mysteries Opened or Scriptural Views of Preaching and the Sacraments, As Distinguished from Certain Theories concerning Baptismal Regeneration and the Real Presence* (New York: Harper and Brothers, 1844), 87–88.

29. Ibid., 86.

30. Ibid., 106.

31. Chorley, *Men and Movements*, 204, 219–21.

32. Ibid., 22.

33. Michael Taylor Malone, "Levi Silliman Ives: Priest, Bishop, Tractarian and Roman Catholic Convert" (Ph.D. diss., Duke University, 1970), 10–20.

34. Ibid., 47, 51–52.

35. S. L. Ollard, *A Short History of the Oxford Movement* (London: A. R. Mowbray, 1932), 123.

36. Malone, "Ives," 201, 243.

37. Levi Silliman Ives, *The Obedience of Faith: Seven Sermons Delivered in His Visitations to the Churches of His Diocese, 1848–9* (New York: Stanford and Swords, 1849), 32, 36.

38. Ibid., 104.

39. Ibid., 49–84.

40. The female seminary continues as St. Mary's Junior College.

41. Malone, "Ives," 88, 100, 104.

42. Ibid., 172–75.

43. [George Badger], *An Examination of the Doctrine Declared and the Powers Claimed by the Right Reverend Bishop Ives in a Pastoral Letter to the Clergy and Laity of His Diocese by a Lay Member of the Protestant Episcopal Church in North Carolina* (Philadelphia: H. Hooker, 1849), 14.

44. John Henry Hopkins, *The Law of Ritualism Examined in Its Relation to the Word of God, to the Primitive Church, to the Church of England, and to the Protestant Episcopal Church in the United States* (New York: Hurd and Houghton, 1866), 52.

45. [Benjamin Moore], *A Catechism Designed As an Explanation and Enlargement of the Church Catechism Formerly Recommended by the Bishops and Clergy of the Protestant Episcopal Church in the State of New York to Which Are Added the Omitted Parts of the Original Catechism of Bishop Innes As Republished by Bishop Seabury*, ed. William Rollinson Whittingham (Baltimore: Joseph Robinson, 1851), 66–76.

46. Malone, "Ives," 215–19, 292.

47. Ibid., iv.

48. William Meade, *Companion to the Font and Pulpit* (Washington: J. & G. S. Gideon, 1846), 77–78.

49. Cummins, *George David Cummins*, 339–40.

50. John Johns, *A Memoir of the Right Rev. William Meade, D.D., Bishop of the Protestant Episcopal Church in the Diocese of Virginia* (Baltimore: Innes, 1867), 204–27.

51. [William R. Whittingham and the editor of *Southern Churchman*] *The Doctrine of Baptismal Regeneration As Held by Cranmer, Latimer and Ridley; and As Taught in the Book of Common Prayer: A Discussion between Bishop Whittingham and the Southern Churchman* (New York: John A. Gray, 1860), 3.

52. William Rollinson Whittingham, *Fifteen Sermons by William Rollinson Whittingham, Fourth Bishop of Maryland* (New York: D. Appleton, 1880), 160.

53. Johns, *Meade*, 300–322.

54. Ibid., 322–79.

55. Chorley, *Men and Movements*, 269–70.

56. John D. Ogilby, *An Outline of the Argument against the Validity of Lay-Baptism* (New York: D. Appleton, 1842), 29.

57. Ibid., 10; Bird Wilson, *Memoir of the Life of the Right Reverend William White, D.D., Bishop of the Protestant Episcopal Church in the State of Pennsylvania* (Philadelphia: James Kay, Jun., and Brother, 1839), 36.

58. *Journal of the Proceedings of the Bishops, Clergy and Laity of the Protestant Episcopal Church in the United States of American, Assembled in a General Convention . . . 1844* (New York: James A. Sparks, Printed for the Convention, 1844), 239–42.

59. S. R. Johnson, *A Contribution to the Doctrine of the Atonement* (New York: James Potts, 1865).

60. Alvin Skarden's biography argued that Muhlenberg was a mediating figure who did not fit into either the high-church or the evangelical party. I have accepted that interpretation here and in *A History of the Episcopal Church*. See the final chapter of Alvin Skarden, *Church Leader in the Cities: William Augustus Muhlenberg* (Philadelphia: University of Pennsylvania Press, 1971).

Allen C. Guelzo has recently challenged this interpretation, depicting Muhlenberg as squarely in the evangelical camp. See Guelzo, *For the Union*, 61–65.

61. William Augustus Muhlenberg, "Muhlenberg Memorial," in *Documents of Witness: A History of the Episcopal Church, 1782–1985*, ed. Don S. Armentrout and Robert Boak Slocum, 208–11 (New York: Church Hymnal, 1994), 210.

62. Alonzo Potter, ed., *Memorial Papers: The Memorial: With Circular and Questions of the Episcopal Commissions; Report of the Commission; Contributions of the Commissioners; and Communications from Episcopal and Non Episcopal Divines* (Philadelphia: E. H. Butler, 1857), 155, 175, 261.

63. Bowen, *Victorian Church*, 97–98.

64. John H. Hopkins, *The Case of the Rev. Mr. Gorham against the Bishop of Exeter Considered: Address to the Clergy of the Diocese of Vermont* (Burlington: E. Smith, 1849), 12–13.

65. Ibid., 7.

66. C. W. Andrews, *Review of the Baptismal Controversy with a Statement of the Argument for Revision of the Office for Infant Baptism*, 2d ed. (Philadelphia: The Episcopalian, 1869).

67. Craik's grandfather, who was also named James, was born near Dumfries in Scotland in 1730. He studied medicine at the University of Edinburgh and emigrated to Virginia, where he served as a doctor with the colonial forces led by George Washington during the French and Indian War. Dr. Craik and Washington became friends, and during the Revolution Washington designated him surgeon general in the Continental Army. Dr. Craik served as Washington's family physician up until the time of Washington's death.

Dr. James Craik and his wife, Marianne Ewell, had six sons and three daughters. Their son George Washington Craik, who was also a physician, was the father of the Rev. James Craik. For further details see Gay Montague Moore, *Seaport in Virginia: George Washington's Alexandria* (Richmond: Garrett and Massie, 1949), 184–92.

68. Guelzo, *For the Union*, 106.

69. James Craik, *The Incarnation: A Supplement to the Divine Life and the New Birth* (Louisville: John P. Morton, 1873), 24.

70. Bowen, *Victorian Church*, 323.

71. Stephen Prickett, *Romanticism and Religion: The Tradition of Coleridge and Wordsworth in the Victorian Church* (Cambridge: Cambridge University Press, 1967), 162.

72. Frederick Denison Maurice, *The Kingdom of Christ of Hints Respecting the Principles, Constitution, and Ordinances of the Catholic Church*, from the 2d London ed. (New York: D. Appleton, 1843), 549–51.

73. Frederick Denison Maurice, *Theological Essays*, from the 2d London ed. (New York: Redfield, 1854), 185.

74. James Craik, *The Divine Life and New Birth* (Boston: E. P. Dutton, 1869), 104–6.

75. Samuel Roosevelt Johnson put Craik's *Divine Life* on his reading list for students at the General Seminary. Craik served on the board of the University of the South (Sewanee) and may also have influenced William Porcher DuBose, the school's incarnational theologian.

76. Potter, *Memorial Papers*, 155–56.

77. See Guelzo, *For the Union*, 74–86, for a detailed account of the Cheney trial.

78. Cummins, *George David Cummins*, 330–31.

79. *Papers on the Proposition of "The Nine Bishops"* (Philadelphia: Claxton, Remsen and Haffelfinger, 1871), 14–15.

80. Horatio Potter, *A Pastoral Letter to the Clergy and Laity of the Diocese of New York* (New York: Pott and Avery, 1869), 8, 19.

81. Ibid., 19.

82. [Alfred Lee], *Review of the Bishop of New York's Pastoral Letter of December 1869 by One of the Nine* (Philadelphia: Claxton, Remsen and Haffelfinger, 1870); Thomas Vail, *Suggestions on Church Comprehensiveness and the Request of the Nine Bishops, Being Part of the Annual Address on May 11, 1870* (Lawrence, Kans.: Journal Company Book and Job Printing House, 1870).

83. Chorley, *Men and Movements*, 406.

84. Richard M. Spielmann, *Bexley Hall: 150 Years, A Brief History* (Rochester, N.Y.: Colgate Rochester Divinity School/Bexley Hall/Crozer Theological Seminary, 1974), 28–29.

85. *Journal of the Proceedings of the Bishops, Clergy and Laity of the Protestant Episcopal Church in the United States of American, Assembled in a General Convention . . . 1871* (Hartford, Conn.: Printed for the Convention at the Church Press, 1872), 92.

86. Ibid., 283.

87. John Johns, "Bishop Johns' Letter in Reply to the Letter of the Rev. Mr. Latane," in *Four Documents*, [ed. Alfred Lee], 32–43 (Philadelphia: I. R. Weldon, n.d.), 36.

Allen Guelzo is critical of McIlvaine at this point, regarding him as misinterpreting the whole turn of events at the General Convention meeting. Guelzo bases his conclusion on the House of Deputies' response to an antiritualist resolution passed by the bishops rather than on the Whittingham resolution. Guelzo's sympathy is with the evangelicals who would withdraw from the denomination to form the Reformed Episcopal church. See Guelzo, *For the Union*, 68.

88. *Journal of the General Convention* (1871), 193, 272.

89. Spielmann, *Bexley Hall*, 29.

90. Guelzo, *For the Union,* 113–14.

91. James Craik and James De Koven, *The Holy Eucharist: A Correspondence between the Rev. Dr. Craik, of Louisville, and the Rev. Dr. De Koven, of Racine College* (N.p.: n.p., n.d.).

92. John Henry Hopkins [Jr.], introduction to Mahan, *Collected Works,* xxxvii.

93. *Journal of the General Convention* (1871), 224.

94. In her account of the schism Diana Butler inverted the order of McIlvaine's death and the formation of the Reformed Episcopal church. There are some advantages to this approach. For example, it enabled her to end her work with the death of her principal character. The approach obscures the connection between the two events, however. McIlvaine was a formidable champion of a continued evangelical presence in the Episcopal church, and his death made departure of the restless evangelicals more likely. See Butler, *Against the Whirlwind,* 207–14.

95. Samuel M. Smucker, *History of All Religions; Containing a Statement of the Origin, Development, Doctrines, Form of Worship and Government of All the Religious Denominations in the World* (Philadelphia: Crawford, 1883), 327–31.

96. *The Book of Common Prayer and Administration of the Sacraments and Other Rites and Ceremonies of the Church, together with the Psalter or Psalms of David, according to the Use of the Episcopal Church* (New York: Church Hymnal, 1979), 876–77.

INDEX

ROBERT W. PRICHARD is the Arthur Lee Kinsolving Professor of Christianity in America at the Protestant Episcopal Theological Seminary in Virginia. He is the author of *A History of the Episcopal Church*, *The Bat and the Bishop*, and *Readings from the History of the Episcopal Church*.